Stones, Bones, and Ancient Cities

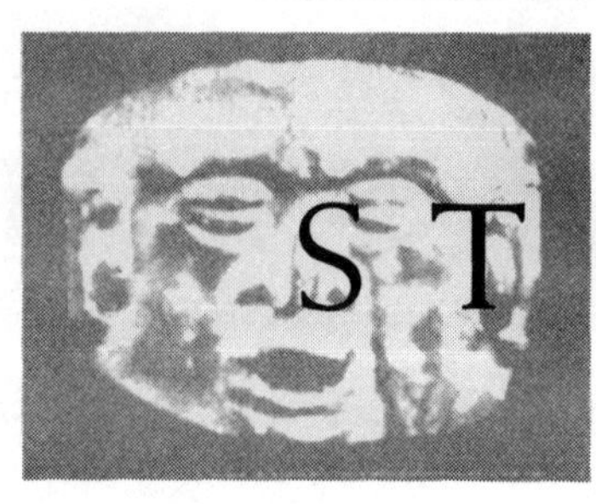STONES,

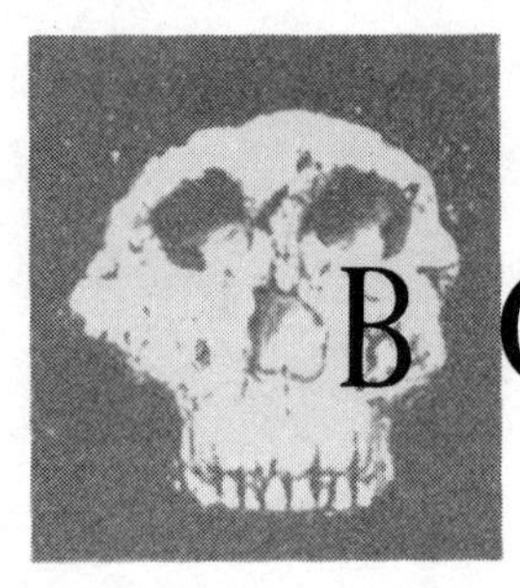BONES, *and*

ANCIENT CITIES

Lawrence H. Robbins, Ph.D.

St. Martin's Press New York

 For information, address St. Martin's Press, 175 Fifth Avenue, New York, N.Y. 10010.

DESIGN BY JUDITH A. STAGNITTO

Library of Congress Cataloging-in-Publication Data

Robbins, Lawrence H.
Stones, bones, and ancient cities : great discoveries in archaeology and the search for human origins / Lawrence H. Robbins.
p. cm.
Includes bibliographical references and index.
ISBN 0-312-07848-X (pbk.)
1. Antiquities. 2. Archaeology—History. 3. Civilization, Ancient. I. Title.
[CC165.R62 1990]
930—dc20 92-3449
CIP

First Paperback Edition : July 1992
10 9 8 7 6 5 4 3 2 1

For Dan, Brian, Michael, and Mark
and in memory of Mark Lynch

Contents

Preface

The roots of this book are many. As a student, I was drawn into archeaology by two classic works that captured the adventuresome side of archaeological discoveries—C. W. Ceram's *Gods, Graves and Scholars* and Geoffrey Bibby's *Testimony of the Spade*. An interest in the past was also kindled by my older brothers, whose imaginations knew no bounds.

More specifically, the idea of the book grew directly out of a course that I developed at Michigan State University called Great Discoveries in Archaeology. The course was aimed at nonspecialists in archaeology and was developed in response to a feeling that most of the standard courses in archaeology were missing most of the subjects that greatly interested the general public, ie., the spectacular finds. The class was successfully launched with TV shows, films, and slide presentations to back up the lectures. The one major obstacle was the lack of a suitable book for the course. The old standbys, while still being fascinating books, were badly out of date. Some of the new ones that were available were not balanced in the way that I wanted. For example, they did not go sufficiently into the human origins area, which technically falls mostly in the domain of physical anthropology. These are the reasons I decided to write this book.

My book is primarily about four areas: 1) The spectacular and important finds and the way they were made. 2) The personalities concerned with many of these discoveries. 3) The reaction to the finds and their impact on both science and the public. 4) Changing interpretations about the discoveries.

Any book of this kind is about other people's work, and mine is no exception. Without the field research and reports of many scholars, an overview of important discoveries in the field would not be possible. The full scope of this is reflected in the bibliography of this book, and I am naturally grateful to all of those who have provided the basic information that I have drawn on in this work. I am also grateful to many students and colleagues who have encouraged me in writing *Stones, Bones, and Ancient Cities*. Some of them have provided source materials for me and feedback on early versions of chapters. I would especially like to acknowledge the enthusiastic support given by the late Mark Lynch when this book was just an idea. I also want to thank Joseph Chartkoff, Russell Skowronek, and Kathryn Egan for providing important sources. Other help obtaining source material was provided by W. E. Wendt, J. D. Lewis-Williams, Gerald S. Hawkins, Brian M. Fagan, Anna Sofaer, J. A. Holman, J. E. Reyman, O. Bar-Yosef, F. Hassan, T. N. Huffman, and Lillian Phenice. John C. Trever, one of the central figures in the discovery of the discovery of the Dead Sea Scrolls, helped with my account of the scrolls. Special thanks are also due to Sergio Chávez for background information on the Inca and Machu Picchu. In addition, I am very grateful to Elsa Soms, who translated the old German script of Hans Reck's work on Olduvai Gorge. I fondly remember Simon Munyao, Noah Gachugi, and Peter Mwara, who once shared a moment of discovery with me at Lothagam. Certainly, that moment helped to stimulate an interest in the personal experiences of others in the process of discovery. There are other archaeologists whose sites I have visited, or from whom I have learned much in conversations, particularly in Africa. Among them are the late Glynn Isaac, Ronald Clarke, and James Denbow.

This book could not have been written without the help of my wife, Pat (Martha Robbins), who has gone over the manuscript in great detail and has made many important improvements in it. Thomas Strange kindly provided useful comments on Chapter 4. Special thanks are also due to Ed Stackler of St. Martin's Press for help in the production of the book. The toleration of my four children for lost time due to "Mom and Dad's work" is deeply appreciated, and a word of thanks is owed to Sunny the Parakeet, for not landing on the computer keyboard except on rare occasions. Finally, like others who write about other peoples' work, I am responsible for any errors that may appear.

Introduction

Many of us long for the chance to become explorers or pioneers. Our restless spirits seek the opportunity to discover the unknown, while rediscovering the ways of the past. Yet there are few real geographical frontiers left to explore on our planet. This book is about one that remains: the frontier that lies beneath the earth. This is not the fictional world at the earth's core created by Edgar Rice Burroughs or H. G. Wells, but the frontier of knowledge about the human past that has been sealed by the dust and decay of time.

Slowly and persistently, this frontier is being penetrated and decoded by archaeologists and other scientists. Much of what they find is not at all spectacular, but, pieced together, adds to our knowledge of the ordinary activities of ancient people. Although this more methodological information is often just as important, public attention has naturally focused on the spectacular finds and major breakthroughs in knowledge. After all, there is only one King Tut's tomb, one Altamira, and one Lucy.

Not all of the discoveries were made by professional archaeologists. Some were made by children, others by modern multidisciplinary expeditions. There were achaeological pioneers who "dreamed the impossible dream" about finding sites that few believed really existed and then went out and found them.

There are many fascinating examples of great discoveries in archaeology. It would take a lifetime of research and an encyclopedia-length book to do justice to them all. In addition, archaeologists would not all agree on what the greatest discoveries were. A rich tomb laden with gold may rank far down the list of importance in comparison to the development of a new way to microscopically examine the edges of 500,000-year-old stone tools and determine how these tools actually were used. In this book we will capture the spectacular, as well as some of those breakthroughs that rank high on archaeologists' lists of important finds, but which do not always reach the top newspapers.

Stones, Bones, and Ancient Cities

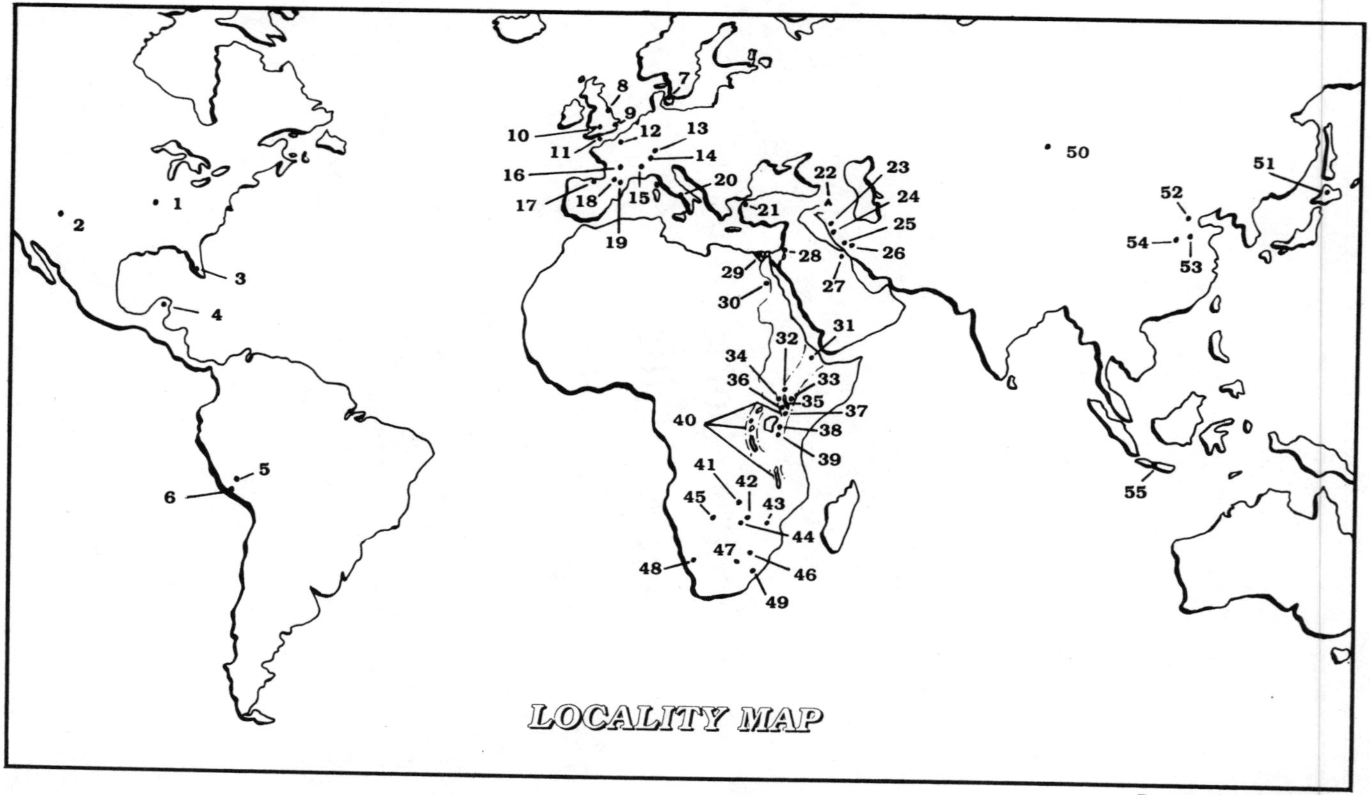

LOCALITY MAP

1 2 3 4 5 6 7 8 9 10 11 12 13 14 15 16 17 18 19 20 21 22 23 24 25 26 27 28 29 30 31 32 33 34 35 36 37 38 39 40 41 42 43 44 45 46 47 48 49 50 51 52 53 54 55

Drawing by Pat Robbins

1 Cahokia
2 Chaco Canyon
3 Little Salt Spring
4 Chichén Itzá
5 Machu Picchu
6 Nazca
7 Skudelev
8 Star Carr
9 Sutton Hoo
10 Stonehenge
11 Mary Rose
12 Abbeville
13 Robenhausen
14 Obermeilen
15 Paladru
16 Lascaux, Regourdou, La Mouthe
17 Altamira
18 Montespan
19 Les Trois Frères
20 Pompeii, Herculaneum
21 Hissarlik, Troy
22 Mt. Ararat
23 Shanidar
24 Nineveh
25 Ali Kosh
26 Susa
27 Ur
28 Dead Sea Scrolls, Qumran
29 Rosetta
30 Valley of the Kings, Tutankhamen
31 Hadar
32 Omo
33 East Turkana
34 West Turkana
35 Lake Turkana
36 Lothagam
37 Namoratunga
38 Olduvai Gorge
39 Laetoli
40 Rift Valley
41 Gwisho
42 Zimbabwe rock art
43 Great Zimbabwe ruins
44 East Botswana
45 San: Northwest Kalahari
46 Sterkfontein
47 Taung
48 Apollo 11
49 Giant's Castle
50 Pazyryk
51 Ainu
52 Zhoukoudian
53 Anyang
54 Qin-Shi-Huang Tomb
55 Solo River, Pithecanthropus

1

LINKS THAT ARE NO LONGER MISSING

The Most Ancient Frontier

It is unusual for a book about archaeological findings to include a discussion of the search for human fossils, to combine descriptions of such landmark discoveries as those of Machu Picchu, the lost city of the Incas, and the painted cave of Lascaux with accounts of the exciting quests for the very origins of humanity. Yet the milestones of human-origins research have helped to put the other discoveries in a broader context. Ancient tools become more interesting when one considers the hands that made them—hands that eventually evolved the capability of producing advanced technology and works of art.

Let us start with the first major discoveries of ancient fossils and proceed chronologically to more recent finds. We will be able to compare some of the pioneer discoveries with those that have been made very recently with the benefit of modern technology and large-scale funding. It will be impossible to conclude which of the finds ranks as the most important, because each provided critical new information at the moment of discovery and publication. We will see how not one but many missing links were revealed as the story of evolution unfolds.

BOUCHER DE PERTHES AND THE DAWN OF THE SEARCH FOR HUMAN ORIGINS

One of the most important breakthroughs in the history of archaeology was made by a French customs agent. Jacques Boucher de Perthes did not find a spectacular tomb, decipher a dead language, or discover a lost civilization hidden in tropical rain forests. In fact, he never found a human fossil. Yet he was one of the first to demonstrate convincingly that human ancestors had lived at the same time as animals that are now extinct. De Perthes' findings were far-reaching, because he demonstrated to a skeptical scientific audience that humans were older than had previously been believed.

Like many archaeological discoveries, de Perthes' were helped along by construction projects. During the 1830s there was much construction near the town of Abbeville in northern France, where de Perthes worked. This work exposed sections of ancient river deposits along the valley of the Somme, where de Perthes collected flint tools and bones of extinct animals such as elephant, rhinoceros, and hippopotamus. De Perthes argued that the animals and tools were associated and belonged to a remote period of time. Since none of these tropical animals inhabited Europe, de Perthes believed that the environment of France must have differed radically at the time when the stone tools were made. Initially, his views were rejected, and he was seen as someone who was out of touch with reality. Some critics argued that the Somme River deposits that had produced the artifacts and bones were recent in terms of age. De Perthes countered that if the deposits were really recent, he should be finding the bones of domesticated animals. In other words, he should have found cows instead of elephants. To this persuasive argument he added the cogent point that there were no metal tools, pottery, or other obviously recent implements; only *flint* tools were found. All the artifacts belong to what is now recognized by archaeologists as the Paleolithic period, or Old Stone Age, and the fossils date to the Pleistocene epoch, or Ice Age.

De Perthes' claims troubled his colleagues because they seriously challenged the prevailing beliefs of the early to mid-nineteenth century, which interpreted the age of the Earth and humankind in terms of the biblical account of the Creation and flood as described in the Book of Genesis. The world was thought to be quite young. In 1636, Archbishop James Ussher of Ireland had calculated from the life spans of individuals mentioned in the Old Testament that the Earth was created in the year 4004 B.C. To this exact date, John Lightfoot added that the Creation took place at 9:00 A.M. on October 23! The Ussher-Lightfoot chronology was accepted widely. Intellectually, there was little, if any, room for the serious belief in the coexistence of early humans and extinct animals before the period of the biblical flood. Yet this is what de Perthes claimed. Not surprisingly, de Perthes commented that some of his critics saw him as one who was heading down the road toward heresy.

Nonetheless, Boucher de Perthes continued to search in the gravel of the Somme and to publish his views despite overwhelming criticism. Interestingly, this ability to persist in the face of great opposition characterizes a number of other famous discoveries. The finding of the first major "missing link," the discovery of the legendary city of Troy, and the uncovering of King Tut's tomb are all classic examples that follow this pattern. De Perthes himself states, "The truth is not the work of anyone; it was created before us and is as old as the world; often looked for, but more often denied; one finds it, but one does not invent it."[1] Perhaps this statement should stand as a message to those who attempt to change prevailing opinions. No doubt there have been a large number of failures or successes that were never personally realized. On the other hand, science is normally built on verifiable evidence, and there have been many totally unfounded theories that have no claim to credibility.

De Perthes' great persistence finally produced results. The critical point came in 1858, when Hugh Falconer, an English geologist, visited France and personally viewed the sites and evidence. Falconer was convinced by what he saw and urged two of his associates, Joseph Prestwich and John Evans, to come to France and see for themselves. Although Prestwich was very skeptical, he changed his mind after actually viewing the evidence. One of the most convincing finds was a flint tool that had only recently been discovered and that was left *in situ* seventeen feet below the ground surface.

In 1859 Prestwich presented a scholarly paper to the Royal Society of London describing and verifying de Perthes' discoveries. The Royal Society included a "who's who" of the leading scientists in England, and Prestwich was highly respected by them. The main point of the paper was that the flint tools recovered at Abbeville were authentic; they had been made by humans and were found in an undisturbed geological context in association with extinct animals. The information was very carefully presented, and the audience generally accepted Prestwich's conclusions. De Perthes had managed to outlast the opposition. Eighteen fifty-nine, the year that de Perthes' findings were accepted, marks the birth of Stone Age archaeology. This was a significant year in other respects as well.

It was the year that Darwin's masterpiece *The Origin of Species* appeared. In this work, Darwin avoided the issue of human evolution. It was not until 1871, when *Descent of Man* was published, that he discussed his famous theory. Darwin postulated that humans were ultimately descended from apes, though he was careful to say that no living species of ape was a human ancestor. This point is sometimes overlooked, or at least misunderstood, by some antievolutionists who argue that since chimpanzees are alive at the present time, we could not be descended from them. While chimps are biologically our nearest living relatives, neither Darwin nor any modern evolutionist would claim that chimps were, in fact, our ancestors; however, their ancestors were very close to ours between about 10 million and 6 million years ago. Of course, Darwin did not have the benefit of modern biochemical studies and fossil evidence to demonstrate this point. Darwin also believed that humans originated in Africa. As will be shown, this was a remarkable bit of prophecy, given the fact that there were no early human fossils known from Africa in 1871. In fact, the scanty fossils that were available at that time included the Neandertal and Cro-Magnon remains, both European finds. They were clearly not apelike in their characteristics, though Neandertals did have large eyebrow ridges and a number of other archaic features. (Neandertals are generally considered an early form of *Homo sapiens* that lived between about 100,000 and 40,000 years ago, and Cro-

Magnon is an example of *Homo sapiens* that lived in what is now France in late Ice Age times, about 20,000 years ago.)

Darwin was not bothered by the lack of evidence to support his ideas about the role of Africa in human evolution, since nobody had seriously looked in the areas most likely to yield fossils. Nevertheless, Darwin believed that fossil remains would one day be found that would connect "man with some extinct ape-like creature. . . ."[2] This was none other than the so-called "missing link," a fossil that would bridge the gap between our ape ancestors and the first protohumans.

SPOTLIGHT ON THE FAR EAST

An amazing story in the annals of anthropological discoveries concerns a fossil known as Java man. Imagine quitting a well-paying job at a university in order to carry out a search on the other side of the world for something that most people did not really believe existed—and then finding it!

As a youth, Eugène Dubois sometimes searched for fossils that were in the ancient chalk deposits in the Netherlands. Perhaps this childhood experience helped to spark an interest in evolution. Most accounts of the work of Dubois state that he was strongly influenced by the ideas of Ernst Haeckel, who had published *Natural History of Creation* in 1866. This was five years before Darwin's *Descent of Man*. Like Darwin, Haeckel postulated that there was a connecting link between humans and apes. The last three stages in Haeckel's complex evolutionary scheme consisted of anthropoid (humanlike) apes, apemen, and modern humans. He had even gone so far as to name the hypothetical ape-man, calling it *Pithecanthropus allalus*, meaning ape (*pithe*) man (*anthropus*) without speech (*allalus*). Haeckel reasoned that this early ape-man would not have been developed enough to have had language.

While it is clear that Dubois used Haeckel's terms, fresh research done by Bert Theunissen on the work of Dubois downplays the influence of Haeckel as the driving force in his personal quest to find a fossil ape-man. Although Theunissen is not certain what motivated

Dubois to embark suddenly on a search for the "missing link," he suggests several factors that may have been instrumental. The background follows: Dubois was trained in medicine and became a lecturer in anatomy in 1886. Theunissen feels that Dubois developed a strong initial dislike for teaching. In addition, he became upset with one of his former teachers concerning a jointly published paper. Dubois felt that his own ideas were being downplayed in this paper. Dubois himself states that this was one of the reasons why he wanted to go to the Far East. Whatever the case may have been regarding the factors that motivated him, his decision to resign from the University of Amsterdam had a major impact on our knowledge of human evolution. The odds of finding a needle in a haystack were far better than what Dubois faced when he resigned his job so that he could hunt for the elusive fossil. The remarkable fact is that he found it —or found at least what would have to be considered the missing link of the nineteenth century.

Unable to raise money for his expedition or to secure official backing from the Dutch government for his work, Dubois enlisted in the Dutch army in 1887 as a medical officer. He saw this as a means of getting to the Dutch territories in the Far East in what is now Indonesia. Dubois believed that the fossil would be found in the Far East because its warm, tropical conditions were what one would theoretically expect as having been the habitat of early human ancestors. Another important fact was that apes, including gibbons and orangutans, lived in the area. Darwin had stated that humans were descended from apes and Dubois was aware of the fact that fossil apes had been found in the Siwalik hills area of what was then northern India. In addition, Haeckel had argued that humans most likely originated in southern Asia.

At first Dubois was stationed on Sumatra. The Sumatra phase of his work was arduous. He relates how he searched in the forest for caves, camping temporarily under rock shelters. He became very sick with high fevers on several occasions. Some of his workers deserted him and local people were reluctant to help him find caves because they were convinced he was after gold or other valuable deposits. This would have been enough to discourage most workers, but Dubois was very persistent. Meanwhile, a human skull had been found on the island of Java at Wadjak. While the skull proved to be of *Homo sapiens*, it suggested that Java might be a productive area to search. Although Java and Sumatra are islands, it should be mentioned that they had once been connected to the southeast Asian mainland due to low sea levels during the Ice Age. Therefore, early humans could have walked to these areas now isolated by the sea.

Theunissen presents an insightful analysis of Dubois' work on Java. One of the most important finds was made in 1891 when an engineer working for Dubois found a skull cap at the locality of Trinil. Apparently Dubois did not make any of the key finds personally. Dubois was quite excited by this find but was convinced the skull fragment was from a fossil chimpanzee. He named it *anthropopithecus*. The next year a fossil thigh bone was found that demonstrated the animal had walked upright. Therefore, Dubois added *erectus* as the species name (*Anthropopithecus erectus*). Later on he decided to change the name. According to Theunissen, one of the reasons for this dramatic change in ideas was that Dubois found that he had initially underestimated the brain size of the skull. New calculations demonstrated that it was much larger than an ape's. He then renamed it *Pithecanthropus erectus*, and considered the find "as a link connecting together Apes and Man . . ."[3] Dubois used Haeckel's name of *Pithecanthropus*, but changed the species designation of the ape-man to *erectus*, which meant that it had walked upright like humans rather than quadrupedally like apes. There were no face, hands, feet, or other major diagnostic parts of the body, and there were no other comparative early human specimens available from other sites. Because Dubois had recovered relatively little data, he would have a difficult time convincing the experts about the status of *Pithecanthropus*. Nonetheless, he strongly believed that he had discovered a missing link. The femur was very similar to a modern human femur and clearly demonstrated the presence of upright posture and bipedal locomotion. However, the skull cap revealed that the brain was significantly smaller than a present-day human's, but about twice the size of an ape's brain. Dubois' claims were opposed by many leading authorities. Some of his opponents argued that the skull belonged to a giant ape, possibly a relative of the gibbon. Dubois countered that this was a ridiculous assumption because an ape with a *Pithecanthropus*-sized brain of 900 cubic centimeters (cc.) would have had a body three times the size of a gorilla's. Dubois maintained that such an animal could not have lived in the trees like the acrobatic gibbons of southeast Asia. Other skeptics, pointing out that the leg and skull cap were found about fifteen meters apart, questioned whether they were really associated parts of the same animal.

The heated arguments about the status of *Pithecanthropus* continued, and Dubois became increasingly upset by them. Toward the end of the century, Dubois found a rather unusual way to resolve the problem: He is reported to have hidden the bones beneath the floor of his house in Holland! In great contrast to his previous behavior, Dubois would not let any scientists see the finds, and he is said to have imagined that thieves were trying to break into his house to steal the fossils. Nobody was allowed to see them until 1923, when Dr. Ales Hrdlicka, an anthropologist from the U.S. National Museum, arranged to meet Dubois, whom he described as "a big-bodied and big-hearted man." Hrdlicka writes, "He had all the specimens in his possession brought out from the strong boxes in which they are kept . . . and then permitted me to handle them to my satisfaction."[4]

Was *Pithecanthropus* an ape, a human, or something in between? The debates continued. What was needed to settle the argument was more complete information, and, luckily, new data were slowly forthcoming from the hills southwest of Beijing (Peking) in northern China. Near the town of Zhoukoudian (Choukoutien), local inhabitants had been collecting fossils that were sold as "dragons' bones" to traditional pharmacists, who ground the bones into powder for medicinal purposes. In 1921, several scientists were informed about a place known as Dragon Bone Hill. One of them, John Gunar Andersson, a geologist, noticed broken pieces of quartz in the deposits. Since the source of the quartz was some distance from the site, Andersson reasoned that the rocks had been brought to the site by humans. On that basis he believed that human fossils would eventually be found in the deposits. He was right, but it was not until 1927 that a human tooth, a molar, was found by Birgir Bohlin, a Swedish scientist. The fossilized tooth was studied by Davidson Black, a Canadian anatomist, who named it *Sinanthropus pekinensis*. He kept the tooth in a custommade container that hung from a gold chain. Obviously, little could be said in a comparative sense on the basis of a single molar tooth except that it appeared to be human. However, in 1929 Pei Wenzhong, who was in charge of the digging operations, found a skull, a find of great importance. As the work progressed, a very large collection of human fossils was unearthed from Zhoukoudian. Comparisons clearly revealed that Peking man was a close cousin to *Pithecanthropus erectus* from Java. If Peking man was human, so was the Java find.

This idea became more credible when additional bones were found on Java by G. H. R. von Koenigswald—notably the partial skull of *Pithecanthropus* 2. Working as a paleontologist in the 1930s, von Koenigswald had stimulated interest in his quest for fossils by offering rewards for significant finds and by holding festivals with "native orchestra and dancing girls." In 1937 von Koenigswald was shown where a fossil skull fragment had been found along a river bank, a little less than fifty miles from where Dubois' original finds had been made. With great excitement, von Koenigswald offered to pay his local workers for each additional fragment they could find by combing the slope. Much to his dismay, he discovered that "Behind my back they broke the larger fragments into pieces in order to increase the number of sales!"[5] Luckily, the pieces could all be reassembled. The skull was very similar to the original find but was more complete—a fact that helped to prove that Dubois' find was, indeed, an early form of human. Dubois, however, did not share von Koenigswald's excitement, having changed his mind about the whole issue. Ironically, Dubois was now convinced that what he had found was an ape and even attempted to discredit the find made by von Koenigswald.

In the same year that the new Java find was made, the work at Zhoukoudian stopped abruptly when the Japanese invaded China. It is fortunate that plaster casts and drawings were made of the key specimens from Zhoukoudian, because the originals, which included the fragments of at least forty individuals, were lost in the chaos that followed the invasion. It was widely believed that the boat that was carrying the fossils to safety was sunk in the Beijing harbor. Tragically for students of human evolution, the priceless data vanished.

Many years after nearly all authorities had assumed that the fossils were lost, hope has been rekindled that they might be found again. When the United States and mainland China started to thaw their relations with each other after years of nonrecognition on the part of the United States, a physician in New York disclosed that he had been a U.S. Marine officer responsible for the fossils at the time of the Japanese invasion of northern China. The doctor stated that the fossils had not been put on the boat that was sunk. He believed that they were, more than likely, still in China near the scene of the attack, where they may have been lost in the moments of confusion that accompanied the invasion. The doctor implied that a careful search of the area might lead to the fossils' rediscovery. Alternatively, the possibility was raised that the fossils had been removed from the country following the invasion. In the growing hope that the Beijing skulls would soon be found, a generous reward was offered for the return of the fossils. There have been some leads, including some photos that were used as evidence, but the whereabouts of the original fossils are still unknown.

Fortunately, Chinese scientists have found some additional fossils at the site, including part of a skull, recovered in 1966, that actually fit the plaster cast of a broken specimen found in the original work carried out in the 1930s! But these new fossil finds are relatively rare when compared with the original discoveries. Nonetheless, this new research has furthered our understanding of Zhoukoudian.

The main fossil locality was at Zhoukoudian, a large cave that had been gradually filled with about forty meters of deposits. It has been possible to distinguish thirteen layers, several of which have been dated. The most recent date from the upper three layers is about 230,000 years old (uranium-series method), while layer ten is approximately 460,000 years old (fission-track method).[6] Interestingly, recent studies, based on six relatively complete skulls, have suggested that the brain size of Peking man increased through time. Some evolutionary developments are also evident in the stone artifacts. These artifacts became smaller through time as new techniques were used to make the tools. Studies of fossil pollen grains have indicated that the ancient climate was similar to the temperate conditions found in northern China today, where winters are very cold. Generally, the landscape contained upland pine forest, deciduous forest, and areas of steppe in the lowlands. Some of the pollen was from edible plants, such as walnuts and hazelnuts, and there were also burned hackberry seeds found in the ash layers. In addition to wild plants, Peking man ate a wide variety of animals, most of which consisted of two kinds of deer.

There is general agreement that the Beijing and Java finds are closely related, and anthropologists now place them in a single group known as *Homo erectus*. The names *Pithecanthropus* and *Sinanthropus* are now used mainly for historical purposes. Specimens of *Homo erectus* are not very numerous, but more discoveries have been made since the pioneer efforts of Dubois and others. *Homo erectus* was widespread geographically: Remains have been discovered in Africa, Asia, and Europe. In Europe, stone hand axes made by *Homo erectus* have been found as far north as the southern part of England and northern France. These early humans lived from approximately 1.6 million years ago to about 200,000 years ago. The oldest *Homo erectus* fossil is a skull discovered in Kenya in East Africa that dates back to 1.6 million years ago. Many would conclude that *Homo erectus* originated in Africa and eventually moved to Asia and Europe. That the kinds of tools made by *Homo erectus* appeared much earlier in Africa than they did in other parts of the world supports this assumption. It is estimated that *Homo erectus* spread out of Africa about a million years ago.

Homo erectus averaged about five to five and a half feet in height and had a small brain, about three-quarters of the average modern size. Footprints found in East Africa and in southern France, along with skeletal evidence, show that *Homo erectus* could walk upright as efficiently as can modern people. There is debate about the language capabilities of *Homo erectus*, but I believe that some form of speech was present. This view can be supported if we briefly review the main cultural achievements of these early human ancestors. First of all, *Homo erectus* knew how to use fire. As mentioned earlier, hearths were found at the Zhoukoudian site, and there is other evidence of fire at several sites in Europe and Africa. The earliest evidence for fire consists of several hundred burned animal bone fragments from Swartkrans cave in South Africa. The deposits are estimated to date to between one and 1.8 million years ago. Comparative experiments based on burning modern antelope bones have revealed that the temperatures of the early fire at Swartkrans were similar to temperatures measured in present-day fires made from local species of South African trees.[7]

Homo erectus also used wooden spears (remarkably, at least two broken spears have survived) and cooperative hunting techniques.

Some of his stone tools were also made according to regular patterns, such as skillfully flaked hand axes found on many sites. Hand axes were most likely used for butchering animals, as well as for other functions. A final point that should be mentioned about the cultural status of *Homo erectus* is that some of the broken skulls found at Zhoukoudian may have resulted from the practice of cannibalism centering on the ritualistic eating of brains. It is difficult to imagine that all these activities were carried out without some form of language.

It was widely believed after the finds from Java and northern China gained acceptance that Asia was the birthplace of humanity. The main stumbling block to this viewpoint was provided by the Piltdown skull, which was found in England in the opening years of the twentieth century. Piltdown, with its large brain and primitive jaw, was an enigma. It simply did not match the Far Eastern skulls, which had much smaller brains and less primitive jaws. As it turned out, the "enigma" was resolved when the Piltdown remains were later shown to be a hoax. An ape's jaw had been filed, stained, and buried in ancient deposits along with a relatively recent human skull. Some think that Piltdown was a joke that was carried too far; others believe that the hoax came about because of deep-seated personal and professional jealousies among certain scientists. There are still arguments about who was responsible for the Piltdown forgery and what motivated that person.

A MONKEY'S SKULL IN SOUTH AFRICA VINDICATES DARWIN

Just four years before the first Beijing skull was found, another, even more significant fossil was discovered near Taung railroad station in South Africa, to the south of the Kalahari Desert. Nearly 2 million years ago, the skull of a monkey was incorporated in limestone deposits deep within a cave in the face of a cliff. In the early 1920s, the cliff was quarried for the limestone, and, about fifty feet below ground level, the monkey's skull, along with other fossils, was blasted out of the cliff. Had the quarrying not taken place, or had the dynamite blasted the skull to pieces, our knowledge of human evolution might have been very different. Fossil monkeys were rare in

Africa, and the discovery of one near the edge of the Kalahari Desert was unprecedented.

The skull was brought to Raymond Dart, an anatomist at the University of Witwatersrand in Johannesburg. A colleague who was going to the Taung area for geological work brought back additional fossils in a heavily encrusted matrix. One of them revealed the negative impression of a brain of what Dart first believed was another monkey. Part of a lower jaw was visible in another piece of rock that, Dart noticed, fitted onto the piece with the brain impression. Dart worked diligently, slowly chipping away at the encrusted fossil. After several months of work, the face of the animal was uncovered. When considered together, the face, jaw, and brain impression indicated to Dart that the animal was, in fact, not a monkey. In addition, the animal clearly contrasted with any of the living apes or, for that matter, any known fossil ape or human. The animal's dentition was strikingly humanlike. The shape of the dental arcade (rows of teeth) was evenly rounded, rather than in parallel rows like that of a chimpanzee. Dart reasoned that since only the first permanent molar tooth had erupted, the skull belonged to a juvenile individual about six years old. In 1925, Dart announced that it belonged to "an extinct race of apes *intermediate between living anthropoids and man*."[8] He dubbed his discovery *Australopithecus africanus*, which meant southern ape of Africa. Dart believed that *Australopithecus* was more advanced than any living ape and was, in fact, similar to what one would expect "in an extinct link between man and his simian ancestor." He felt that *Australopithecus* was a kind of man-ape, that is, a humanlike ape. Dart went on to state that the fossil evidence had verified that Darwin had been right in postulating that Africa was the birthplace of humanity.

At first, Dart's claims were rejected widely in a manner that followed the pattern of the de Perthes and Dubois finds. For example, Sir Arthur Keith, a prominent British anatomist, called Dart's interpretation of *Australopithecus* "preposterous."[9] Keith argued that *Australopithecus* was no more than "an extinct relative of the chimpanzee and gorilla." Furthermore, he maintained that the Java find was, in fact, "the only known link between man and ape, and this extinct type lies on the human side of the gap." One of the major difficulties in attempting to resolve the arguments about the status of *Australo-*

pithecus centered on the juvenile skull. Skeptics questioned interpretations given without any knowledge of what an adult skull looked like. Because an infant-chimpanzee skull looks more like a human skull than the skull of an adult chimp, it was reasoned that perhaps an adult *Australopithecus* skull would show much stronger resemblances to an ape. Another problem was that there were no other bones that could be used to compare *Australopithecus* with humans and apes. The discovery of bones of the leg, foot, and hip would have had a critical bearing on resolving whether *Australopithecus* walked upright or, like apes, quadrupedally. Further search was underway.

Sterkfontein is another limestone quarry, located about forty-five minutes' drive from Johannesburg near the town of Krugersdorp. A 1935 sightseer's guidebook to the greater Johannesburg area actually stated: "Come to Sterkfontein and find the missing link." As remarkable as it might seem, a year later Robert Broom did just what the guidebook suggested. Broom, a physician and paleontologist, was a follower of Dart's controversial views. Broom relates that he asked the director of the Sterkfontein quarry to keep a close watch for fossils that might be like the Taung child. One day the quarry director handed him a "blasted out natural brain cast of an anthropoid."[10] The director asked him, "Is this what you're after?" In a matter-of-fact way, Broom replied, "That's what I'm after." After a careful search, Broom found more of the cast as well as pieces of the skull and teeth. This was the first adult *Australopithecus* skull. Later on, more finds were recovered from the site. One of the best-preserved skulls was discovered when Broom literally blasted it out of a piece of solid rock! The new material from Sterkfontein, which also included the remains of a pelvis, strongly supported Dart's position. Eventually, five different *Australopithecus* sites were located in South Africa. As work progressed, carried out by Dart, Broom, and others, it became apparent that there were at least two distinctive kinds of australopithecines (a collective or group name that is commonly used). One kind, *Australopithecus africanus*, was about four feet in height and had a brain about as large as that of a gorilla. The other kind, which most authorities believe belongs to a different species, is often known as *Australopithecus robustus*. It was somewhat larger and had much more massive jaws and molar teeth. The robust examples are also known for the prominent ridge, or crest, on top of the skull, which is lacking on the more gracile *A. africanus* specimens. The ridge was where strong muscles attached to the top of the skull, much as is seen in a large male gorilla. The two species were never found together at the same sites, and stratigraphic and faunal evidence indicated that the robust ones were more recent in age. However, the actual age was unknown, since none of the deposits could be dated.

Clearly, both kinds of the australopithecines had walked upright. They were not apes, nor were they humans. I like to think of them as protohumans. They are classified as members of the zoological family known as Hominidae and are commonly called hominids by anthropologists. This is the family to which we belong, as well as all of our ancestors from the time that they diverged from the apes somewhere in Africa.

As more South African early hominids were discovered, important questions were posed. How old were they? What was the evolutionary relationship between the two species of *Australopithecus*? Was one of them the ancestor of *Homo erectus* and subsequently, in the remote sense, ourselves? These questions were debated by anthropologists through the 1950s and 1960s and are still the source of much discussion. Later, I will return to these questions after additional discoveries have been introduced that have an important bearing on them.

The monkey's skull at Taung opened up the search for human origins in Africa. No longer could scientists dismiss Africa as a center of early hominid evolution. But the search shifted in intensity from the South African limestone quarries to East Africa, where the most exciting discoveries have been made in the last few decades. These finds have revolutionized what is known about human origins.

OLDUVAI GORGE

The East African search started in what is now the northern part of Tanzania at the site of Olduvai Gorge. Olduvai is a remarkable place that resembles a smaller version of the Grand Canyon cut into the edge of the vast Serengeti Plain. About 300 feet of deposits have been exposed through a combination of faulting and stream erosion. There are five main beds, consisting of variable amounts of lake, stream, and volcanic deposits. These beds contain an abundance of stone tools and fossil animals, as well as hominid remains. Frequently, the remains of bones and artifacts are found littering the eroded slopes of the gorge, and the sites can be located by excavating into the adjacent deposits. The gorge can be considered an important standard for measuring human evolution through time. The base of Bed I is about 1.8 million years old, while the upper part of Bed V, near the top of the gorge, chronicles events that are only about 17,000 years old. Olduvai is a unique site in terms of the length of time covered and the abundance of remains, and it is considered one of the most important archaeological sites known. The little-known details of its discovery are a story in themselves.

In the opening years of this century, Olduvai Gorge was a long way from the main areas of colonial settlement in what was known as German East Africa. There were no roads, and the immediate area was basically unexplored. Much of the Serengeti was inhabited by the Masai, a proud and independent people who were feared by many. In addition, lions, leopards, buffalo, rhino, and other big game thrived on the Serengeti Plain, which is still famous for large herds of animals.

In 1911 a German entomologist named Kattwinkel was collecting butterflies when he accidentally wandered into the gorge. He found some fossil animal bones and carried them back across the hot, dry Serengeti. These fossils were transported back to Germany, where they aroused great curiosity about the area. Hans Reck, a geologist, was sent to East Africa to locate Olduvai and to search for more fossils. Reck was given a crude explorers' map of the region, with the approximate location marked, and some photographs taken by Kattwinkel.

Reck set out through the rugged East African landscape in 1913 with a large group of Africans who assisted in carrying his supplies. Reck walked through what he described as "a hell of heat," where the rocks were actually so hot that he burned his fingers while climbing over them.[11] Water was scarce and often, when it could be found, not good to drink. His route led to the slopes of the extinct crater Ngorongoro. This massive volcano is in some respects like a lost world. The rim of the crater is covered by thick forest and is often shrouded in fog and clouds. Reck climbed the crater searching for Adolf Siedentopf, a German settler who lived a hermitlike existence on Ngorongoro. Reck felt that he might learn more about Olduvai from Siedentopf, but the latter was much feared, as his reputation closely matched the literal translation of his name, which is "boiling pot." He treated Ngorongoro as his own private kingdom and went out of his way to exclude others. According to Reck, when local herdsmen were not quick enough in answering Siedentopf, he shot at their feet! Reck, however, was careful enough in his behavior so as to get along very well with the quick-tempered Siedentopf. While the settler did not actually know where the gorge was, he did have a vague recollection that Kattwinkel had come from an area known as the Balbal Depression, which was situated to the west of the crater. Siedentopf provided two Masai guides to take Reck to the west side of the volcano, where there was a freshwater spring.

After leaving the volcano's slopes, Reck headed for the open plains. Filled with the anticipation of finding Olduvai, he moved hastily ahead of his helpers, leaving most of them behind. This was a lucky move for Reck, because lions attacked his main camp that night and ripped the window screen of his tent to shreds.

Visibility on the open grasslands of East Africa can be almost unlimited when the view is not obscured by dust or shimmering, miragelike reflections that look like small lakes. As Reck crossed the plains, he began to wonder whether he would ever find Olduvai in such a vast and deceptive area. His doubts quickly faded when he noticed a canyon in the distance, etched into the dry landscape like a dark ribbon. But when he actually compared his view of the gorge with Kattwinkel's photographs, the two scenes simply did not match. With considerable disappointment, he followed the gorge only to find that it ended abruptly. When he climbed over the rim onto the adjacent plains, he saw only "the wide blanket of Serengeti . . . without any gorges . . . scornfully sneering." As Reck traveled farther, the plains became "more and more romantic and sinister."

Soon he came to another valley, where he found an overlook marked heavily with rhinoceros tracks. The view troubled Reck because he had the sensation that he had already been to the place. Then it suddenly dawned on him to look again at Kattwinkel's photos. Much to his surprise, the photos matched the landscape perfectly. Hans Reck had reached his destination after traveling about 200 kilometers, in about two weeks. This is quite remarkable, given the general conditions and the available information.

Reck spent several months at Olduvai collecting fossils, studying the geology, and generally exploring. He lived off the land by shooting wild game. He remarked that usually about two wildebeests would last for about a week in his camp of approximately fifty people. There was a muddy water hole at the gorge that his crew shared with a pride of lions, and other animals which fouled the water. Reck, however, had his personal fresh water brought daily from a distant spring.

Olduvai did not disappoint Reck. The fantastic gorge yielded hundreds of animal fossils. Toward the end of his stay at Olduvai, Reck discovered human remains that he believed were associated with the extinct animals; he had found the bones of an anatomically modern human. This find was of great interest because the deposits were surprisingly old to contain modern human bones. Later on, other researchers demonstrated that Reck's skeleton was actually a burial, in which the burial pit had intruded into the ancient deposits. We now know through radiocarbon dating that the skeleton is only about 17,000 years old, but Reck had no way of knowing this when he found the remains.

Reck's Olduvai expedition was a great success. He planned to return to the site but was prevented by the outbreak of World War I. The fossil-laden beds of Olduvai Gorge would lie fallow until 1931, when a new expedition would reveal more of the gorge's secrets. This one was led by Louis Leakey, who had met Reck previously in Germany. Leakey, the son of missionaries, had been raised in Kenya among the Kikuyu people. Most anthropologists feel that he knew more about the Kikuyu than any other person of European descent; he spoke their language well enough to dream and think in it. Leakey was educated at Cambridge University in England, where he studied anthropology. Interestingly, Leakey's mentors at Cambridge strongly advised him not to follow through with his plans to return to East Africa to look for human ancestors, because at that time it was believed widely that humankind had originated in Asia. (This was before Dart's surprising announcement of the discovery of *Australopithecus africanus* in South Africa.) Fortunately, Louis Leakey was rather like Dubois and de Perthes in sticking to his convictions.

In many ways he was even more tenacious, especially in maintaining his interpretations of the fossil record in the face of severe criticisms.

Leakey's first expedition to Olduvai included Hans Reck, A. Tindell Hopwood, who was a leading authority on fossils from Britain, and Captain J. Hewlett, a noted hunter. In addition, there was a staff of eighteen Africans. Leakey decided to drive to Olduvai despite Reck's advice that it would be impossible to reach the gorge through the rough terrain. They had to stop frequently to let the overheated engines of their heavily loaded trucks cool down. It was a difficult drive, but they managed to reach Olduvai in about four and a half days.

Leakey's description of the 1931 Olduvai expedition is punctuated with excitement. He reports that their camp was surrounded at night with the glowing eyes of hyenas and lions. On another occasion during the trip he relates that when Reck and Hewlett "were on duty with a water party they had a pitched battle with some lions, while on another occasion I was charged point-blank by an angry rhinoceros and had to kill it in self defense."[12] The Olduvai area is still very much alive with animals: I won't easily forget being routed from the gorge by a rhinoceros while working there as a student.

Leakey's first expedition to Olduvai was as productive as it was personally thrilling for him. A large number of fossils were unearthed, as well as early stone tools. While no human fossils were discovered, the finding of tools was very important proof that early humans had lived at Olduvai. Louis Leakey felt that it would only be a matter of time and patient searching before human fossils would be found.

Subsequent expeditions to Olduvai were also rewarding and sometimes adventurous. The archaeological sites were of special interest. Never before had so many sites of such great antiquity been found in one area. In contrast to most of the early sites known from Europe, the artifacts and associated animals' bones had not been disturbed greatly or redeposited by the action of rivers. Louis Leakey and his wife, Mary, realized that the careful excavation of these sites afforded the potential to recover information on aspects of early human behavior that was previously unknown. They were pioneers in the development of modern field methods for excavating early hominid occupation sites. They often used the step-trench method, by which one digs carefully into the side of the hill until a significant cultural layer is encountered and then exposed on a horizontal surface. After mapping the position of all the bones and artifacts, a vertical step is formed as one proceeds down the slope from the edge of the previous occupation surface in the search for underlying older levels. The completion of the excavation reveals a section through the deposits where the various layers are exposed like huge steps down the hillside. In this fashion, the data from the various sites can be compared, and one can gain a more complete picture of the range of different activities carried out by early hominids as well as study cultural changes through time. "Culture," in this sense, refers to a related tradition of toolmaking.

The oldest deposits at Olduvai (Bed I and lower Bed II) contained a new stone-artifact tradition that was simpler than any other and that is still recognized as the oldest Stone Age culture. Known as the Oldowan, it is characterized by flaked pebble choppers and flake tools that have been shaped along their edges. While we give these tools specific names, in most cases we do not know their exact use. Such tools were most likely used for cutting meat, scraping, pounding, and possibly working crudely in wood. The Oldowan tools were made from volcanic rocks and quartz, both of which were available in the immediate area. In contrast to the Acheulian (handaxe culture) that follows, the tools are unstandardized in terms of formal shape characteristics, and there is also no evidence suggesting the use of fire or wooden spears. The Oldowan artifacts have provided a logical antecedent for those of the more widespread Acheulian and have extended our knowledge of protohuman tool-making abilities back to nearly 2 million years ago. In fact, in the Afar triangle of Ethiopia, Oldowan tools have been discovered which may be as much as 2.5 million years old.

Along with the tools at Olduvai lie many broken bones of extinct species of tortoise, pigs, antelope, giraffe, elephant, and equids, as well as other animals. Were these bones the leftovers of early hominid meals? To what extent were the earliest hominids at Olduvai hunters? An interesting story centers on this issue. Pat Shipman and other researchers, using scanning electron microscopes, have found cut marks on some of the fossil bones.[13] These match marks produced experimentally on modern bones by using sharp-edged stone flakes similar to those used at Olduvai. This tells us that the meat was butchered, but Shipman has also found carnivore tooth marks and other evidence implying that the animals were probably first killed by big cats such as saber tooths, lions, and leopards and that the early hominids scavenged from them.

A particular Oldowan site known as DK I, one of the oldest in the gorge, is dated to about 1.8 million years ago. Excavations uncovered a circle of volcanic rocks that measured about fourteen feet in diameter. According to Mary Leakey, these rocks were intentionally brought into the site and were most likely used to reinforce the base of a shelter in which branches were used as a superstructure. After such temporary shelters are abandoned, the flimsy superstructure eventually deteriorates and only the outline of stones is left. I have seen similar shelters in use recently in parts of northern Kenya and Uganda. On the other hand, I have also seen roughly circular patterns of stones that have been formed naturally by the uprooting of trees. If Mary Leakey's interpretation is correct, the circle could be considered the world's oldest artificial structure, albeit a very simple one. More importantly, from the social viewpoint, it suggests that a related group of hominids used the shelter as a temporary camp. Near the circle was a dense scatter of Oldowan tools, along with broken animal bones. Many of these bones were probably splintered for their marrow. The DK I site was situated very close to the edge of a large, ancient lake. Impressions of roots found in the deposits at the site are very similar to root imprints left by papyrus plants at the shore of a small lake that still exists near Olduvai.

Before continuing with the story of the discoveries at Olduvai, some further comments about L. S. B. Leakey are of interest. He was one of the most colorful personalities in human origins research; there are many stories about his work in the bush. I will add a brief one here. Long ago, I remember going with him as a student to the site of Laetoli in northern Tanzania. We encountered a bush fire that blocked the track we were following in the Landrover. Leakey ordered us out of the vehicle while one of his assistants ran through the smoke to indicate the route. Leakey calmly drove through the smoke while we safely walked around the smoldering area and joined him. He was an energetic field worker who had an uncanny natural intuition about where to search for fossils. Through the years, he always seemed to have the knack for announcing new landmark fossil finds much as a magician pulls rabbits out of a hat. Usually, the finds were given new names and were often viewed as the earliest of our ancestors. Others argued about his interpretations, and his theories were often seen as farfetched. He was very forceful about promoting his own ideas while at the same time encouraging others to be open-minded. Leakey has also been cast as being possessive or territorial about his research by making it difficult for others to work in the same area. On the other hand, he helped to pave the way for the first multidisciplinary project in human origins research in East Africa. In addition, Leakey was the spark that stimulated Jane Goodall's famous study of chimpanzees and Dian Fossey's mountain gorilla project.

While Louis Leakey was the driving force who personally popularized Olduvai Gorge, he did not make the most famous fossil discovery at the gorge. It was Mary Leakey who found it in July 1959 while searching the slopes of Bed I. In fact, Louis Leakey was sick and resting in his tent when his wife found the fragmented remains of an early hominid skull. The excitement of the discovery soon brought Louis Leakey out of his tent and restored his health. The skull was pieced together and was named *Zinjanthropus* (East African man). Further study of the skull has convinced most experts that *Zinjanthropus* is really a special East African version of a robust australopithecine now called *Australopithecus boisei*. This in no way diminishes, however, the historical importance of the discovery. It was sensational news, especially because it was the very first protohuman fossil found in deposits that could be dated. Unlike those of the South African sites, deposits surrounding *Zinjanthropus* were of the wind-blown volcanic variety. The newly developed potassium-argon technique dated the volcanic tuff as being an astonishing 1.75 million years old. Since this was the first date on an australopithecine site, it was of tremendous importance. It nearly doubled the time span that many authorities had suspected for the likely age of the australopithecines. This early date actually made many evolutionists more comfortable, for it greatly extended the amount of time for humans to have emerged from their more apelike forebears.

Furthermore, the date was significant because Oldowan tools were found at the site, and this meant that the ability to make stone tools was considerably older than many anthropologists had believed. At first, Louis Leakey believed that *Zinjanthropus* was responsible for making the Oldowan tools. This was a most important conclusion, since none of the South African sites had revealed clear associations between australopithecines and tools. There were, in fact, serious arguments about whether or not australopithecines were capable of making stone tools. Although the association between *Zinjanthropus* and tools appeared to settle the problem, future discoveries at Olduvai caused Leakey to change his mind about who had made the Oldowan tools.

In 1960, Jonathan Leakey, one of Louis and Mary's sons, found a new site in Bed I that was actually lower in the deposits than the *Zinjanthropus* site. Here, Jonathan discovered some skull fragments and the lower jaw of a child who was about twelve years old at the time of death. The bones of the "pre-Zinj child," along with some similar specimens found elsewhere at the gorge, impressed the Leakeys as being more modern or humanlike in appearance than *Zinjanthropus*, yet the new finds were at least as old, if not older. The new fossil hominids were called *Homo habilis* (handy man). The genus name *Homo* was an immediate indication that Handy man was a closer relative to *Homo sapiens* than any australopithecine, such as *Zinjanthropus*. Louis Leakey was convinced that *Homo habilis* was the true remote ancestor of ourselves, whereas the australopithecines, as a general group, were side branches in the human evolutionary tree —an experiment that failed. Thus, a logical conclusion was that the slightly larger-brained and more human-looking *Homo habilis* was the real maker of the Oldowan tools. Hence, the popular name "Handy man."

The reaction to *Homo habilis* was similar to what happened in the case of other landmark fossil discoveries. Many anthropologists disagreed openly with Leakey's interpretation. They did not accept *Homo habilis* as a new kind of hominid that was significantly different from at least some of the australopithecines. The opposition claimed that a close inspection revealed that the *Homo habilis* remains fell within the expectable range of variation of the South African *Australopithecus africanus* fossils. An immediate consequence of this view was that *Homo habilis* was really an East African version of *Australopithecus africanus*. Was this a case of new wine in old bottles? As will be shown, *Homo habilis* gained credibility when more convincing evidence was found east of Lake Turkana. Moreover, the pendulum has also swung in the direction of accepting *Homo habilis* as the most likely tool maker in Bed I at Olduvai. While the debate continued, one point was overwhelmingly clear: The work at Olduvai had pushed the dawn of humankind back to nearly 2 million years ago. The exciting finds at Olduvai stimulated a host of new questions. Paramount among them was whether the roots of our earliest ancestors could be traced back still further into the past.

It was becoming clear that the most likely place to search was in the great Rift Valley. This is a giant crack in the earth that extends from the Red Sea area through much of eastern Africa. The Rift was formed over an extensive period of time by faulting, a product of movement of the continental plates and spreading of the sea floor. This faulting, together with erosion, exposed sites like Olduvai, which would otherwise be deeply buried. Much of the Rift Valley, notably the part that extends from northern Kenya through Ethiopia, had not been explored scientifically when *Zinjanthropus* was discovered in 1959.

THE LAKE TURKANA BASIN

Sometimes sites are discovered by a combination of clues and good luck. We have already seen how "dragons' bones" led to the discovery of Zhoukoudian. The site of Lothagam is another case in point. In 1965 I was searching for archaeological sites near the western shore of Lake Turkana, which is a Rift Valley lake in northern Kenya. The area that I was exploring was essentially desert, inhabited by the nomadic Turkana people. There were few roads, and bandits and cattle raiders were still active in the area. One day a local schoolteacher visited my camp, which consisted of two tattered British Army tents, a drum of gasoline, and another of water. He asked me what I was doing and told me that I ought to look on the other side of a hill known as Lothagam. Although he had never been there, tribal elders said that there was a place where bones could be found that were "hard as stone." I could see the tip of the hill sticking out like a ship across the desert, and it looked as though it might intersect with the ancient beach deposits of Lake Turkana. It was worth a chance.

Together with a crew of three Kenyans, I drove across the dry Turkwel River valley in a rickety old Landrover. We drove through about fifteen or twenty miles of shifting sand dunes only to find that the way around the hill to the alleged fossil site was virtually blocked by sand and extremely rugged terrain. From a distance, Lothagam looked like one hill, but, in fact, there were two. We thought that we could find a short cut to the other side by attempting to pass between the hills via a maze of narrow erosion gullies. The steep-sided gullies eventually became impassable right in the middle of the hills. Dejectedly, we got out of the vehicle and climbed over the gullies to have a closer look at the barren, moonlike landscape of the interior of Lothagam. Much to our surprise, we found that we were right in the middle of ancient lake beds strewn with bones, shellfish, and artifacts.

Underneath the lake beds were much older red-colored deposits that contained fossils. My job as an archaeologist was to investigate the artifact-bearing lake beds, which proved to be about 7,500 years old. I reported that the underlying red beds should be researched by specialists in earlier fossils. Brian Patterson, a paleontologist from Harvard University who was working in a nearby area, subsequently investigated the early beds at Lothagam; he determined that they were between 8 million and 5 million years old. This was the period that theoretically covered the time when many believe that the first protohumans separated from their ape ancestors—clearly an important gap in the record. Patterson's group found many new fossils at Lothagam. The most notable was a jaw fragment that has proved to be a real bone of contention. Some of the experts see it as protohuman and, as such, the oldest (dated to about 5.5 million years), while others say it belongs to an ape. In an attempt to clarify the situation Henry M. McHenry and Robert S. Corruccini compared measurements of the Lothagam specimen with both living and fossil apes as well as with australopithecines and other hominids. Their statistical analysis supported that the specimen is intermediate between the ape sample and hominids. Perhaps it represents a transitional form. Lothagam is one of those enigmas, but it may be that more complete evidence will be found there.

Meanwhile, plans were underway to investigate another area known as the Omo Valley, located to the north of Lake Turkana in southern Ethiopia. Fossils had already been collected at Omo in 1932 when a French expedition visited the area. The Omo expedition, which began in 1967, was international in scope. The driving force behind it was F. Clark Howell, who headed the American team. There was also a French contingent directed by Camille Arambourg, who had done the original work in 1932, and a Kenyan group led by Richard Leakey, another son of Louis and Mary Leakey. The Omo expedition contrasted with most of the earlier research on human origins. First of all, it was supported by substantial research grants that resulted in an abundance of equipment, including four-wheel-drive vehicles, boats, an airplane, and even a helicopter. In addition, the Omo project was multidisciplinary in the sense that it involved the cooperation of scientists from different fields, such as geology, paleontology, and archaeology. I think the expedition signaled the end of an era in human-origins research. The days when a single researcher could follow an educated guess and work independently of others on a shoestring budget were mostly over. The well-funded, multidisciplinary approach greatly increases the chances of finding fossils, and, almost as important, it increases the amount and validity of the information about dating, paleoenvironmental conditions, and other factors.

At Omo, a great many fossils were found, such as early forms of elephants, pigs, antelopes, and other animals, along with numerous australopithecine remains. While the Omo work yielded nothing as spectacular as the skull of *Zinjanthropus*, the overall data obtained were in many respects more important, particularly in regards to dating. The fossil deposits sampled a period of time that had not been dated previously. Potassium-argon dates on the volcanic layers showed the main part of the Omo sequence to be between 1.5 and 3 million years old. This pushed the dates of our remote ancestors even further into the past than did the deposits of Olduvai. Furthermore, it provided a sample of well-dated animals, especially pigs and elephants, that could be used as a comparison for other sites. In other words, here was a means of cross-dating in the event future sites were discovered that contained similar animals. Finally, some stone artifacts were recovered that dated back about 2 million years, making them slightly older than Bed I at Olduvai.

The Omo expedition contained the seeds of further discoveries. Richard Leakey, the director of the Kenyan team, was flying in a small plane from Nairobi to the Omo Valley when he noticed what appeared to be extensive exposures of deposits over the remote northeastern shore of Lake Turkana. Leakey followed up on his aerial view with a visit to the exposures and found that they were exceptionally rich in fossils. Subsequently, the East Turkana area became the "hot spot" for the human-origins search, and many of the key discoveries of the 1970s were made there. Richard Leakey had learned much by growing up in East Africa and working at Olduvai and other sites. He carried on the family tradition of being a skillful field worker and a master of organizing expeditions to remote areas. A permanent field station was eventually constructed along the lake shore at Koobi Fora, including an airstrip, quarters for visiting scientists, a field laboratory, and other facilities. Here, ongoing work could be conducted without the periodic disruption of closing down a temporary camp, packing everything in trucks, and deserting the area. Another great strength of the East Turkana work was that, through the years, the National Museum had developed a staff of Kenyans who specialized in finding human fossils. These "hominid hunters," led by Kimoya Kimeu, found a very large number of fossil hominids. In fact, most of the East Turkana hominid remains were found by them rather than by the visiting scientists or expedition leaders.

The most spectacular find was made by Bernard Ngeneo, one of the hominid hunters. It consisted of the skull of a hominid known as KNM ER 1470. (All specimens are given a museum number in Kenya, and a permanent marker with this number is placed on the site of discovery. This is done to ensure that the site can be relocated in the event future questions arise about the find.) The new skull possessed a braincase significantly larger than that of any known *Australopithecus* (775 cc. versus 500 cc. for *Australopithecus* and about 1,330 cc. for present-day humans).[14] Several other characteristics, such as the angle of the face, appeared to be more modern in comparison to *Australopithecus*. Hominid 1470 was a good candidate for the *Homo habilis* group and was much more complete than the controversial evidence from Olduvai. Furthermore, the dating of the skull was very exciting. It was found below a layer dated at 2.6 million years, and it was estimated that the skull was nearly 3 million years old. Few of the experts would have guessed that the *Homo* lineage could be this old. An additional point of great interest was that a well-preserved, robust *Australopithecus* skull was discovered higher up in the deposits and found to be less than 2.6 million years old. Taken together, the new finds from Lake Turkana supported the contentions that (1) *Homo habilis* really was a valid species distinct from the australopithecines and (2) *Homo habilis* was older than the australopithecines in terms of ultimate roots. Both strongly supported the theory that *Homo habilis* was indeed, a "true" human ancestor, while the australopithecines, as a group, were side branches in human evolution that became extinct.

A serious problem developed, however, regarding the dating of 2.6 million years. Scientists who had worked extensively with the fossil animals at Omo compared their findings with the East Turkana animals, and the results differed. The kinds of animals at Lake Turkana thought to be 2.6 million years old were too recent for that age, according to the Omo scientists. They suspected that the East Turkana dates were wrong. For this reason new samples were obtained and dated by a different lab using a more refined potassium-argon technique. The new results were internally consistent and indicated an age of about 1.8 million years instead of 2.6 million years. This reduced the age of hominid 1470 considerably and weakened the argument that *Homo habilis* was much older than the australopithecines.

A large number of other hominid fossils have been recovered from East Turkana, including more fragmentary remains of *Homo habilis* as well as robust australopithecines. Another significant discovery was a relatively complete *Homo erectus* skull similar to those found in the Far East. This Lake Turkana skull is 1.6 million years old and, together with a new find from the opposite side of Lake Turkana, is one of the oldest known examples of *Homo erectus*. The new West Turkana find is quite unusual. It was discovered in August 1984 by Kimoya Kimeu, who noticed some bones eroding from deposits on the northwest side of the lake at a place called Nariokotome. Excavations by Richard Leakey uncovered the nearly complete skeleton of a twelve-year-old *Homo erectus* boy who died about 1.6 million years ago. This is far and away the most complete *Homo erectus* skeleton known. Because of its completeness, it is possible to reconstruct the size of the boy and estimate his probable height as an adult. Large for twelve years old, the boy stood about five feet, four inches tall and weighed about 150 pounds. Leakey and his associate, Alan Walker, have speculated that fully grown the youth from West Turkana would have been at least six feet tall.[15] This new specimen hints that *Homo erectus* may have been much larger than many anthropologists have thought.

The northwest Turkana basin continues to yield other exciting finds. In 1985, Leakey's team returned to the sun-scorched landscape and found two *Australopithecus boisei* specimens, a skull and a partial jaw. The skull is similar to the *Zinjanthropus* find from Olduvai. The new West Turkana fossils are the oldest examples of *A. boisei* known, dated at about 2.5 million years.

In addition to the wealth of new fossils, an abundance of Early Stone Age archaeological sites have been found at Lake Turkana. Some of these are Oldowan sites, including an intriguing hippo-butchery site about 1.8 million years old. This is one of the earliest sites known at which a large and dangerous animal was butchered. Was this animal actually killed by the early hominids, or was its carcass found and eaten? More than likely the latter explanation is true.

In an effort to determine just how the Oldowan tools were used, archaeologists Lawrence Keeley and Nicholas Toth have examined Lake Turkana stone artifacts about 1.5 million years old under incident-light microscopes. Keeley pioneered techniques in the 1970s that showed that distinctive polishes indicating meat cutting, hide scraping, and woodworking are produced on the edges of stone tools. The Turkana specimens revealed characteristic polishes for cutting wood, plants, and meat. Since wood and plants are perishable, microwear analysis such as this can be of major significance in revealing possible uses for such ancient tools.

ETHIOPIA AND THE DISCOVERY OF LUCY

As the work continued at Lake Turkana, other sites were being discovered. A French geologist, Maurice Taieb, was working in the isolated Afar Triangle in Ethiopia when he found extensive fossil deposits. In 1972 he invited Donald Johanson to join him in exploring the area. Johanson was working as a graduate student in paleoanthropology on the Omo project and was eager to visit the Afar with Taieb. The Afar region, especially in the Hadar area, was exceptionally rich in well-preserved fossils, some of which might be 3 million years old. If the dating assessment proved correct, the Afar would be a most promising place to investigate because no hominid fossils had been dated specifically to this period. Following the exploratory trip, an international (American and French) expedition was organized, and the search for human ancestors was underway. In 1973, during the first expedition, Johanson relates that he was surveying when he "kicked at what looked like a hippo rib sticking up in the sand. It came loose and revealed itself, not as a hippo rib, but as a proximal tibia—the upper end of the shinbone—of a small primate."[16] This was the first of many significant hominid discoveries made at Hadar. Further study revealed that it was a knee joint. This was a lucky find, because it showed that upright posture and bipedal locomotion were well established by about 3 million years ago.

The 1974 season proved to be very important. The first discoveries included several hominid jaws. Then, on the last day of November, Johanson reported feeling lucky. As they started to return to camp after visiting one of the fossil localities known as 162, Johanson noticed a bone lying on the surface of a gully. It was part of a hominid arm. Close inspection revealed more hominid bones lying nearby, including a piece of a skull. Johanson relates excitedly:

> We stood up and began to see other bits of bone on the slope: a couple of vertebrae, part of a pelvis—all of them hominid. An unbelievable, impermissible thought flickered through my mind. Suppose all these fitted together? Could they be parts of a single, extremely primitive skeleton? No such skeleton had ever been

> found anywhere . . . In that 110 degree heat we began jumping up and down. With nobody to share our feelings, we hugged each other, sweaty and smelly, howling and hugging in the heat-shimmering gravel, the small brown remains of what now seemed almost certain to be parts of a single hominid skeleton lying all around us.

This was the discovery of the famous Lucy, named after a popular Beatles song. Lucy was the most complete protohuman skeleton known. She was estimated to be between 3 and 4 million years old, based on potassium-argon dating of volcanic deposits. Lucy stood about three and a half feet in height, and study of her skeleton reaffirmed that bipedal locomotion, a human trademark, was well established by that early date. This was indeed an incredible find. The chances of a relatively complete skeleton being preserved for so long are very slim, and the chances of finding one like this are even less. But this find was nearly overshadowed by discoveries made the following year at AL 333.

It all started one morning when some hominid teeth were discovered. The following day, more bones were found on the same site. Careful comparison of the body parts represented indicated that they had belonged to several different individuals. Because of the likelihood of finding even more bones, efforts spanning two field seasons were concentrated on this site. Remains of at least thirteen early hominids were found at this site. Never before had such a large number of early hominids been found at a single locality in such close proximity. These fossil hominids were dubbed the "first family," though it has not been established that they were actually related. No one is certain how they died, but it is clear that this was not a cemetery, because intentional burial of the dead was not practiced until the time of Neandertal man, which is much later. Johanson speculates that the deaths may have resulted from a group being caught in a flash flood. Such floods are not unusual in East Africa. I have seen a dry river bed suddenly become an impassable, raging torrent while the sun still shone. Heavy rain falling outside the immediate area produced a flood, which rolled down the river as a moving wall of water. Anyone caught in such a flood would drown, yet the chances of a large number of bodies being deposited in the same area would seem slim.

A great many protohuman fossils have been recovered from Hadar, which is probably the most prolific of all the early hominid sites. Detailed study of the Hadar remains by Johanson and Tim White, the latter from the University of California, indicated that they were not quite like any other species that had been described. According to Johanson and White, the shape of the jaws and slight projecting nature of the canine teeth were much more apelike than was the case with other species.[17] The two researchers saw striking similarities between specimens from Hadar and ones discovered by Mary Leakey at the site of Laetoli in northern Tanzania. Johanson and White concluded that they had discovered a new species, which they called *Australopithecus afarensis*. The new species included only the remains from Hadar and Laetoli. Potassium-argon dating revealed that the fossils of *Australopithecus afarensis* were approximately 3.6 million years old at Hadar and 3.7 million years old at Laetoli. The dates revealed that the new species was about 1.5 million years older than the other kinds of australopithecines and *Homo habilis*. The early dates and the primitive features of the dentition implied that *A. afarensis* was getting us increasingly closer to the time when the protohuman lineage diverged from ape ancestors. Johanson and White have argued that their new species was the common ancestor to both *Australopithecus africanus* and *Homo habilis*. (In this view *A. robustus* is a later offshoot of *A. africanus*.) This interpretation means that *Australopithecus afarensis* is the earlier ancestor, while *Homo habilis* is a later step along the way, situated between *A. afarensis* on the one hand and *Homo erectus* on the other. If we carry this one step further, most authorities believe that *Homo erectus* is the direct ancestor of early *Homo sapiens*. This new interpretation is in direct conflict with the view of Richard Leakey, who believes that *Homo habilis* is our true remote ancestor. Bitter arguments have followed, which rival those experienced by Dart back in 1925, when the first *Australopithecus* was discovered. Mary Leakey, for example, has maintained that the Laetoli remains should not have been included in the new species. She viewed them as an early form of *Homo*, more advanced than *Austra-*

lopithecus. This of course, would support the contention that *Homo habilis* was our earliest ancestor.

Much of the interpretation of early hominid evolution ultimately depends on the dating of the fossils and how the various species compare with one another in age. We have seen how the dating of skull 1470 from East Turkana was challenged and that its approximate age of 3 million years was reduced to less than 2 million. Lucy and the other *A. afarensis* remains at Hadar are undergoing the same treatment. Reanalysis of the dating has implied that she is only about 2.9 million years old, rather than 3.6 million.[18] The more recent date creates some problems for the new theory of the primacy of *A. afarensis* as a remote ancestor. The problems are underscored when we consider the fact that South African *Australopithecus africanus* sites such as Sterkfontein may be about the same age as the Lucy remains. If *A. afarensis* is the same age as *A. africanus*, the new species from Hadar cannot be the ancestor of *A. africanus*. Critics have also pointed out that the primitive dental features of *A. afarensis* are really not outside the range of physical variation of *A. africanus* specimens from South Africa. This might lead us once again to the conclusion that we are seeing new wine in old bottles. Perhaps *A. afarensis* is really an East African version of *A. africanus*.

It is not an easy task to decide which of these alternatives is correct. While the data itself is based on precise comparative measurements, the interpretations are ultimately tied to arbitrary decisions about where to draw the dividing line between different species of fossil hominids. One investigator might take a narrow view of where to draw this line while another might want to accommodate more variation within a single species. These differences in approaches to the same data base then fuel arguments about evolutionary relationships between groups. In contrast, the definition of living species is based on the concept of reproductive isolation—this is directly observable. If two closely related groups of animals either cannot or do not interbreed they are considered to belong to different species. Obviously, this definition cannot be strictly applied to the fossil record except where groups are separated by either time or space. In the case of the early hominids in question, the dating situation is by no means crystal clear. For these reasons, coupled with the incompleteness of the record, I feel that it is difficult to completely support any of the above interpretations. If I were placing a bet on which explanation is correct I would put my money on a broad-based view that says that one of the australopithecines is almost certainly ancestral to *Homo habilis*. I would then eliminate *A. robustus* from the picture because of its unique dental characteristics and other specialized features. At this point I would say that one of two options is the most likely interpretation. 1.) *Australopithecus afarensis* is the ultimate remote ancestor of the *Homo* lineage via *Australopithecus africanus*. 2.) *Australopithecus afarensis* and *Australopithecus africanus* are actually members of the same widely varying species and this group as a whole should be considered as ancestral to the *Homo* lineage. While option 1 may have the strongest support, I wouldn't like to defend this position in court. To go further would be like betting on the Kentucky Derby without knowing the previous track records of the horses, in this case the uncertainties of some of the dates and the gaps in the record. These controversies are far from resolved. Future fieldwork resulting in the discovery of more complete skulls anywhere from 4 to 5 million years in age might provide some answers, and there is every reason to believe that such discoveries will be made.

In 1981 researchers from the University of California initiated work along the Awash river in the Afar Triangle. They found a piece of hominid skull, along with an abundance of fossil animals in 4-million-year-old deposits. Surprisingly, plans for more intensive follow-up research were stymied when the Ethiopian government suddenly refused to allow any more foreign workers to carry out human origins research. This was a real bombshell, considering the great promise of the area and heightened interest in the subject.

The Ethiopian government banned foreign researchers because of concerns about what they believed were past violations of their antiquities laws. However, an underlying cause was rooted in the fact that, prior to the 1981 project, certain researchers attempted to exclude others from continuing in the area. One of the individuals concerned actually had to leave the country because of unverified rumors linking him with the U.S. Central Intelligence Agency.[19] This was not the first time a promising new area of excavation was closed to outside scientists. Even the excavation of King Tut's tomb was halted during a period of rising Egyptian nationalism, as we shall see in Chapter 3.

Several years after the closing of the Afar Triangle, a new opportunity appeared on the horizon for Johanson and his colleagues: Olduvai Gorge. The Leakeys' work at Olduvai had drawn to a close. In 1986, the new work at Olduvai yielded a partial skeleton of what is believed to be *Homo habilis*. The remains are estimated to be about 1.8 million years old. This discovery, made by Tim White, has provided the first detailed picture of what a *Homo habilis* skeleton was like. One of the surprising points is that the arms were very long, suggesting that this hominid was an adept climber.[20]

FOOTPRINTS THROUGH TIME

History has a way of repeating itself, although not necessarily in exactly the same way. The enormously successful recovery of hominids in East Africa had been triggered by Mary Leakey's discovery of *Zinjanthropus* at Olduvai in 1959. Not far from Olduvai is the site of Laetoli. This site was originally discovered in 1935 when a local Masai man who was working at Olduvai informed Louis Leakey that fossils could also be found at Laetoli. The man guided Leakey and his associates to the site. Although numerous animal fossils were found, the site did not seem as promising as Olduvai and was not intensively researched. In 1974, however, George Dove, the owner of a nearby safari lodge, found that the Laetoli deposits were more extensive and richer in fossils than had previously been suspected. Mary Leakey was called to the scene and recognized the potential importance of the new exposures. A large quantity of early hominid jaw fragments were recovered, as well as many animal fossils. The deposits also included volcanic ash approximately 3.7 million years old. This date pushed our ancestors back in time even further. As mentioned previously, Mary Leakey originally believed that the jaws from Laetoli should be considered part of an early member of the genus *Homo*, while White and Johanson included the very same fossils as *Australopithecus afarensis*. More recently, Mary Leakey has noted similarities between the Laetoli hominids and the gracile forms of australopithecines.[21]

In 1976, a unique discovery was made quite by accident at Laetoli. Several of the researchers were amusing themselves by throwing dried animal dung at one another, and while bending down one of them noticed animal tracks in the volcanic ash layers. Subsequent investigations revealed the ancient trails of a wide variety of animals, such as elephant, rhinoceros, giraffe, pig, hyena, monkey, and bird. Many of the tracks were very clear and could be readily identified by a local man who was a skilled animal tracker. There was even an insect trail as well as spattering marks from raindrops. In 1977, some tracks that looked human were found. As nothing like this had ever been found in such ancient deposits, there was considerable discussion about whether the tracks were really made by hominids. As luck would have it, more tracks were found in 1978 that convinced even the most skeptical.

The tracks were indeed amazing. No one would have expected to find early hominid footprints; it is rare enough to find their bones, which are certainly more durable than tracks. Unique conditions led to the preservation of the tracks, which were eventually traced for more than eighty feet. When hominids walked over the area, the ground was wet and covered by ash from a nearby volcano. This ash contained carbonate, which hardened around the prints as the ground dried out. The tracks were eventually covered by further deposition of ash. Erosion then exposed the section of footprints that was ultimately discovered. Scientists subsequently excavated more of the tracks. According to Louise Robbins, an anthropologist and footprint expert, there was evidence of three hominids.[22] One left tracks that averaged a little under seven inches in length. Robbins, using a formula established for estimating stature from footprint size, judged that this hominid was about four feet in height. Another individual appeared to be surprisingly large, with footprints averaging about ten and one-half inches long. If the assessment is correct, this hominid was about five feet, nine inches tall. This does not seem likely to me because stature estimates based on measurements of bone of australopithecines are much smaller than this. The third hominid walked in the tracks of the second one, and this one was about five feet tall and left tracks that were just under eight and one-half inches in length. Were these hominids part of a social group walking together? Louis Robbins implies that they might have been walking together, but others have persuasively argued that there is no way to demonstrate that this interpretation is correct. Despite these arguments, several detailed studies have shown that the heel impressions along with the way body weight was being transferred was already the same as is seen in modern humans. This leads to the most important conclusion that bipedal walking, an essential human characteristic, was already well established nearly 4 million years ago.

We have come a long way since Boucher de Perthes opened the doors to a new frontier. We can only imagine what de Perthes, Darwin, and others would have thought if they knew about the wealth of fossil hominids, the early tools, and the reasonably well-dated time sequence that is now available. No doubt they would have been amazed by the mass of information that is now common scientific knowledge.

Where do we go from here? My guess is that an enormously rich frontier remains, especially in the blank area in the time sequence, from 4 to 6 million years ago. The Awash River, Lothagam, and perhaps other, unknown sites may help us to resolve some of the conflicting interpretations that are now being debated.

2

THE FRONTIER OF CAVE ART

The total darkness was almost oppressive. I breathed a sigh of relief when the guide's light returned. He pointed to a narrow crawlway that led off to the side of the main chamber in an inconspicuous place. I inched forward into the space and looked at the wall. There in front of me was the painting of a woolly mammoth. These Pleistocene (Ice Age) elephants had become extinct in southern France more than 10,000 years ago, yet here I could see one painted in great detail by someone who had actually seen, and most likely hunted and eaten, these animals. For a brief instant, I felt as if the Ice Age had returned. I was standing in the Bernifal Cave, one of many Paleolithic art sites in France.

This chapter examines one of the most impenetrable, but at the same time one of the most thought-provoking, frontiers beneath the earth. My guess is that many archaeologists, if pressed, would confide that they have intentionally avoided researching Paleolithic art because of the almost insurmountable difficulty in drawing verifiable conclusions from the data. For the most part, the paintings cannot be treated with the same rigor and objective approach as a collection of stone tools or broken pieces of pottery. The behavioral data that may be encoded in the paintings is anything but clear cut, whereas artifacts, which were used for definite purposes, are not usually as abstract and problematical. In most cases, interpretations are highly subjective, and critics can always counter almost any argument by stating: "We will never really know what was in the mind of the painter." I find that this element of the unknown, while difficult to challenge, is one of the motivating forces that make the subject so intriguing.

Progress in penetrating the rock-art frontier has been slow but nonetheless quite exciting. The major historical discoveries were punctuated with the thrill and suspense that are found naturally in the dark recesses of caves not penetrated by humans since the end of the Pleistocene. The initial discovery of cave art resulted in a rejection that was as powerful as those that characterized the quest for human origins. Experts refused to believe that the paintings were ancient.

DISCOVERY OF EUROPEAN CAVE ART AND THE APOLOGY OF A SKEPTIC

In the middle of the last century, few, if any, scholars would have seriously entertained the idea that Stone Age peoples were capable of painting the animals that they hunted with such a profound sense of realism as is seen in the caves of France and Spain. Stone Age archaeology was just beginning at that time. Pioneer investigators who followed on the heels of Boucher de Perthes' major breakthrough in 1859 were only beginning to unravel the complex, cultural sequences of the Stone Age that were buried deeply beneath the natural rock overhangs in southern France. Two of the most active researchers were Édouard Lartet, a lawyer turned professional archaeologist, and Henry Christy, a wealthy English banker. Lartet and Christy worked together at many key sites in the archaeologically rich Dordogne region, laying the foundations for much of the Stone Age culture classification that is still being used today. They remained unaware, however, of the numerous painted caves that surrounded them.

Shortly afterward, in 1868, not far from the northern Spanish coast, a hunter was following his dog along the slope of a hill known as Altamira when the dog suddenly vanished into the brush. Faint barks could be heard from beneath the ground where the dog had forced its way into a hole following an animal. The hunter enlarged the hole to rescue the dog and found, much to his surprise, that the dog had penetrated the blocked entrance of a cave. This cave was on the summer estate of a nobleman, Marcelino Sanz de Sautuola. Several years passed before the news of the cave reached de Sautuola, who was himself a budding archaeologist. Well acquainted with the newly discovered Stone Age finds made in caves and rock shelters in neighboring parts of France, he was eager to investigate the cave on his property.

De Sautuola began a systematic investigation of Altamira by first clearing away the debris that blocked the main passageway, then excavating a pit near the entrance, where he uncovered blade tools, bone artifacts, and broken animal bones. For the most part, the remains were comparable to those found by Lartet and Christy in France. De Sautuola would have been amazed to find that, after radiocarbon dating became a reality many years later, his tools would be dated to about 13,550 B.C.[1] The assemblage, and others like it, are called Magdalenian and date between approximately 17,000 and 10,000 B.C. They belong to the Upper Paleolithic time period (39,000–10,000 B.C.).

In the Altamira cave there was a crawlway that led to an alcove on the side of the main passageway. When de Sautuola started to dig in this area in 1879 his young daughter, Maria, entreated him to let her join him in the cave. Little Maria wandered about the cave happily while her father worked, his eyes riveted to the growing pit in the expectation of uncovering some remarkable new artifacts.

Suddenly, the silence was broken by Maria's loud exclamation: "*Toros pintados!*"[2] which means "painted bulls." Her father was astonished to see paintings of extinct bison in the flickering light of the cave. Maria had made one of the most important discoveries in the history of archaeology. Nothing like it had ever been found in Europe, and de Sautuola realized quickly the great importance of the paintings. As soon as possible, he rushed to Madrid with the news and informed a geologist friend. Together, they returned to the cave, where further exploration revealed more paintings, supporting the original discovery.

The case that the Altamira paintings were painted by prehistoric humans seemed to be crystal clear. The cave had been sealed until the hunter had found it. The archaeological deposits buried in the floor belonged to the Stone Age and included bones of some of the same kinds of extinct animals shown in the paintings.

De Sautuola published a report announcing the find in 1880. Despite the clear circumstances surrounding the discovery, the leading experts in archaeology rejected the report. Altamira was seen as a fraud or, at best, the paintings were believed to be recent. One prominent artist, E. Lemus y Olmo, wrote:

> By their composition, strength of lines and proportions, they show that their author was not uneducated; and though he was not a Raphael, he must have studied nature . . . they [the paintings of Altamira] are simply the expression of a mediocre student of the modern school.[3]

Most of the critics didn't bother to see the site. Édouard Harlé, a noted French paleontologist, did go to Altamira but felt that the paintings were recent. One bit of evidence used to support this point of view was that there was no soot on the cave wall. How could the paintings have been done by Stone Age peoples whose primitive torches would surely have darkened the walls? It was even alleged that the paintings were by an artist who had been a guest of de Sautuola. The situation at Altamira was compounded by the prevailing assumption that Stone Age hunters were primitive and could not have painted such refined pictures.

De Sautuola received essentially the same kind of treatment accorded Boucher de Perthes, only in this case de Sautuola died before his views were vindicated. About twenty years would elapse before the Altamira art was accepted by the scientific community. We have seen that most of the landmark discoveries that were at first rejected, like Java man and *Australopithecus africanus*, were not acceptable to most authorities until more evidence was recovered in indisputable contexts. Recall, for example, that the finds made at Beijing helped to verify that Dubois' Java man was indeed a hominid. I think that the case of the cave art is even more complex than that of the skulls. A skeptic could always maintain that cave paintings were recent or, in fact, faked, unless a geologically sealed site was discovered that no one could have entered since Ice Age times. The likelihood of finding such a cave is next to nothing. While Altamira was actually a sealed cave, about ten years had elapsed between the time it was reopened by the hunter and Maria de Sautuola's discovery of the paintings. Skeptics claimed that the paintings were done during this interval.

Luck has often played a significant part in archaeological discoveries, especially in the area of cave-art finds. In 1894 a local villager in Tayac, in southwestern France, was digging a potato-storage cellar. Much to his astonishment, his cellar penetrated a cave system that had been hidden by rocks. This cave was called La Mouthe. While few people other than cave-art enthusiasts have heard of it, it is a very special site. Shortly after its discovery, Émile Rivière, an archaeologist, began to explore the interior of the cave. He uncovered Ice Age deposits containing reindeer teeth, stone implements, and a seashell that must have been transported a considerable distance. Later on, in April 1895, a local youth squeezed into a narrow crawlway that had not been investigated previously. He found some engravings on the wall that, significantly, included the drawing of an extinct bison. Rivière's report of this find, which is not available in English, is worth translating. He writes:

> These engravings are not only apocryphal, but . . . it is not possible for me to doubt their antiquity . . . I understand very well that all new discoveries demand, before being accepted, serious scientific discussion. . . . But my conviction has been made; the engravings of La Mouthe are prehistoric. . . . They extend underneath the stalagmite . . . and partly under the red sand.[4]

No doubt, Rivière recognized that it would be almost impossible to argue against the antiquity of an engraving that had been covered by a crust of stalagmite formation. Rivière then bolstered his case by noting that he had found the remains of a reindeer antler and a bear near the engraved bison. These were both Ice Age occupants of southern France. He was sensitive to the problems surrounding Altamira, so he was very careful in how he marshaled his evidence. Luckily, his excavations were visited by some of the founding fathers in Stone Age archaeology. The Abbé Henri Breuil, a French priest, was one of the visitors. Breuil, a young man at the time, would come to dominate the field of Stone Age art for the next five decades. Another important visitor was Émile Cartailhac, whose powerful voice had come thundering down against accepting the art of Altamira, concerning which he had written, "Take care! You can't play games with French Prehistorians."[5] After visiting La Mouthe and Pair non Pair, another recently discovered art site, Cartailhac became convinced that the Paleolithic art was authentic. This caused him to reverse completely his position about Altamira. Cartailhac actually followed through with a classic apology, written in 1902 in a paper entitled "Caves ornamented by designs: The cave of Altamira Spain, Mea culpa of a skeptic." In it, he reviewed the history of Altamira and noted that he had "been mistaken for 20 years and there is an injustice that clearly needs to be corrected." After further discussion he emphatically states, "*We have no reason to be suspicious of the antiquity of the paintings of Altamira*. . . . It is necessary to accept the reality of a fact and I say this out of concern for the honorable M. de Sautuola." This signaled the acceptance of Paleolithic art as a legitimate field of study.

ABOUT CAVE ART

I believe it would be helpful at this point to present an overview of cave art in general, which will enable us to put these and other discoveries in context. Known prehistoric cave art is concentrated in the limestone country of southwestern France and northern Spain, where there are now reported to be at least 150 sites.[6] While most of the major sites were discovered over thirty years ago, some new caves featuring engravings of extinct animals have been found as recently as 1987 by cave explorers in the Dronne River Valley in France. Some isolated sites are known from farther afield, such as in

Italy and the Soviet Union. And, as will be discussed later on, there are other unrelated, but extremely interesting, Stone Age art traditions in Africa.

The Upper Paleolithic art believed to be the oldest consists of engravings, possibly dating back to as much as 30,000 B.C., found at rock-shelter sites in France. Some of these early engravings are said to depict female sex organs. The cave paintings are nearly impossible to date precisely because they are not associated directly with materials that can be subjected to radiocarbon dating. Such materials (most typically, charcoal) are recovered commonly in habitation sites where people actually lived, but most of the painted caves were not inhabited. As far as I am aware, there is no sound way to date the paintings on the cave walls. In some cases, it is possible to match particular art styles evident in the caves with pictures engraved on bone tools found in nearby habitation sites at which the specific layers are radiocarbon dated. In addition, there are style changes within the Upper Paleolithic art traditions. Very often one picture was painted on top of another. Thus, by examining large numbers of paintings, one can deduce which style is earliest and construct a relative sequence of changing art styles. When the various kinds of such indirect evidence are put together, it appears that most of the paintings were executed between approximately 20,000 and 9,000 B.C. In my opinion, a good ball-park estimate for the main period of the cave art would be between about 15,000 and 10,000 B.C.

In most cases, these Upper Paleolithic "art sanctuaries" were in the dark interior of the caves, away from the entrance. Light was most likely provided by dishlike stone lamps that were fueled by melted animal fat. Some of these lamps have been recovered in painted caves and in nearby occupation sites.

Paints were made from natural iron minerals that, when reduced to powders or used in lumps, produce various shades of red, brown, yellow, and black. The powdered coloring material was probably mixed with animal fat or blood, which served as a binding medium. Painting could have been done by using brushes made from animal hair or frayed sticks. In some cases, it seems as if the paint had been blown through a bone or reed tube, which resulted in a spray-gun effect. Some support for this idea is seen in pictures of "negative" hand prints, where the paint, applied directly around the hand, produced an outline of the hand on the cave wall. (This interpretation has been questioned by some critics.)[7] Outlines and shadings could have been made by using lumps of pigment as natural crayons. The engravings were most likely done with sharp-edged flakes or, perhaps, specialized stone tools called *burins*. Such chisel-like tools were also used to shape and engrave bone and antler artifacts.

There are a great many abstract signs, but most of the paintings are of animals, notably horses, bison, wild cattle, woolly mammoths, woolly rhinoceroses, deer, reindeer, musk oxen, ibexes (mountain goats), boars, lions, and bears. Sometimes there are even fish and birds. Horses, bison, and wild cattle make up about 60 percent of the animals, with the horse being the most frequent. Interestingly, reindeer, one of the most important food animals of Upper Paleolithic peoples, are represented by only 3.8 percent of the animals.[8] In fact, paintings of large animals such as mammoths are overrepresented in comparison to actual finds of the butchered remains of these animals excavated from habitation sites. In contrast to the large number of animals, paintings of humans are relatively rare and are generally poorly done. This is usually attributed to a theory that Paleolithic peoples considered an identifiable painting of a person a target for voodoolike black magic.

THE ALTAMIRA PAINTINGS

Let us return now to Altamira. Prior to the collapse of the entrance, this area received enough sunlight to make it suitable for a temporary camp. This is where de Sautuola and several other archaeologists who followed him excavated and found both artifacts and the bones of bison, wild horses, reindeer, red deer, bears, mammoths, and other kinds of animals. There were even some shellfish and seal bones brought from the nearby Atlantic coast. Whether the occupants responsible for the artifacts and bones were also the painters is unknown, but this is a distinct possibility because some engraved bones with pictures of deer were recovered, along with lumps of pigment and grindstones. Margaret Conkey, a specialist on paleolithic art, has suggested that Altamira was an aggregation site where smaller sub-groups of a hunting and gathering society reunited into a larger group at certain times of the year. Perhaps important ceremonies were conducted in the cave when this happened.

Next to the habitation area is a chamber that, at the time of the original research, had a low ceiling. Here is where the art was first noticed by Maria de Sautuola. These spectacular paintings are among the most famous in archaeology, leading some authorities to dub the site the "Sistine Chapel" of prehistory. Represented are the bison, horse, deer, and ibex, along with abstract signs that vaguely resemble bows and barbs. Altamira is well known for its striking polychrome paintings in which black, red, and yellow were sometimes employed to color a single animal. Polychrome art is usually believed to be a hallmark of the Magdalenian culture.

Of all the animals depicted at Altamira, the bison have engendered the most discussion and debate. Some of these fascinating animals are shown with hairs bristling and tails sticking out, suggesting that they are enraged. One of them was painted lying down with its legs bent upwards. At first glance, this animal looks as if it has been disemboweled, with part of its intestines pulled out in a gory expression of death. These "enraged and dead" animals have been used to support the theory that cave art was done as a magical aid to hunting. The artists are viewed as attempting to control the bison herds and to ensure successful hunts by ritually killing the animals on the walls of caves. This theory of sympathetic magic has been criticized heavily, largely because most of the animals depicted in cave art are not being hunted symbolically—there are very few animals that are clearly depicted as being wounded or dead, and paintings of weapons are not associated with most of the animals. Maybe Upper Paleolithic peoples wanted to show live animals so that there would, in fact, be an ample supply of them. More recently, research has pointed to some close similarities between the condition of some of the Altamira bison and the characteristics of modern female wild bison in the process of giving birth. This remarkable transformation in ideas from death to birth underscores the problems in interpreting cave art.

Notable abstract symbols or signs of Altamira include the barbed and bowlike designs, some elliptical and others resembling windows with bars on them. Many of these, as well as other abstract signs, are found at other caves. The chance of the same signs being repeated in numerous caves at random is almost nil. What do they mean? Hunting-magic theorists see some of them as representations of wounds, weapons, or traps, but clearly there are many other examples that cannot be put into the mold of hunting paraphernalia. One researcher, André Leroi-Gourhan, has done an extensive statistical analysis of the signs and animal paintings in a large number of caves.[9] He has concluded that they are sexual symbols and part of a larger male-female symbolism in the art as a whole. On the other hand, some of them look much more like parts of plants, and it has been suggested that such symbols are indicators of specific seasons of the year.[10] One interpretation even goes much further afield by suggesting that there are some striking similarities between some of the signs in Paleolithic art and those symbols used in a number of ancient writing systems, although this viewpoint is not meant to imply that Upper Paleolithic peoples had developed a form of writing comparable to that used in the early civilizations of the Near East.[11] Most recently, a very challenging view of the abstract signs has been presented by J. D. Lewis-Williams and T. A. Dowson. One of the main points in their analysis is that certain of the signs such as zigzags and gridlike designs are reported to be seen by all people when they experience the initial stages of hallucination. It is known that shamans ("medicine men") often claim to achieve contact with the spirit world through hallucinations when they enter a trance. This is especially true among the peoples of hunting and foraging societies. The two researchers conclude from their study of the signs, as well as other kinds of data, that Upper Paleolithic art is related to shamanistic traditions. Though this interpretation is illuminating, the problem of the abstract signs remains to be solved.

SOME UNDERGROUND ADVENTURES

Le Tuc d'Audoubert

Several major discoveries of cave art have centered on underground adventures that would have impressed Mark Twain, whose account of Tom Sawyer's cave exploits is an American classic. That some of the most important discoveries were made by teenagers makes the comparison between fact and fiction even less remote.

The first episode begins in an isolated part of the French Pyrenees in the summer of 1912, only ten years after Cartailhac's "Mea culpa of a skeptic." This is when the three teenaged sons of Count Bégouën decided to explore a small underground river called the Volp, which disappeared into the side of a hill near their summer home. On a raft made from crates and gas cans, they floated into the darkness of the cave. The stream led them to a natural docking area, where they beached their raft and continued exploring part of the cave on foot.

That fall, the brothers returned with a young friend, François Camel, to explore more of the cave. After retracing their float trip, they worked their way carefully along the floor of the cavern. This time, they floated and hiked about a quarter of a mile from the entrance and came to a small cliff. They climbed it carefully and found themselves in a gallery with some spectacular cave formations and, even more exciting, engravings and traces of paintings. Further exploration led to a chimneylike passageway leading upward. Slowly and with great effort, the boys twisted their way through the chimney while holding tightly to the rocks on the sides of the narrow space. It was a difficult climb, although only about forty feet. Now they had reached a remote part of the cave, where they found themselves in a room with a low ceiling. They couldn't go any farther because the passage itself was blocked by stalactite pillars, but the position of the cave formation hinted that the passage might continue on the other side of the pillars. There was only one way to be sure. Max Bégouën and François Camel chipped away at the formations and broke a space through the pillars that was barely large enough to crawl through. They slipped into the unknown, entering a part of the cave that was last seen by humans in the Ice Age. Their dim light revealed tracks and claw marks of cave bears, almost giving the impression that these extinct beasts might still be lurking in the dark corners of some chamber. Bones of bears and other animals added an eerie quality to their experience. This was further heightened when they noticed footprints of Stone Age peoples that had survived for more than 10,000 years in the moist environment and stable temperature of the cave.

As far as I am aware, this was the first discovery of the footprints of Ice Age humans. Such finds are extraordinary, as we have noted already in the case of the 3.7-million-year-old (pre-Ice Age) hominid tracks from Laetoli in East Africa. The Stone Age hunters who visited Tuc d'Audoubert must have had an easier way of getting into the cave, but all traces of it have vanished, and the trail of footprints is not long enough to locate where the ancient entrance might have been.

About one-half mile from the entrance of the cave, the boys were amazed to discover a group of four clay bison that had survived intact since the Upper Paleolithic. The largest was about two feet long. This was an outstanding find: Sculptures of such antiquity had never been found before. In the history of art, the bison of Tuc d'Audoubert are still considered among the oldest lifelike clay models. While their exact age is not known, they could be as much as 15,000 years old.

Why would somebody make models of bison deep inside a cave that was used by bears and, possibly, hyenas and Pleistocene lions? The Abbé Breuil, in his classic work *Four Hundred Centuries of Cave Art*, concluded that they were made for fertility purposes in order to increase the number of animals. This idea can be neither confirmed nor rejected on the basis of any factual data. Other researchers have pointed to the large number of human footprints and have posited that the deep heel marks in the cave floor bear witness to a dance performed during initiation rites, in which the bison may have been ritual objects. This argument was fostered by an analysis of the footprints concluding that they were made by a group of adolescents, presumably the young initiates. Certainly, the dark chamber of a cave would be a dramatic natural stage for an initiation ceremony, especially if part of the routine was to create an atmosphere of suspense. Nevertheless, this interpretation has been criticized heavily on the grounds that the analysis of the footprints is questionable and that the association between the footprints and the bison is circumstantial.[12]

The Bégouën brothers' days of cave exploration and archaeological discoveries had not ended. Just two years later, in 1914, they made another exceptional find. Near the Tuc d'Audoubert cave was a mysterious sinkhole, where the winter snowfall melted quickly because warm air issued from the ground. Was there another cave entrance beneath the steep-sided natural pit?

The Bégouëns and François Camel decided to climb into the sinkhole. Since the drop into the pit was about seventy feet, it was necessary to use a rope for the descent. Slowly, and with great care, they climbed into the dark pit, not knowing where their adventure would lead them. When they reached the bottom, they realized they had, indeed, found another cave system. As time passed, Count Bégouën, who was waiting at the top of the pit, began to wonder about the wisdom of the adventure. The count would have been even more anxious if he could have seen the boys jumping adroitly over a forty-five-foot-deep hole in the cave floor. Several hours later, Count Bégouën was relieved to hear voices in the distance, but, surprisingly, they did not come from the sinkhole below him. The boys had found that one of the passages, which led to a nearby cave they had already explored, provided an easy exit for them.

Further exploration of the cave system below the sinkhole, now known as Les Trois Frères in honor of the three Bégouën brothers, demonstrated that the site was significant. It revealed an abundance of engravings and paintings now thought to have been fashioned between 20,000 and 15,000 B.C. Notable artwork includes mammoths, rhinoceroses, reindeer, some very fine lions, and several snowy owls. One of the most widely discussed pictures in all of the Paleolithic caves is the so-called sorcerer of Les Trois Frères, originally copied and described by the Abbé Breuil.

The sorcerer was placed in a special area about twelve feet above the cave floor. It can be reached only by a "secret corridor climbing upwards in a spiral."[13] From its lofty position, the sorcerer is described as presiding over a vast number of engraved animals located in an area dubbed the "sanctuary." Breuil presents the sorcerer as a man disguised in an animal skin with a bearded mask, deer-antler headdress, and a wolflike tail. The sorcerer is about two and one-half feet long and has been both engraved and painted black. Breuil states that it is the only painted figure in the immediate vicinity of the engravings.

It should be mentioned that reinvestigation of the sorcerer many years after Breuil's work does not show some of the details depicted by the abbé.[14] The face, for example, is not as clear as shown in Breuil's picture. In fact, recent work by Robert Bégouën and Jean Clottes has revealed that the tracings of the Abbé Breuil varied considerably in quality. However, the two researchers also note that the methods available to the Abbé Breuil were poor compared to what is currently used in studying cave art. Despite these problems, Breuil's presentation of the sorcerer had a significant influence in supporting the theory that rituals conducted by shamans, or medicine men, were performed in the caves. As originally conceived, this interpretation was rooted in a rather freewheeling use of ethnographic analogies in which the behavior of present-day hunting peoples is used to support an interpretation of ancient finds. For example, some aboriginal Siberian hunters have shamans in their societies who wear antler headdresses reminiscent of the one shown in the painting.

Among most hunting societies (e.g., Eskimo, Shoshoni Indians, San [Bushmen]), the shaman is a special person who is believed to have the ability, often through a trance, to make direct personal contact with the spirit world for the purpose of curing the sick, controlling the habits of animals, rainmaking, and performing other vital activities. In some cases, the shaman believes he is transformed into an animal, which gives him great power. Considering this, it is possible that the sorcerer of Les Trois Frères was not a man in disguise, but an artist's literal rendition of such a metamorphosis.

Work has been renewed at Les Trois Frères in the 1980s, led by Robert Bégouën and Jean Clottes. Many new engravings, including bison, horses, and other animals, have been found by carefully cleaning the mud from the walls. Use of sophisticated photographic techniques along with the making of casts of the engravings has revealed new details not seen by the Abbé Breuil and has also picked up some of his mistakes. For example, close scrutiny of an engraved lion originally described by the French priest as having multiple heads and tails has revealed evidence for one less head, and, surprisingly, one of the tails has turned out to be a human arm. New investigations have also been confirmed that the adjacent cave of Enlène served as the entrance of Les Trois Frères during the time of the Magdalenian culture. Another interesting point about the neighboring cave is that it has yielded one of the largest concentrations of Upper Paleolithic engraved stones that has ever been excavated. Clearly, much will be learned from these caves in the future as the work goes on.

Montespan

Not far from the Trois Frères region, the Garonne River winds its way through the foothills of the Pyrenees. The village of Montespan lies nestled in these hills. Late in the summer of 1922, local villagers led Norbert Casteret to the base of a hill where an underground stream disappeared into a cave. Casteret, an avid spelunker, was well acquainted with the Bégouëns' work at Les Trois Frères and envisioned another possible discovery in the cave at Montespan, but there was a major obstacle. Villagers claimed that the cave could be entered only for a short distance because the roof sloped and eventually touched the stream. It was impossible to go farther, they said, because there was no room to breathe.

On the other hand, Casteret was aware that the climate had been very dry during parts of the late Ice Age. Frost-cracked rocks, soils, and animal bones bearing witness to cold and dry climatic conditions had been noted by archaeologists excavating the layers of French rock-shelter sites. If the conditions had been dry, Casteret reasoned, the Montespan stream had probably been much lower during the period when cave artists lived in southern France. Maybe people had entered the cave at that time. Casteret concluded that Montespan was indeed worth exploring on the chance that one could find dry chambers farther in the interior of the cave. This, however, was a risky business.

Casteret went into the small entrance and waded into the icy stream and the dark interior of the cavern. Just as the villagers had predicted, he soon found that the ceiling was too low to continue and, just ahead, the chilling water was up to the roof. Certainly this would have stopped most explorers, but Casteret was an exceptional swimmer and gambled that he might be able to hold his breath long enough to reach areas ahead that had higher ceilings. He dived into the subterranean stream and, amazingly, emerged where there was a small air space. Casteret captures the drama of this situation:

> Where was I? I had not the slightest idea. The darkness was absolute. Without doubt I had passed through a siphon tunnel. Immediately I turned around and dived toward the spot from which I had come, for nothing is more dangerous than to lose one's sense of direction in such a case.[15]

The following day he returned with candles and repeated his dive. He was able to work his way along the narrow air space for several hundred feet to where the cavern opened into a large chamber. Further exploration led to another dead end, where the water prevented access. Once again Casteret plunged beneath the stream and like a veritable cave fish swam blindly underwater for an even longer distance. He emerged from the stream and followed the cave system via narrow passages and crawlways. Finally, after spending half of the day underground, aided only by candlelight and his own fortitude, he found his way back to the entrance.

Casteret was convinced that Montespan was well worth additional work. He returned the following summer when the stream was at its annual low point. Together with a friend, he penetrated a gallery that was about twice the length of a football field. Casteret relates that they had to crawl most of the way through this gallery. Here, in the inner reaches of Montespan, the flickering candlelight slowly revealed sights that had not been viewed since the Pleistocene. Casteret found a large clay model of a bear along with other clay animals. There were also engravings on the wall of horses, bison, ibexes, and possibly a hyena. This art, it is now judged, could be nearly 15,000 years old.

Like the Tuc d'Audoubert bison, the Paleolithic clay statues are unique, but they are no less puzzling. What was the purpose, if any, of modeling a clay bear in such a remote part of a cave? The animal was headless, but nearby Casteret found the skull of a real Pleistocene bear. Since it is most unlikely that this was a chance association, several writers have concluded that the skull was once part of the model. Brueil, for example, posited that the bear skull was once propped up by a stump that has long since rotted away. He went on further to say that there could have been a skin covering the model. Casteret has emphasized that the clay bear was pock-marked with holes. Similar holes were also observed on some of the engravings, as well as on the adjacent wall of the cave itself.

When the pieces of the Montespan puzzle were put together by early researchers, the picture that emerged was that of a ritual hunt. The clay bear and the animal engravings were killed symbolically by spearing, as evidenced by the holes. The ritual guaranteed the hunters success on future hunts and, more than likely, protected them from dangerous encounters with bears. This is the hunting-magic theory again, and Montespan is considered a major case in support of it. Critics, on the other hand, have been quick to point out that the site is not well documented and that the alleged spear holes may, in fact, be natural.[16]

There is certainly more than one way to look at Montespan. When we spin the wheel of ethnographic case studies far enough, it stops at the traditional peoples of northern Asia such as the Samoyed, the Tungus, and the Ainu. Almost all such northern hunters have been noted to have elaborate cults and rituals centering on the brown bear. Among the Ainu of northern Japan, the bear was viewed as the master spirit in nature, presiding over all other animal spirits. When a bear was killed, the hunter was required to apologize to the spirit of the bear and address it with special terms. The bones of the bear were then put in a special place, such as the fork of a tree, to appease the bear's spirit. Improper treatment of the bear was believed to offend the master spirit of nature and was thought to disrupt the natural world that the Ainu depended upon to secure food. The Ainu also had a ceremony for killing a pet bear. It is plausible that Upper Paleolithic hunters also treated the bear with special deference.

Lascaux

One of the most famous discoveries of Paleolithic art was made near the village of Montignac in the Dordogne region of France. Lascaux cave was accidentally found in September 1940, but there are several different versions of the discovery. The account most widely quoted asserts that four teenagers led by Marcel Ravidat were hunting in the woods near the estate of Lascaux. The *London Illustrated News* of 28 February 1942 reports that they were tracking a wounded bird when their dog disappeared into a hole that had been hidden by brush. They dropped some stones into the hole and reasoned from the sound that the bottom was not far below. After enlarging the hole, Ravidat and the others squeezed in, rescued the dog, and had a look around. The flickering light produced by the few matches they had brought revealed the entrance to a large cave. Another account about Lascaux, written by Georges Bataille, claims that the above story was fabricated by the youths in response to interviews by the press. He reports that they had actually planned to explore the hole after an old woman had insisted that it marked the entrance to a medieval passageway. In this version, Ravidat enlarged the hole and "plunged straight in head first."[17] In yet a third version, the boys found a mysterious hole where a tree had been uprooted. They enlarged the opening and worked their way down into a slippery passage of wet clay using a flashlight.[18]

The cave of Lascaux was another one that had not been entered since the close of the Ice Age. The youths found painting after painting of magnificent animals illuminated by their dim light. Ravidat relates, "Our joy was beyond description; a bunch of wild Indians doing a war-dance wouldn't have equalled us."[19] Apparently the youths kept their find a secret for almost a week while they explored the cave with a homemade torch fashioned from a bicycle pump. They finally decided to disclose their secret to Leon Laval, the local schoolmaster. Laval was skeptical, but after a personal visit to the site, he quickly notified Abbé Breuil while the boys carefully guarded the cave entrance. Breuil arrived, and his expert opinion confirmed the news that an important new cave-art sanctuary had been found at Montignac.

Lascaux cave was eventually opened to the public for guided

tours. Lights were installed and a walkway was constructed. Laval, the schoolmaster, was appointed conservator of the site and Marcel Ravidat became one of the guides. This seems a pleasant ending because several discoverers benefited personally from their find, but all did not go well for the cave art itself. No one had guessed that the cumulative effect of opening and closing the cave for thousands of tourists would change the stable atmospheric conditions in the interior that had preserved the paintings for thousands of years. It was Ravidat who first noticed that a mold known as "green sickness" was causing the paintings to deteriorate. The cave was closed to the public in 1963. The mold was removed with formalin and antibiotics, but, unfortunately, a formation of calcite deposits (white sickness) has prevented the cave from being reopened. The French, not at all discouraged, constructed a meticulously built artificial cave next to the original, where the paintings have been reproduced faithfully.

Lascaux, like Altamira, is one of the few painted caves that have been radiocarbon dated. Some charcoal in one of the stone lamps found in Lascaux is about 17,000 years old, and cultural remains found are of the early Magdalenian period.

The Lascaux paintings represent the zenith of Upper Paleolithic artistic achievement. There are said to be about 600 paintings and hundreds of engravings in this cave alone.[20] A trip to Lascaux is like visiting an Upper Pleistocene version of a zoo. Wild cattle and horses are especially prolific. Many were done in a lively polychrome style, and some are very large, up to at least fifteen feet in length. Some of the other animals include red deer, ibexes, wolves, bears, some engraved lions, and a rhinoceros. In addition to the animals, there is a wide range of abstract signs, some of which are also seen at other sites.

Several of the paintings are especially noteworthy. First is the "unicorn," an obvious misnomer because this animal actually has two horns. The face is squared, the belly sags, and there are some oval patterns on the skin. Clearly this animal has no living counterpart, and it is unique to Lascaux. Some authorities think that it is a human wearing an animal-skin disguise, perhaps to get closer to animals during a hunt. On the other hand, it could be a mythical animal that was never intended to be taken as a realistic picture.

A red-and-black horse at Lascaux has been depicted widely as a classic example of Paleolithic art. It is very fat and has a featherlike symbol painted on its side. Is this horse pregnant, or does it simply reflect the fact that hunting peoples often prefer animals that are fat? Is the sign a representation of a projectile, a symbolic wound, or a plant symbolizing a bountiful pasture?

An interesting fact about the European cave art is that there are few paintings that show groups of animals interacting with each other or with people. In addition, there is no background, such as water, trees, or hills. The focus is on individual animals. Lascaux has one of the most notable exceptions to this rule—the painting often referred to as the "well scene," or "shaft of the dead man." This picture was painted at the bottom of a steep-sided shaft roughly sixteen feet deep. The edges of this natural pit were worn smooth by the ancient hunters who climbed in, possibly by using a rope. A carbonized piece of rope was found in the cave. The chamber at the base of the shaft, or well, has a painting of a disemboweled bison with bristling hair, reminiscent of the one at Altamira. Directly in front of the bison's horns lies the slanted figure of a "dead man" who has a birdlike head and an erect penis. Beneath the man is a stick with a bird's head and a spear thrower (a device used by Australian aborigines to increase distance and accuracy). Opposite the dead man is a rhinoceros who is charging away from the scene while defecating. Possible traces of human hand prints have also been noted.

The "decoding" of this scene has been very imaginative. Breuil felt that it was depicting a man who was killed while hunting. He concluded that the enraged rhinoceros had probably gored the bison to death because the man's weaponry was too puny to have done so. I can't help wondering whether the Lascaux "dead man" is not dead at all but rather a depiction of a man in trance state possessed by an animal spirit, in this case a bird. Human figures are often drawn poorly in Paleolithic caves in comparison to animals. Maybe they were intentionally done this way to indicate spirit possession or trance.

What about some of the other items in the shaft of the dead man? Breuil compared the enigmatic bird-headed stick to posts used by Eskimos in association with funerals. The abbé also suspected that careful excavation of the cave floor might actually uncover the remains of the dead hunter. Leroi-Gourhan, mentioned previously in connection with sexual symbolism, suggests that the bird-headed stick and the spear thrower are male symbols, while the entrails of the bison are female symbols.[21] Another investigator, Alexander Marshack, has maintained that the bird on the stick and other objects reflect seasonal concerns. He concludes that the shaft of the dead man was most likely used over a long time during the appropriate season for recounting stories and myths that were significant to the group. It is interesting to see how the same information can lead to such completely different results.

SOME EXAMPLES FROM AFRICA

One serious problem in most research on European cave art is that there are *no* societies that have been observed by anthropologists that can serve as direct, historically related models for what Upper Paleolithic societies were like. Virtually all of the comparisons based on anthropological case studies of hunting and foraging groups are drawn from distant and unrelated peoples who live in environments that contrast substantially with the late Ice Age scene in western Europe. This is why many of the interpretations have been so varied and speculative. Because of this problem, it is enlightening to review some examples from Africa, the source of a number of anthropological case studies that figure prominently in the interpretation of prehistoric art. Here, the linkage between past and present has been forged.

Some of the most important interpretations of prehistoric art have been made recently in Africa, yet this information has reached only a small audience of experts because of the overwhelming concentration on European art. African rock art, which includes both paintings and engravings, is not related to European cave art. The former is widespread geographically, with notable concentrations in the Saharan mountains, East Africa (especially Tanzania), and at many locations in southern Africa. At first it may seem surprising that southern African art was seen by Europeans at least a century before Cartailhac and his French colleagues accepted the landmark European site of Altamira. In a matter-of-fact way, the famous explorer Sir John Barrow describes rock art in the interior of South Africa in 1797–98 as work that was "too well executed not to arrest attention."[22] Barrow was giving an account of his journey into the land of the Bosjemans (Bushmen). The art initially viewed by Barrow included paintings of zebra, antelope, ostriches, baboons, and various symbols. He was very impressed by the paintings and concluded that such finely executed work "could not be expected from savages. . . ." Barrow attributed these paintings to the Bushmen. The primary reason the African art was noticed more quickly was that its sites are more abundant than the European sites and are usually easier to see. The pictures were generally painted on rock overhangs located in the open instead of being hidden inside caves.

In the case of African art, one does not have the accounts of incredible underground adventures that typify the pioneering days of discovery in the European caves. While this is true, I would guess that some harrowing stories could be collected from researchers who have worked in remote areas. In search of rock paintings I have nearly stepped on a large puff adder and had my path blocked by a spitting cobra, hooded and poised for the attack.

African rock art can be every bit as impressive as European cave art, although it could be claimed that one does not get the same feeling of awe that is inspired by viewing the painting of a long-extinct animal in a remote part of a cave. Nevertheless, some African paintings can also be inspirational, as well as relatively inaccessible. On a recent Botswana National Museum expedition to the remote Tsodilo hills in the vast Kalahari Desert, we saw numerous, richly painted rock outcrops. One painting of a rhinoceros could be seen from the base of a hill, but we had to climb straight up, mainly hand over hand, for about 200 feet over very steep terrain to reach the narrow ledge next to this painting. There was a sheer drop below the ledge. The view of the rhinoceros from this dizzying position was spectacular. The impact of the painting was intensified when a kudu (large antelope) appeared from the bushes directly below us. I thought then of the long-vanished painter, who may have witnessed a similar scene while completing his work.

Southern African art contrasts markedly with the European art in a number of general ways. As noted previously, the African art was executed mainly on rock-shelter walls and rock outcrops. Another notable contrast is that humans were painted frequently in the African art, and they were often shown in groups. These human figures are often very graceful and natural, although there are also highly stylized humans and a wide array of human-animal combinations such as antelope-people, crocodile-people, and the like.

Many different species of animals were depicted, though none are recognized as extinct forms. Antelope such as eland and kudu are very prevalent. There are also giraffes, zebras, elephants, rhinoceroses, baboons, lions, and other animals. More rarely there are fish, snakes, and river crabs. Similar to European art, however, an intriguing part of the African art includes a wide variety of abstract signs and symbols such as circles, dots, rectangular enclosures, lines, and so on.

San Rock Art

Most of the southern African art was probably done by San-speaking peoples. In popular accounts they are known as the Bushmen. This, however, is a derogatory term. They are one of the most intensively studied hunting-and-foraging groups in the world. The San, along with the related Khoi peoples, were the original inhabitants of much of southern Africa prior to the influx of Bantu-speaking farmers, whose descendants include the vast majority of people now living in southern Africa. Tragically, the San were nearly destroyed as a people when the Dutch colonists, who settled in the Cape region of South Africa, moved into the interior. At present, the San are found mainly in the Kalahari Desert in Botswana, just to the north of South Africa, and in adjacent parts of Namibia. Their traditional lifestyle, which was based on hunting and foraging, is disappearing quickly.

None of the San paint rock shelters today, but there is solid evidence that they were painting in some areas until the time of historic contact with Europeans. First, there are some scenes in the art that depict historic events, showing horses, wagons, and Europeans. Second, when the San in South Africa were slaughtered by the Europeans, a few of the victims were carrying painting kits. All of this means that some of the more recent paintings are probably only a few hundred years old. In fact, most authorities judged that even the earliest of the southern African rock art is no more than 6,000 years old.

This opinion was shattered in 1969 by findings made in an obscure cave located in the Hun Mountains in Namibia. Deep in the occupation layers of the cave known as Apollo, 11 several painted slabs were recovered, and the layer containing the slabs was found by radiocarbon dating to be between 28,450 and 26,350 years old.[23] These are among the oldest dated paintings in the world, much older than those for sites such as Altamira and Lascaux. In addition, some engraved stones have been found recently in South African sites dating to about 10,000 B.C.[24] It is clear that we have not yet established how old some of the southern African rock art really is, though experts still assume that most of it was done within the last few thousand years.

What does the southern African rock art mean? Can it be decoded, or is there any hidden meaning? For the most part, interpretations have been quite general. Some of the art is thought to be narrative. That is, there are some well-known paintings that are believed by many to depict events such as particular hunts, funeral rites, honey gathering, and dancing. There are many other paintings, however, that cannot be explained so easily. Were they of mythological significance, or were some of them done for the sheer enjoyment of painting? Many of the questions about African rock art could have been answered if someone had sought out a few of the painters at the time of European contact. After the San were heavily decimated and the tradition of painting had ceased, there was almost no way of getting direct information. The San population in South Africa disappeared quickly, and it seemed as if the information about the paintings was also lost.

Wilhelm Bleek, a German linguist, was well aware of the fact that the San were headed toward extinction, and he had the foresight to collect information about their traditions and language. In the 1870s he obtained permission to interview some southern San who were then prisoners in Cape Town, South Africa.[25] While Bleek worked on the language, his sister-in-law, Lucy Lloyd, recorded myths. Thousands of hand-written pages on folk traditions were collected on many different aspects of southern San customs. When these collections were recorded, no one realized that some of this information would, one day, contribute to a new understanding of the lost tradition of rock art.

For a long time, these documents gathered dust in the library and only occasionally attracted the attention of scholars. Nearly a century had passed when J. D. Lewis-Williams, a South African rock-art specialist, began to research the Bleek-Lloyd documents as well as another nineteenth-century source recorded by a magistrate. A careful sifting of the primary documents revealed some very important clues to the interpretation of some of the rock paintings that Lewis-Williams had studied in the Drakensberg Mountains of eastern South Africa. Spurred on by the success of his historical research, he interviewed the !Kung San (the exclamation point indicates a click sound) of the northwest Kalahari and found them very cooperative and interested in his work. He noticed striking similarities between what he had gleaned from the nineteenth-century sources and what his informants were reporting from the Kalahari. Together, the two sources blended into a powerful tool for analyzing the art that he had recorded in the Drakensberg area.

Much of the pertinent material centers on the importance of the eland, which is the world's biggest antelope. The San have a very special relationship with this animal. It is a symbol in almost all of their major cultural transitions, such as girls' puberty rituals and marriage. The eland is also seen as an important source of power for San spiritual leaders in their efforts to cure the sick, make rain, or otherwise influence the divine. These people enter a state of trance by means of a trance dance, during which they frequently experience nosebleeds and hallucinations. Finally, the spirit of the fallen dancer is believed to leave the body, fly through the air, and become transformed by spiritual power into an animal, often an eland.

Careful study of the nature of the dance and the trance-state has led to a new appreciation of some of the most puzzling characteristics of the San paintings. These include lines that connect human figures, animals, and people with "bloody noses," "flying bucks" (antelope), and people with hooves and antelope heads. The new interpretation views the enigmatic lines as lines of force symbolizing the supernatural power or potency of medicine men in trance. Researchers even suspect that some of the zigzag lines reminiscent of a malfunctioning television are depictions of the initial stage of hallucinating, reported to be a universal characteristic experienced by people entering a state of trance.

An example of how Lewis-Williams has applied this information to the rock art is seen in the photograph showing South African rock art from Kamberg. The half-human figures with either horns or hooves symbolize spiritualists in trance who have been transformed into antelope. The figure who bends over with outstretched arms is said to have a posture typical of trance dancers. The eland has a bristling coat, which Lewis-Williams views as being symbolic of death as described by San. The San view the state of trance itself as a form of "dying." Thus in this picture, Lewis-Williams sees a "clear link between the death of eland and the 'death' of trancing medicine men . . ."[26] The dancer who is touching the eland is receiving the animal's power.

Lewis-Williams has concluded that the southern African paintings are not to be understood as literal narratives of particular events but as parts of a complex system of metaphors. He believes that trance power is the most important aspect of the interpretation of the art. If this analysis is correct, it can cause one to wonder whether there also may be series of hidden meanings associated with the European cave art.

Namoratunga: The People of Stone

Not all of the African rock art was done by San-speaking hunter-foragers. Some of it was the work of Bantu-speaking farmers, as well as other groups who were cattle herders. In parts of eastern Africa there were pastoral Neolithic peoples who began to keep cattle, sheep, and goats by about 2,500 B.C. Some of these people were ancestral Cushitic speakers, and they also practiced rock art.

A very interesting case of interpreting some of this pastoral art is seen at the Namoratunga site, which is located in a remote desert region of northern Kenya. Namoratunga, which means "people of stone" in the local Turkana language, has been radiocarbon-dated to about 335 B.C. It includes more than 1,000 rock engravings, clustered on several hills and on large upright slabs that demarcate graves. These engravings depict a wide range of geometric designs such as circles, sunbursts, and ladderlike patterns. There were no other sites like it in the immediate area, and the Turkana claimed no relationship to the site.

Mark Lynch, who was excavating the graves that were associated with the stones, solved the puzzle of the Namoratunga engravings in 1975. On his way back to camp, as he watched a young man herding a bull through the scrubby vegetation, Lynch noticed that the back of the bull was branded with a pattern of lines that matched one of the symbols on the ancient rock engravings. That night in camp he watched, with great interest, as Turkana elders drew the same symbols in the sand. Their similarity to rock engravings was striking.

Lynch then recorded about 142 different symbols from the Namoratunga engravings. Turkana elders recognized about 70 percent of these symbols as brands used by their people to indicate ownership of livestock. Although the Turkana were not connected historically to the site, Lynch reasoned that, through the years, they preserved elements of a widespread pastoral heritage, as evidenced in the retention of many of the same brand symbols. Furthermore, among the Turkana and other societies, brand symbols are passed down from father to son. When Lynch excavated the graves at Namoratunga, he found that only males had decorated gravestones. A strong case can be made, therefore, that ancient Namoratunga people were also patrilineal.

But that is not all. At Namoratunga there are two distinct cemeteries and associated areas of rock art. The first one, which is the largest, includes 162 graves. This cemetery is diamond-shaped, with each point of the diamond oriented toward one of the four main compass directions. Lynch discovered that within each part of the diamond, the placement of the graves also correlates significantly with these directions. The spatial distribution of the engravings on the rock outcrops adjacent to the largest cemetery also match the compass directions. In addition, the outcrops differ significantly in the kinds of designs they contain. All the data, when analyzed, implies that the cemetery was divided into separate burial areas, perhaps for different kin groups within the larger society, and that each part of the cemetery had its own distinctive rock-art area.

The idea that one could link together the meaning of the rock art, the organization of a cemetery, and the nature of ancient social organization was not apparent when the work was initiated at Namoratunga. These conclusions were based on a combination of luck and skillful analysis. By excavating only representative graves chosen by a random-sampling method, Lynch discovered the patterning in the cemetery itself, as well as data on the burial positions and the relationship between marked gravestones and male burials. The analysis of the engravings on the rock outcrops was done separately and utilized several statistical methods to test for correlations. Then the two bodies of data (those on the cemetery and the engraved rock outcrops) were compared. Lynch's study reflects methodological and analytical breakthroughs in archaeology that began in the 1960s and are continuing at present. The major advances centered on the development of more sophisticated problem-solving approaches that are, in and of themselves, as vital to archaeologists as the pioneering discoveries made at Altamira and other historically significant sites.

3

THE BURIAL FRONTIER

From Wildflowers to Gold Coffins

The uncovering of burials continues to provide one of the central and most glamorous themes in archaeology. For example, on September 14, 1988, the discovery of what has been described as the richest prehistoric tomb in the New World was announced on page one of *The New York Times*. This find, made near Sipán in coastal Peru, features numerous items of gold as well as a story of intrigue involving tomb robbers and a gunfight. The tomb is linked to the Moche culture and is estimated to be about 1500 years old. Public attention has been captivated by the rich grave furnishings and monumental effort invested in the ancient burials of divine kings and other prominent people. While the story of Tutankhamen is the most notable example of a high-profile burial site, there is also much to be learned from the first simple burials of the Neandertals. We will begin with them and then review some burials that are among the greatest of archaeological discoveries.

THE NEANDERTALS OF SHANIDAR CAVE

Humans are the only animals that bury their dead, and the oldest human graves were made by Neandertals. About forty Neandertal graves have been found, almost all of them in Europe and the Middle East. Neandertals thrived between about 100,000 and 40,000 years ago, though most of their remains date to the start of the last glaciation of Europe (70,000 to 40,000 years ago). Because artifacts and food were frequently placed in the graves, possibly destined for use in a future life, anthropologists postulate that Neandertals believed in a spiritual existence after death. Therefore, these oldest graves are also thought to document the dawn of religious beliefs more than 60,000 years ago.

The Neandertals were the first of our ancestors to attain modern brain size. In fact, some feel that the average size of their brains was even larger than the average modern brain. Neandertals were characterized by low cranial vaults, large brow ridges, a massive face (especially the sinus cavities), and the lack of a chin. Below the head, their skeletons were essentially like ours, except that they were powerfully built people who seemed to have undergone a great deal of physical exertion.[1]

Were the Neandertals our ancestors? This question merits further discussion before looking at the Shanidar burials. An early reconstruction of the Neandertals based on a skeleton found in France gave the impression that Neandertals walked in a stooped fashion and had many primitive characteristics. This reconstruction was shown to be in error, principally because the skeleton was arthritic. Unfortunately, however, the stereotype of Neandertals as highly primitive cave men was perpetuated for decades. As a result, there has been a tendency to view the Neandertals as a side branch in our evolutionary tree that withered away, unable to compete with anatomically modern *Homo sapiens*. This view was seriously challenged, especially during the 1960s and 1970s when many anthropologists became convinced that the Neandertals were, in fact, our direct ancestors. They were generally accepted as an early form of *Homo sapiens* and were classified by the different subspecies name of *Homo sapiens neandertalensis*. It was widely believed that the evolution of

Neandertals into modern humans occurred shortly after 40,000 years ago.

The issue of the evolutionary relationship of the Neandertals to ourselves, which seemed to have reached a final solution, was not to be put to rest. Another view surfaced in 1987 and has since gained momentum. The latest view is supported by data far removed from the typical field setting where fossils are found. Instead, it centers on discoveries in molecular biology made by Rebecca L. Cann and her coworkers. They have been researching mitochondrial DNA, which is found outside of the cell nucleus and is only carried by females. There are known to be differences among present-day human populations in the structure of mtDNA that are the result of mutations that have occurred over an extensive period of time. By comparing samples of the mtDNA from different populations it has been possible to trace the divergence of the mtDNA through human females back to a theoretical point of origin represented by a single woman. The greatest diversity in mtDNA is evidenced in Africans, notably in samples taken from the !Kung San, who live in the Kalahari desert of Botswana. The researchers have also calculated what they believe to be the divergence rate for the mtDNA and have estimated when it first appeared. Current results indicate that *Homo sapiens* originated in Africa, most likely between 100,000 and 200,000 years ago. This would predate the time of the Neandertals. This view, based on molecular biology, would have profound implications if independently substantiated by the fossil record. First, in a remote sense, it would mean we are all descended from an original *Homo sapiens* population that migrated from Africa at an early date. Secondly, this would add new credibility to the argument that Neandertals were a side branch that in one way or another disappeared. In this version, the Neandertals would have faded out of the picture when the more advanced newcomers from Africa spread into the area. This is called the "out of Africa theory" and it is the subject of much debate. Some researchers see too much continuity between the Neandertals and anatomically modern *Homo sapiens* to accept this theory while others see just the opposite. I think the issue will be greatly clarified when we recover more complete skeletal remains from Africa that are firmly dated to the period in question. Now, on to examine the remarkable finds at Shanidar cave.

In the summer of 1951, Dr. Ralph Solecki was looking for cave sites in a remote part of the northern Iraqi mountains near the Turkish border when he was informed about a large cave that still had people living in it. It was located on a mountain known as Baradost, which overlooks the Greater Zab River, a tributary of the Tigris. Intrigued, Solecki searched for it, accompanied by an armed escort because that part of northern Iraq was a troublesome political area inhabited by the fiercely independent Kurds. After a considerable climb up the hot slopes of Baradost Mountain, Solecki found Shanidar Cave. He writes that he "felt a twinge of excitement" as he approached the site. "It looked bigger and bigger as we came close."[2] Shanidar was not disappointing, to say the least. The cave had deep deposits, traces of fire, and room for a large group of people. The deposits extended from fairly recent occupation, back through the Upper Paleolithic, and on into the Middle Paleolithic—the time range of the Neandertals.

The first Neandertal discovered at Shanidar, Sh. I, was a man of about forty years, buried under a pile of stones. He was apparently killed by a rockfall, due to one of the frequent earthquakes in the area, that fractured the ceiling of the cave. This man had arthritis and was blind in one eye. There was also a healed wound on his skull. Moreover, his "right arm, collarbone, and shoulder blade had never fully grown from birth." In addition, there is evidence that the end of the arm had been amputated before the man died. The amputation is thought by some writers to indicate a form of surgery by the Neandertals, though perhaps it resulted from an encounter with a dangerous animal. This man was clearly handicapped for a long period in a society that was based entirely on hunting and foraging for wild foods. He may not have been a very productive hunter, limited to the use of one hand; one would expect, therefore, that there was enough food available to support this person and that the group went out of its way to care for a handicapped individual. Certainly, this example places the "brutish" Neandertals in a different light, making them worthy ancestral candidates for *Homo sapiens*.

Altogether, Solecki's team recovered the remains of eight Neandertals, one of which ranks among the most extraordinary specimens ever recovered. This skeleton, named Sh. IV, was found when Solecki decided to draw a profile of the wall of the excavation, a standard archaeological procedure. While cleaning an area prior to doing the drawing, Solecki noticed some white, powdered material that looked like disintegrated antler. Subsequently, he found some bones, which he thought were from animals. He showed one of them to T. D. Stewart, who was the excavation team's physical anthropologist from the U.S. National Museum. Stewart recognized immediately that the bone in question was from part of a human leg. Further work with this lucky find slowly revealed the remains of an adult male Neandertal who had been buried on his left side, facing west. Eventually, the work uncovered four individuals who had been recovered in the same general area—the man, two women, and a child. The remains of Sh. IV (the man) were in a very poor state of preservation and started to crack during the excavation. For this reason, preservative was applied, and the whole complex was plastered and removed in a block. This would enable Stewart to work on it in a lab under better conditions.

Before removing the skeleton, soil samples were taken from the immediate area. This is a standard procedure in archaeology that is done in the hope of recovering paleoenvironmental data through later laboratory analysis. Under the right conditions, microscopic pollen grains can survive for thousands of years and provide detailed information about the environment in which ancient people lived. In such cases, the pollen can be identified and the overall vegetation pattern can be reconstructed. Solecki tells us that he was not optimistic about recovering any data from the samples. The big surprise came eight years later, after Mme. Arlette Leroi-Gourhan, a pollen expert, analyzed the soil.

Two of the samples, taken less than sixteen inches from Sh. IV, contained a great amount of pollen, while other samples had much less. Leroi-Gourhan writes, "A remarkable fact was that instead of the normally isolated pollen grains found in caves, many of them appeared to be clustered in groups which contained from two to more than 100 pollen grains."[3] From the nature of the evidence, Leroi-Gourhan concluded "that complete flowers (at least seven species) had been introduced into the cave at the same time." This would not have been a haphazard event, because one of the species of flowers was a hollyhock, which cannot be gathered at random in a mixed clump of other flowers. It had to have been picked individually. The fact that the scale of a butterfly wing was found in the sample tells us that flowers were brought into the cave rather than the pollen having been simply blown into the cave by the wind. The butterfly, or at least part of it, must have been attached to the plant. Another point supporting this conclusion is that some of the clusters of pollen "have retained the form of the anther of the flower." According to Solecki, the flowers were brought into the cave about 60,000 years ago. More specifically, the blooming period of the flowers suggests the burial occurred sometime between late May and early July.

Why did the Shanidar people bury this man with wildflowers? Nothing like this had ever been found before, and it was a bit mind-boggling given what most people thought about life in Neandertal times. Was it done to show respect for the dead or to decorate the body with something considered to be beautiful? No one knows the answers to these questions, but it is interesting that all of the flowers come from plants that have important uses as traditional folk medicines in Iraq. Indeed, most have multiple uses. For instance, one is used to treat stomach problems, another asthma, and the hollyhock for toothaches as well as other remedies. Were these medicinal plants used to bring the person spiritually back to life in another world? We can only speculate about this. It is not uncommon for people who live close to nature to have extensive traditional knowledge about the plants around them. We archaeologists who collect and make a record of the uses of plants that grow around our sites have often found that most of the plants have some kind of traditional value as medicine, food, or sources of material for making something. Probably our remote ancestors also explored various uses of plants. In any case, the Shanidar flower burial is unique, and it demonstrates how completely unforeseen information can be obtained through routine sampling of soils in the field. If this had not been done, the microscopic clues to a completely different side of the life and death of Neandertals would have remained unknown.

PAZYRYK: FROZEN TOMBS IN SIBERIA

Reconstructing the details of life in prehistoric times is based upon a very incomplete record, because most materials, such as wood or skin objects, decay quickly and are never found. Occasionally, however, sites are found at which the preservation is excellent, such as the desert caves of the Dead Sea region, certain wet deposits, and frozen soil. The amazing discovery of Ice Age woolly mammoths with skins preserved in the icy regions of Siberia is a case in point.

As far as I am aware, the first frozen site associated with humans was discovered in June 1865, when Dr. Wilhelm Radloff was exploring the Altai Mountains in southern Siberia, a little more than one hundred miles north of the Chinese border and not far from the western edge of Mongolia. At the time of Radloff's explorations, Russian archaeology was in its infancy, and nothing was known about the rugged Altai region, which was inhabited by independent groups of pastoralists. Radloff tells us in his journal that he encountered a great number of graves marked by large mounds of boulders concentrated near the Katanda River. Radloff attempted to excavate several of them, but, after removing great blocks of stone and earth, his work came nearly to a standstill. He writes, "In the frozen solid soil here we could only work with the help of fire," and this created a swamplike ooze. "All of the time mud and water flowed into the burial pit so it was only with difficulty that pieces of gold leaf and felt clothing could be collected."[4] The thawing mud of the Katanda graves yielded birchbark, pieces of leather, clothing, felt, furs, and even some wooden tables. Radloff also uncovered numerous graves of horses, complete with bridles and other riding paraphenalia, as well as human skeletons. No one knew how old the graves really were, but Radloff placed them in a remote time that he called the "Old Ice period of the Southern Altai."

We now know that the frozen tombs excavated by Radloff were graves of Scythian chiefs, known as the Yue-Chi to the Chinese who lived to the south of the area and traded with them. These Altai people were part of the loosely related Scythian groups who, at the height of their power at about 600 B.C., ranged from the borders of China across much of central Asia and into the Middle East. The great military success of these and other pastoral nomads was rooted in their speed and mobility on horseback and in a flexible social organization that enabled large groups to coalesce rapidly under the leadership of prominent chiefs.

The follow-up to Radloff's discovery did not begin until 1924, when Sergei Rudenko, a prominent Russian archaeologist, did some exploratory work in a nearby area called the Pazyryk Valley.[5] Rudenko was a natural for this work. He was an avid horseman keenly interested in the customs of the different groups of local nomads. His initial work was interrupted by the outbreak of war, and he wasn't able to return to dig the Pazyryk tombs in earnest until the late 1940s. Because of this delay, Rudenko was able to take advantage of the radiocarbon-dating technique, which was discovered in 1949. He found that the Pazyryk tombs dated to about 430 B.C. Further fine-tuning was made possible by comparing the annual tree rings in the cross sections of the logs used in the construction of some of the tombs. The age of a tree when it was cut down can be determined by counting the annual rings of growth. These annual growth rings in trees, especially in conifers, are somewhat analogous to fingerprints. The size of particular rings varies with the weather conditions of specific years. This enables specialists to match up and overlap the ring sequences of different logs. For example, assume that log A has fourteen annual rings and during the fifth and tenth years of growth very large rings were formed. If the same sequence of large rings can be matched in logs B and C, which are sixteen and eighteen years old, the age of when all of the logs were cut relative to each other can be firmly established. This is the principle that Rudenko used. He established that the first two tombs were constructed in the same year, while the next was built seven years later. Another was made thirty years after that, and the last one was built after yet another eleven years. Finally, by examining the seasonal condition of the horsehair and flowers found in the graves, scientists were able to determine that the burials took place in either early summer or autumn.

The Pazyryk graves also revealed relative social standings. A great many small graves were found containing modest amounts of goods. In contrast, some of the chieftain barrows, or burial mounds, were up to thirty-six meters in diameter and capped by substantial mounds containing hundred of logs and boulders that weighed several tons. They featured large square burial pits with wooden floors. The soils at Pazyryk are not naturally frozen on a year-round basis, yet the graves were encased in ice. Evidently, the deep burial pit capped by logs and boulders had the effect of creating a natural refrigerator. Cold air was trapped at the bottom, and the moisture that seeped in through spaces between the rocks and logs froze. The normal summer thaw was short enough so that thawing in the depths of the tombs was kept to a minimum.

Rudenko slowly thawed the icy graves by pouring hot water on them. The preservation was extraordinary. Each body had been eviscerated, stuffed with plants, and then stitched back together. The brain had been withdrawn through a small hole in the skull. The corpses were placed in hollow-log coffins in specially built burial chambers at the base of the tombs.

Barrow 2 was one of the most interesting of the graves. Here were found two corpses, an old man and a woman about forty years old. They were probably originally buried together in the same coffin, but it appeared that robbers had taken the bodies out and beheaded them to remove twisted metal necklaces called *torques*. The woman's legs and one of her hands were also cut off, probably to remove other jewelry. The man was almost certainly killed in a raid. Rudenko tells us that his scalp had been "cut through from ear to ear through a forelock of hair and then torn off backwards . . ."[6] According to Herodotus, the Greek historian who observed Scythians near the Black Sea, scalping was a common Scythian war practice. Interestingly, the man was also wearing a fake beard. In addition, his skin was so well preserved that it still revealed extensive tattoos covering his leg, arm, chest, and back. They depict many imaginary animals typical of Scythian art.

The Scythian chiefs were buried with some of their finest horses, symbolic of their wealth and prestige. The horses were killed by an ax blow, lowered into the graves on ropes, and arranged with their heads facing east. Rudenko recovered large numbers of horse skeletons, as well as twenty frozen carcasses on which the coats, manes, and tails were well preserved. The horses were mostly chestnut or brown with trimmed manes, carefully braided tails, and ears marked to signify ownership. There were work horses as well as some very fine thoroughbreds. An amazing array of riding equipment was recovered. Applied felt on the saddle covers depicted winged lions and griffins attacking animals such as mountain goats. The saddles were decorated lavishly with gold leaf and fancy leatherwork. Carved wood pendants of animals dangled from the bridles. Several horses were even wearing masks, one of which was capped by deer antlers.

Hundreds of well-preserved artifacts were recovered from the frozen tombs. Among the many highlights were

- The oldest known woven wool carpet. It has been described by Artamonov as having been woven "in an incredibly complicated fashion: in an area of 100 square centimeters (about 15½ square inches) 3,600 knots can be counted."[7] This carpet is approximately six feet square and is richly decorated with bands of horsemen, deer, and other designs.
- Embroidered Chinese silk used as a saddle cover.
- A wooden carriage with spoked wheels that was covered by a canopy decorated with felt swans. The carriage was restored from its crushed condition. It was probably of a ceremonial nature, similar to ancient Chinese carriages. This carriage, which may have been used to bring the bodies to the burial site, was buried with the four horses that pulled it.
- Felt wall hangings that had originally lined the tombs. These were decorated impressively. The largest one, which could easily cover the floor of a large living room, was patterned with horsemen, while others depict stylized birds, floral patterns, and human-lion figures.
- Musical instruments, including a drum and a stringed instrument.
- A wide variety of clothing. Notable finds were a man's shirt, woman's apron, hats, and felt stockings. Rudenko comments that one of the stockings still contained a foot.
- A fine silk purse and bags of fur and leather. One of the pouches still contained cheese. Other wooden and clay vessels are thought to have been used for a

popular, traditional Central Asian brew: fermented mare's milk.

- Food for the afterlife. Pieces of mutton and horsemeat were found.
- Complete kits for inhaling hashish. This included a tentlike frame with an attached leather bag of seeds and a bronze incense-burning pot. The tent served to collect the smoke.

Several authorities have pointed out how closely the Pazyryk burial pattern is illustrated by a Herodotus account from the fifth century B.C. of Scythian funerals near the Black Sea. Herodotus said that when a "King dies, they dig a great square pit." Subsequently, his stomach is "slit open, cleaned out and filled with various aromatic substances, crushed galingale, parsley-seed, and anise; it is sewn up again and the whole body covered with wax."[8] Herodotus also describes transporting the corpse by wagon, the killing of large numbers of horses, construction of tombs of beams, and the heaping up of a huge burial mound. A final observation concerns the Scythian custom of personal purification after the burial. Herodotus wrote that they built a tripod and covered it with felt.

> Then they take some hemp seed, creep into the tent and throw the seed onto the hot stones. At once it begins to smoke, giving off a vapour unsurpassed by any vapour bath one could find in Greece. The Scythians enjoy it so much that they howl with pleasure.[9]

Other writers have commented that Herodotus was probably bewildered by this custom because he wasn't familiar with the effect of inhaling hashish smoke.[10]

THE SUTTON HOO SHIP BURIAL

In 1926, Mrs. Edith M. Pretty purchased a large estate in southeastern England known as Sutton Hoo. This was in a windswept, sandy area cut by the River Deben, which wound its way down to the sea, about eight miles to the southeast.

On the estate, about one-half mile from the river, was a group of large barrows that protruded out of a landscape somewhat similar to the ones at Pazyryk. None of them had been excavated, but there was some imaginative local speculation that they were likely to contain treasure. Supposedly Mrs. Pretty's nephew had even foretold, with a divining rod, that gold was buried in the largest mound.[11] Through the years, Mrs. Pretty's curiosity about the mounds heightened. In 1938, spurred on by friends, she decided to have the mounds excavated and sought professional help from the nearby Ipswich Museum.

The museum sent Basil Brown to do the digging. He began by opening some of the smaller mounds. One of them contained poorly preserved traces of a small ship, which had been looted, while the others contained cremations.

In May 1939, work was initiated on the largest mound, which was about one hundred feet long and nine feet high. This was an ambitious project for Brown, who was working with a crew of only two local helpers. Brown notes in his diary that when one of his workers found a small piece of iron, he "immediately stopped the work and carefully explored the area with a small trowel and uncovered five rivets in position on what turned out to be the extreme end prow or stern of a ship."[12] Thus began one of the greatest discoveries in British archaeology and, in many ways, one of the most problematic.

After a little over a week of excavating, Brown described how he was "continuing the slow excavation work of the ship itself carefully creeping along rivet by rivet. It is now evident however that we are up against a far larger thing than anyone suspected." The outline and impression of the ship had been preserved by the alignments of these rivets, though the wood itself had rotted away. All indications implied that the ship was much larger than the few others that had been found previously in England and about which there was very little information. Clearly the Sutton Hoo find offered a unique opportunity to learn more about ship burials. At first, Brown believed that the find was a Viking ship, possibly similar to ones recovered in Norway. This heightened the potential significance of

Sutton Hoo, because no Viking ships had yet been discovered that had escaped looting. Brown had found traces of a robber's hole that was off-center, but indications suggested that the looters had given up before reaching the burial chamber. Also, it seemed quite clear from the size of the ship that only a king or some other very important person would have been buried in it.

As Brown inched his way to the burial-chamber area, interest peaked and the news of the find spread rapidly among British archaeologists. It became increasingly clear that the work at Sutton Hoo was of national significance, and the government decided to step in. What had started as a low-key local effort mushroomed into a major project headed by Charles W. Phillips of Cambridge University. Brown continued to work on the project, along with several of the leading archaeologists in Britain. They were in a race against time, because the clouds of World War II were gathering over Britain. (In fact, the war broke out a week after the dig was completed, and the artifacts could not be restored and studied until many years later. During the war the Sutton Hoo finds, along with many other important artifacts from the British Museum, were hidden in an abandoned London subway tunnel to protect them from the ravages of German bombing raids.)

Work proceeded in the suspected burial-chamber area, and, relates Phillips, the remains of a sword were uncovered.

> Almost at once gold objects were revealed to the north of the sword blade. These had been covered with a thin layer of wood but were showing through it. In view of their obvious richness and importance it was plainly unwise to leave the objects *in situ* . . .[13]

Among the key finds were a gold belt buckle and a jeweled purse that had thirty-nine gold coins and two gold ingots in it. The coins proved to be from the Merovingian dynasty, which, from A.D. 500 to 751, had extended from France to Switzerland. This dynasty is associated with the early history of the Franks or French state. It was named after King Merovech, but the most prominent ruler was

Clovis I who converted to Christianity following a vow to do so if he was victorious in battle. Returning to the coins, a study of the gold content, which varied according to when they were minted, revealed that most of the Sutton Hoo coins dated from A.D. 600 to 615, with the latest specimen dating between A.D. 620 and 630. The age of the coins, together with other finds, demonstrated that Sutton Hoo was a burial not of a Viking ship but of one from an earlier, Anglo-Saxon period. The Anglo-Saxons were Germanic peoples who entered England in the fifth century A.D., following the Romans.

Other discoveries made in the same general place were mostly in a crushed or fragmentary state. Among them were a shield, a helmet decorated with gold leaf, silver drinking-horn parts, chain-work, silver spoons, a lyre, and a whetstone-scepter. One of the pleasant surprises occurred when a large silver dish was removed. Under it was a silver bowl containing another smaller silver bowl and a series of wooden bottles. A group of leather items were associated with this, including some bags and remains of shoes. This is only a partial inventory of what was uncovered at Sutton Hoo. Nothing quite like it had ever been found before, and the amount of gold and silver made it the greatest archaeological treasure discovered in England.

Sutton Hoo was an interesting and informative burial site, but where was the body? Originally, a few fragments were identified by an anatomist as being human, including a piece of skull, but they turned out to be oak. Phillips wrote in his diary in 1939: "It was agreed by all that although an inhumation had probably taken place in this region of the burial chamber there was no surviving trace of it either in the form of bones or teeth or any local effect." The following year H. Munro Chadwick wrote, in a classic article entitled "Who Was He?": "Indeed the prevalent view now seems to be that the tomb never contained a body—that it was constructed as a cenotaph . . . This is the view that is, and always has been, held by those who took part in the excavation, there has been no change of view."[14] He attributes the story that a body was present to "the imagination of an uninformed newspaper writer." A prevalent view was then fostered that the missing king at Sutton Hoo must have died elsewhere, and, because his body could not be recovered, a full burial ceremony was carried out to commemorate him. Perhaps, they guessed, the missing king was Athelhere, who died in battle and whose body was believed to have been lost in a flood.

More recent detectivelike chemical studies added to the speculation. It was reasoned that artifacts lying near a body might bear chemical traces of the body itself. Test results of the sword revealed unusually high concentrations of phosphates, which easily could have been produced by the decomposition of an adjacent skeleton. Furthermore, analysis showed that some enigmatic lumps of material were originally bone that had been transformed by burning into casts of bone high in ferric phosphate. Was this a human cremation-burial—or perhaps the remains of a roast animal included as an offering of food?

Although the evidence is circumstantial, the leading expert of the subject, R. Bruce-Mitford, believes that a human body was, in fact, buried in the Sutton Hoo ship. The presence of ceremonial shoulder clasps, a scepter, and what is most likely a royal standard suggests that an important king was buried there. Which king was it? Once again, a ninth-century document and other sources referring to Anglo-Saxon kings were consulted, and the dates of the coins were considered. As a result, opinion shifted away from Athelhere to a king known as Redwald, who reigned in East Anglia between A.D. 599 and 624, a time of profound changes when Christianity was spreading to England. Redwald himself was converted but retained pagan customs as well.

The lab work on the Sutton Hoo finds required many years of patience and skillful insights. For example, only rusty traces of what was hardly recognizable as chain were found lying near some bronze cauldrons. A photograph was taken of the position of the chain in the ground, and then the amorphous pieces were removed. It took six months to reconstruct the rusty pieces in the same order as shown in the original field photo.[15] Then a series of X-ray pictures were taken that enabled the technicians to see the actual linkage pattern beneath the crusty exterior. With this information drawings were made, and an accurate model of the original chain was constructed by a blacksmith. From the tangled mass of unrecognizable rusted iron emerged a twelve-foot-six-inch chain, the original of which must have been used to hang a cauldron over a fire from a towering ceiling.

Clearly the Sutton Hoo burial was part of the cultural heritage of England's past, but did it belong to the state or to Mrs. Pretty, who owned the property and initiated the dig? In 1939, a coroner's inquest was held to decide this issue. Long before, Sir William Blackstone (1723–1780), the founding father of English law, had written that any treasure such as coins and gold found "hidden in the earth" belongs to the king if the original owner is unknown.[16] At the time of the inquest, one of the missions of the jury was to determine whether or not the treasure was hidden purposefully by the original owner with the expectation of eventually retrieving it. If this could be proved, then the finds would belong to the state, otherwise they would be the property of the finder. Archaeologist Phillips testified that the amount of communal effort reflected in the Sutton Hoo burial

> makes it impossible that the act of burying a person in a barrow can have been carried on with any real secrecy . . . there can have been no concealment of the fact that many rich and valuable objects were being put in the grave . . . The objects placed with the dead man were for his use in a future life . . . and there was no intention on the part of those carrying out the burial to recover them later . . .[17]

After the court ruled that the treasure indeed belonged to Mrs. Pretty, she donated the entire collection to Great Britain.

THE ROYAL SHANG TOMBS

In 1899, Wang-I-Yang (Wang Yirong), the Dean of Hanlin College, purchased some "dragon bones" to treat an ill member of his family according to Chinese folk tradition. (These were the same sort of medicinal bones, often fossils or old bones found in farmers' fields, that would later lead to the discovery of Zhoukoudian, the famous Peking-man site discussed in Chapter 1.) Before grinding them into powder, Wang scrutinized one of the bones, a turtle-shell fragment, and found some ancient Chinese characters inscribed on it. Although he could not read them, he was intrigued enough to buy out the medicine shop in search for other specimens. Wang had made a significant discovery, but he did not live to see it bear fruit. A year later, he committed suicide.

Eventually, news of Wang's find spread, and more of the mysterious turtle shells were collected from the medicine shops. Once scholars learned how to read them, it was established that they were ancient oracle bones. They were used mainly by members of the elite to predict the weather, determine future health problems, and examine a range of other subjects. The particular questions about the future were written on the shells by specialists and heat was applied. Answers were determined by interpreting the nature of the cracks in the bones. This type of divination, called *scapulamancy*, has been practiced in other cultures using shoulder bones of animals.

In the opening years of the twentieth century, roughly between 1900 and 1925, an avid interest in collecting oracle bones developed, and the dragon bones with writing became expensive curios. Local villagers made a profit digging for them and selling them to professional collectors and dealers.

In 1928, scholars from the Academia Sinica, a science research institute, decided to investigate the most productive places for finding oracle bones, areas near the city of Anyang. A young scholar, Tung-Tso Pin, questioned the local school principal and found that the students sometimes found the oracle bones by digging in a field outside of town. Tung paid a child to take him to the place. He wrote: "The child pointed to a sand heap and stated that oracle bones came from underneath it."[18] Nearby were some freshly dug holes, a testimony to the fact that the child knew what he was talking about. Tung returned to the Academia Sinica animated about his findings at Anyang. His opinion was that excavations "must be undertaken without delay," because there was a great danger that much archaeological information was being destroyed by collectors, whose pits were cutting into the site.

Archaeology was a new science in China, and Anyang was the first major Bronze Age excavation. The work was started in 1928 and has continued for decades. At first, excavations centered on the Bronze Age city of Anyang. Only the looters, who competed with the archaeologists, realized that a royal cemetery existed in a nearby area. Li Chi, and early director of the project, mentions that when each field season ended, there was a great rush by professional looting teams in their destructive search for oracle bones and other treasures. In 1934, rumors began to circulate that some extremely interesting bronze artifacts were recovered by a collector in an area known as the "northwest high ground." The archaeologists quickly followed the lead, and a careful search led to the discovery of royal tombs. Because of the richness of the site and the need to prevent further looting, the excavations shifted from the main Anyang site to the cemetery. The next several seasons saw a monumental work effort, with hundreds of laborers excavating. Sometimes the excavators were endangered by cave-ins while working in the deep tombs. One worker was buried alive and several others narrowly escaped with their lives.

The work at Anyang established that the legendary ruins of Yin, heretofore known only through the writings of a Chinese historian of the first century B.C., were a historical fact. It was the last capital of the Shang kings, between 1384 and 1111 B.C., prior to the rise of the Chou (Zhou) Dynasty. The Shang society signaled the beginning of the Bronze Age in China and stands as one of the world's pristine civilizations, along with ancient Egypt, Mesopotamia, the Indus Valley (Harrapan culture), and the early civilizations of Mexico and Peru. Shang civilization centered in northern China, but its influence extended over a vast area. Hallmarks include a sophisticated bronze technology, writing on oracle bones, walled cities, stamped-earth construction methods, and a pronounced social hierarchy, with the royal dynasty at the top and slaves at the bottom. Modern Chinese archaeologists, who follow a Marxist interpretation of the past, have concentrated on the social aspects of the age and have dubbed the Shang a slave society.

At the Anyang excavations, at least ten royal tombs have been discovered, as well as hundreds of smaller graves. It has been difficult, however, to relate the royal tombs to specific rulers, as is done in Pharaonic Egypt. Historical information provided by the oracle bones is helpful, but it is simply not as rich or specific as the documentary sources provided by Egyptian hieroglyphs.

Shang royal tombs are large square pits, up to forty feet deep. They are laid out along a north-south axis and have ramps leading into them.[19] At each base is a wooden burial chamber with log flooring and a coffin. One of the most striking characteristics about these tombs is the large number of human sacrificial victims found in them. The ancient Chinese were greatly concerned with pleasing the spirits of their ancestors, and this was epitomized at the funeral ceremony of a king, which was marked by extensive sacrificial rites. One of the tombs contained at least 131 people, plus 52 birds and other animals, while another one yielded 164 people. Who were the victims of these terrifying funeral ceremonies? According to Zheng Zhenxiang, as well as other writers, they were most likely war captives who were often decapitated or buried alive. The oracle bones mention the taking of thousands of prisoners by the powerful Shang armies.

There were hundreds of smaller burials that were also sacrificial. Some pits contained large numbers of skulls, while others yielded the skeletons of decapitated victims. Zheng, in a summary of recent work, mentions finds of 191 sacrificial pits, "each containing eight to ten decapitated skeletons. A total of 1,178 skeletons were identified."[20] In addition to humans, some burials of horses, elephants, and chariots are known. One of the chariots was buried with two horses and the driver.

It is unfortunate that almost all of the large royal tombs have been looted. Despite this fact, many bronze works of art have been recovered that were either missed or deemed unimportant to the looters. There are bronze wine vessels, helmets, and spear points, as well as some exquisite objects of jade. The bronze vessels bear the hallmark of Shang Dynasty art—a stylized animal mask.

In 1976 a major discovery was made of an intact royal Shang tomb that was missed by the looters. The importance of the find is underscored by its being the only Shang tomb in which the identity of the dead individual has been definitely established. A large number of wine vessels found in the tomb bear the name Lady Hao, and she is also mentioned on the oracle bones. They have described her as "a royal consort . . . a feudal vassal . . . and . . . as a military commander with the rank of general."[21] In one military campaign, she is credited with commanding thousands of troops. Lady Hao was the most influential wife of an important king. Her tomb was furnished lavishly. Because it was smaller than the looted tombs, it provides a minimal measure of what the others were probably like before they were robbed. Nearly 2,000 artifacts were found, including 210 bronze vessels, mostly for wine.[22] There were hundreds of jade figures of humans, dragons, and other animals. Ivory cups, bronze mirrors, weapons, and tools also accompanied Lady Hao, as did a vast quantity of cowry shells used for money and some sacrificial victims.

Objects from Lady Hao's tomb, along with other Bronze Age works of art from China, including the magnificent clay figures discussed in the following section, toured U.S. museums in 1980 and 1981. They have been viewed by thousands who otherwise would never have had the opportunity to see the originals. In this way, archaeology has helped to further international awareness and understanding.

THE BURIED ARMY OF QIN-SHI-HUANG

The Shang was followed by the Chou (Zhou) Dynasty, which was, in turn, succeeded by an episode of feudal unrest known as the Period of Warring States. One of the rulers who was rising to prominence at the end of this period was a youth who became known as Qin-Shi-Huang. He founded the Qin Dynasty (221–206 B.C.), brought about the end of the Warring States Period, and became the first emperor of China. He is credited with unifying the disparate feudal groups, standardizing the different kinds of money and weights and measures, and building the Great Wall of China. On the darker side, Qin persecuted and killed Confucian scholars and made many enemies with his despotic use of power. Like an ancient Idi Amin, Qin moved from palace to palace to confuse would-be assassins. Even his death was kept secret while his slowly deteriorating body was brought back hundreds of miles in a chariot.

A prominent early Chinese historian, Ssu-ma-Ch'ien (Sima Qian), lived about a century after the death of Qin. He provides an account of the emperor's tomb.[23] Supposedly built by 700,000 laborers, it took nearly four decades to finish. If we can believe the account, Qin's tomb was reputed to be a miniature replica of the universe. The major geographical areas of the earth were reproduced, and the main rivers of China were made out of constantly flowing mercury. Constellations were put in the sky. There were scale-model palaces and sumptuous grave furnishings. Emperor Qin, seasoned by the realities of the era he lived in, was prepared for the inevitable tomb robbers: Crossbows were carefully set with hair triggers to await them. Can this description be true? Qin's tomb is a well-known landmark in Xian province, where it is known as Mount Li. It is a huge, artificial, grass-covered hill that towers over the landscape. It has never been excavated, and most sources claim that it has never been looted.

In 1974, some construction workers were digging a well less than a mile east of Qin's tomb. To their amazement, they uncovered traces of a life-sized, realistic clay army that had been buried for more than 2,000 years. Not since the discovery of King Tut's tomb in 1923 had any archaeological site received such widespread attention. It has been estimated that more than 7,000 clay soldiers and horses were placed in a series of underground chambers to guard the emperor's tomb. (The practice of burying live guards and hundreds of sacrificial victims had ceased centuries earlier.) The remains of the clay army were found in a crushed state, buried beneath fifteen to twenty feet of earth. Chinese archaeologists have been facing a monumental task in excavating and restoring the army, as well as reconstructing the details of Qin's sophisticated military organization.

The first pit was about twice as long as a football field and nearly 200 feet wide. Here about 6,000 troops were placed in battle formation. The leaders were an elite attack force of archers and crossbowmen. Behind them were chariots, each drawn by four clay horses and manned by a driver and a warrior. A dozen foot soldiers protected each chariot. Next came the main body of infantry, armed with spears. The rear of the formation was defended by additional foot soldiers, and the flanks were guarded by a double column of archers. Two years after the original discovery, another pit was located a short distance away. This one contained mostly chariots and cavalry. Further work revealed a third pit, which included commanding officers. They were placed strategically behind the rest of the army. Finally, a fourth pit was found, which was unfinished.

The great amount of skill and effort that went into constructing this pottery army was awesome. Each soldier's body was made individually by the technique of coiling the clay. Parts, such as hands, were done separately and attached to the body. The troops were painted and given distinctive variations in hair, moustaches, and other features. Even the size of the troops was varied intentionally, probably to reflect real-life distinctions in the military. Infantrymen ranged between five feet, eight inches and six feet, one inch tall, while the charioteers were more imposing, averaging about six feet, three inches. The leader of the advance troops was a formidable six feet, five inches.[24]

Qin's clay army was placed to the east of the tomb. Archaeologists suspected strongly that additional remains might be buried on the west side. This supposition was based on the overriding concern in ancient China for achieving balance. Symmetry was an essential consideration in the layout of the early Bronze Age Shang tombs. In 1978, archaeologists were thus test drilling the deep deposits just to the west of the tomb when the drill was reported to have "jammed at seven meters underground. A gold ornament the size of a small walnut was recovered. Excavation brought up a part of a bronze helmet."[25] During the next two years, two bronze chariots were uncovered in the deep deposits, along with horses and a kneeling driver. The workmanship on one of the chariots has been described as consisting of more than 3,000 "separate parts of gold, silver or bronze." The bronzework featured the use of "different proportions of copper and tin according to the parts' different functions." The gear for the horses was silver and gold. After more than 2,000 years of burial, the richly colored paints applied to the chariots still survived. The Chinese suspect that there may be many more finds in the general vicinity.

These new finds tell us that the era of dramatic discoveries has by no means come to an end. Not everything was found in the pioneering days, when each shovelful of earth or slice of the machete seemed to reveal something new. Modern excavations can be even more productive, as archaeologists take advantage of better excavation and laboratory techniques.

THE TOMB OF TUTANKHAMEN

In the history of archaeology, perhaps no subject has stirred the imagination as much as the Egyptian tombs and the almost unbelievable efforts expended in their construction and ornamentation. Unfortunately, virtually all of the major tombs were looted, mostly within a few hundred years after the burials if not sooner. An ancient Egyptian hieroglyphic text of the trial of eight tomb robbers contains this confession.

> We stripped off the gold, which we found on the august mummy of this god, and its amulets and ornaments which were at its throat, and the covering wherein it rested. We found the king's wife likewise; we stripped off all that we found on her likewise. We set fire to their coverings. We stole their furniture which we found with them, being vases of gold, silver and bronze.[26]

The robbers divided the loot eight ways. In this case, the thieves were mainly workers who had banded together, but there is another case that points the finger directly at two high-ranking bureaucrats. No doubt bribery and a variety of other clandestine means were employed by looters.

Sometime around 1500 B.C., Pharaoh Tuthmosis I made a radical decision that abruptly changed the course of Egyptian tomb construction. In an effort to deal with the ever-present threat of tomb robbers, he decided to have his architect secretly construct a hidden tomb in a remote valley situated to the west of the Nile near what is currently the town of Luxor. This secret burial place is now known to Egyptologists as the Valley of the Kings. Tuthmosis I had established a new tradition that would be followed by his numerous successors. Yet in the end, only one of the tombs would escape being ravaged by looters. This was the tomb of Tutankhamen, the boy king, who ascended to the throne when he was only nine years old.

Tutankhamen reigned during the New Kingdom (ca. 1567–1085 B.C.). This was a period that included some exceptionally powerful rulers, as well as some that were mediocre. Tutankhamen followed on the heels of the heretical Pharaoh Akenaten and the queen of legendary beauty, Nefertiti. Akenaten was best known for having instituted a short-lived revolution in religious thinking that changed the official polytheistic system of beliefs to a form of monotheism centering on the solar god Aten. Originally, Tutankhamen's name was Tutankaten, until Akenaten's influence ended and the worship of the high god Amen was rekindled. Tutankhamen was not a notable pharaoh in the context of Egyptian history. He died when he was only eighteen, in about 1350 B.C., and was laid to rest in a secret tomb in the Valley of the Kings. His main claim to fame is that his tomb was found relatively intact.

The discovery and clearing of this, the richest tomb ever found, is an adventure story. The principal characters are Howard Carter, the seasoned excavator, and Lord Carnarvon, a wealthy British nobleman.

Howard Carter got into the field of archaeology by way of the back door. He had almost no formal education and had been raised in a large English working-class family. Nevertheless, he was an exceptional artist. When he was seventeen, Carter was lucky enough to work for some of the leading pioneer Egyptologists, most notably Sir Flinders Petrie. As a young man he quickly picked up the basics of fieldwork and learned Arabic, as well as the rudiments of reading hieroglyphics. It was not long before he had worked his way up to the position of inspector of monuments for Lower and Middle Egypt.

Carter's bureaucratic career folded the day some drunken French tourists demanded to be shown the Serapeum (a labyrinthlike tomb) after it had been closed for the day. Carter was called to the scene, and some shoving and insults were exchanged between Carter's guards and the inebriated Frenchmen. The tourists filed an official complaint against Carter, who obstinately refused to apologize and became even more incensed about the whole affair. This cost him his job. Following his dismissal as inspector of monuments, Carter lived in Cairo as a self-employed artist and resident expert on Egyptian antiquities. His archaeological career awaited his eventual meeting with Lord Carnarvon.

George Edward Stanhope Molyneux Herbert was the fifth Earl of Carnarvon. In some ways, he can be seen as the stereotype of a wealthy English lord. Fond of traveling and sports, he was also an avid sailor, had hunted big game in Africa, and was one of the first Englishmen to own a car. His enthusiasm for driving was his undoing, but it strongly influenced the course of the Tutankhamen story. He was motoring in Germany, where cars were almost never seen, when he suddenly encountered some ox carts in a dip in the road. Lord Carnarvon swerved to avoid the carts, and the car flipped over. His sister, Lady Burghclere, described the aftermath of the wreck. She wrote that her brother was "suffering from severe concussion, his face swollen to shapelessness, his legs severely burnt, his wrist broken, temporarily blind, the palate of his mouth and jaw injured, caked in mud from head to foot." His first words on gaining consciousness were "Have I killed anyone?"[27] Luckily he had not, but his own health was affected severely. The ailing Lord Carnarvon found it necessary to avoid the cool, damp winters of his English estate. In 1903 he began to winter in Egypt, where he became an avid collector of antiquities.

In those days, the antiquities laws were lax. It was easy for a wealthy person to buy artifacts and, with a little more effort, even arrange to excavate sites. Lord Carnarvon quickly became interested in excavating but lacked experience. After seeking help through the Antiquities Department, he was introduced to Howard Carter. The two formed a team in 1907.

Archaeologists had labored extensively in the Valley of the Kings with the great hope of discovering a tomb that had escaped the looters, but all efforts seemed in vain. Carter had also been eager to dig there, but the American millionaire Theodore Davis held the official permit for the valley. During the next seven years, Carter and Carnarvon excavated a number of other sites without great success, while Davis continued to search the valley. Finally Davis completed his work and announced that further work in the valley would be fruitless; nothing of importance was left. Davis claimed he had already found the remnants of Tutankhamen's tomb and that the zone had been excavated thoroughly. This opinion was echoed by Sir Gaston Maspero, the director of antiquities. Nevertheless, in 1914 Carter and Carnarvon were given official license to work there.

Unlike his colleagues, Carter believed that Davis had actually missed the tomb of Tutankhamen. He reasoned that Davis had confused a small pit, perhaps a minor tomb, with Tutankhamen's tomb. He felt that Davis had uncovered some important clues as to the whereabouts of the real tomb, however, such as a broken wooden box and a faience cup with Tutankhamen's name on them. In addition, there was some special funerary equipment containing clay seals with the king's name. To Carter, the location of these finds hinted that the real tomb must lie somewhere near the middle of the valley. Carter devised an excavation strategy based on dividing the suspected area, about two and one-half acres, into a triangle bounded by three other tombs. He was convinced that it was essential to dig down to bedrock (beneath the rubble of previous excavations) in the entire triangle.

The real quest for the tomb was delayed until 1917 because of the outbreak of World War I. During the first phase of the work, Carter and Carnarvon excavated near the tomb of Rameses VI, where Carter casually notes uncovering some "workmen's huts, built over masses of flint boulders, the latter usually indicating in The Valley, the near proximity of a tomb."[28] Most clearly, this was a lead worth following immediately, but Carter decided to move elsewhere in the triangle. Why did he do this and betray his own skill as an excavator? Carter tells us that he had the tourists in mind and moved because he was worried about his expanding excavations "cutting off all access to the tomb of Rameses above, to visitors one of the most popular tombs in the whole Valley." One authority maintains that the real motive for the move was simply that Carter despised tourists.[29] In any event, the result was that the next six seasons were a great disappointment. More and more, it looked as if Davis and Maspero had been right: The valley was exhausted. The two excavators certainly were. The complete triangle had been excavated except for the promising, initial excavation area near the Tomb of Rameses VI.

The dejected Carter and Carnarvon debated whether they should continue in the valley or go elsewhere. Lord Carnarvon had sunk a lot of money into the project, and his health was failing. Nevertheless Carter maintained diligently that his "own feeling was that so long as a single area of untouched ground remained, the risk was worth taking."[30] For this reason, they agreed to do one more season's work in what was literally a last-ditch effort. Howard Carter sums it up: "We had almost made up our minds that we were beaten . . . and then—hardly had we set hoe to ground in our last despairing effort than we made a discovery that far exceeded our wildest dreams."

The first hint of the discovery came on the morning of 4 November 1922, when an uncanny silence was noticed among the laborers. A step had been uncovered accidentally by a waterboy playing in the sand. Ironically, the step was underneath one of the ancient workmen's huts, not far from where the work had started six seasons earlier. With great anticipation, Carter's crew feverishly uncovered step after step until they ended at a sealed door marking the entrance to a tomb. Carter captures the moment: "Anything, literally anything, might lie beyond that passage and it needed all my self-control to keep from breaking down the doorway and investigating then and there." Since Lord Carnarvon was in England when the tomb was located, Carter cabled with the exciting news of the discovery and quickly reburied the entrance pending Carnarvon's arrival.

When Lord Carnarvon returned, the steps were re-excavated, and the door area was uncovered. Excitement and suspense heightened as seals were revealed bearing the name of Tutankhamen. Carter made a small peephole in the door and checked for foul gas. Then, in the dim light, he was spellbound by the first view of the interior. He saw "strange animals, statues, and gold, everywhere the glint of gold."

Carter, Carnarvon, and their crew found the tomb essentially intact, yet further investigation revealed that robbers had entered the tomb shortly after Tutankhamen's burial. Items were in disarray in one area known as the annex. There were even footprints, presumably of the robbers, on one of the boxes. Carter believed that the thieves had been surprised and had quickly dropped a group of gold rings tied to a scarf. There is no way of knowing how this ancient drama had ended, but it is certain, because of the small size of the opening they had made to enter the tomb, that the thieves did not get away with any large objects. Following the robbery (there may have been two attempts, according to Carter), the tomb had been resealed and covered. All traces of it were lost in the dust and rubble of the valley until Carter's diligent search paid off. Howard

Carter, like Jacques Boucher de Perthes, Eugène Dubois, and Louis Leakey, had adhered tenaciously to his convictions in the face of strong opposition and had made a find of fundamental importance.

The contents of the tomb presented a major challenge. First, there was the problem of security. News of the rich discovery had spread, and the threat of robbery was a serious concern. Carter reports that there were three sets of guards in the vicinity at all times: a group of soldiers, guards from the Antiquities Department, and some of his own staff. In addition, a specially constructed, padlocked steel gate was installed at the entrance of the tomb. Second, Carter had to assemble a team of experts to handle the recording, photographing, removal, and preservation of the finds. Finally, there was a need for a field laboratory in the valley. The excavators established one in the tomb of Seti II, which was in an area not frequented by throngs of tourists.

It took about a month of preparation before the actual removal of the objects commenced; the complete clearing of the tomb took nearly a decade. Approximately 5,000 objects were recovered, including furniture, jewelry, elaborately fashioned boxes, statues of wood and alabaster, vessels, musical instruments, and many other rare items. Many of the finds were probably King Tut's household furnishings, while others appeared to have been made specially for the burial during the approximate seventy-day period that was necessary to complete the process of mummification.[31] The work of clearing the tomb was, at times, exhausting. The workers had to labor in hot, cramped spaces, fearful that a clumsy move might destroy priceless works of art that had survived for more than 3,000 years. For instance, in the annex, a pile of about 300 objects had been heaped up by thieves in such a way that they were in danger of falling and crushing one another if disturbed. There was almost no room to work. To solve this problem, the worker who removed the artifacts was suspended by a rope sling, which was controlled by people in an adjacent room.

The burial chamber was one of the highlights in the excavation. It took nearly three months to get through the wall and to dismantle the gold shrines that were found inside. There was a moment of great suspense when Carter opened the third gold shrine and found another shrine within it.

> The decisive moment was at hand! An indescribable moment for an archaeologist! What was beneath and what did that fourth shrine contain? With intense excitement I drew back the bolts of the last and unsealed doors . . . and there . . . stood an immense yellow quartzite sarcophagus . . .[32]

The sarcophagus, which was nine feet long, was intact and outlined strikingly against the background of the gold shrines. An official contingent of notable Egyptologists, government representatives, and others were present at the opening. Once again, the drama was heightened as the massive stone lid was raised with the aid of block and tackle. Some linens were removed, and the audience was stunned when it saw the gold-effigy coffin lid of King Tutankhamen.

There were two more coffins nested inside the first one. The second was also a striking effigy of the king, covered with gold and finely inlaid with cut glass. The third coffin was stuck solidly in the second one because some of the pitchlike unguents used by the ancient Egyptians had spilled and hardened like cement. Eventually, these two coffins were separated by melting the unguents while protecting the coffins with wet blankets to keep them from burning. When the unguents and the linen that covered the third coffin were removed and the outer coffin was lifted, Carter was astonished to find that the entire inner coffin "was made of solid gold!" This exquisite coffin contained King Tut's mummy, wrapped in linen and stained with unguents. The head of the mummy was covered by a splendid gold mask. It was stuck firmly to the back of the head and had to be removed with hot knives.[33] The unwrapping of the mummy itself revealed fine pieces of jewelry, including elaborate pectoral collars made of colored glass and gold, necklaces, gold rings, and thirteen bracelets. There were also amulets and two daggers, one gold and the other iron.

One can easily imagine the priests of the royal necropolis uttering protective incantations during the funeral ceremony. Indeed, there is a long litany of mysterious events and deaths attributed to a curse that supposedly protected King Tut's tomb from defilement. Lord Carnarvon himself died several months after the tomb was discovered. It was rumored that he accidentally pricked himself on an object in the tomb, but the official diagnosis was that his death resulted from an infected mosquito bite. Of course, Carnarvon had been in a declining state of health and had a history of illness. Many sources report that when he died, all the lights went out in Cairo and that his favorite dog howled and dropped dead. Another interesting case concerns Carter's pet canary. One expert wrote that the bird had become a symbol of impending good luck and was affectionately called the "golden bird."[34] Soon after the tomb was discovered, the golden bird was eaten by a cobra. It was a well-known fact that cobras were important to the ancient Egyptians and were widely represented in their art. Was this one sent by the pharaoh as an omen of impending doom? Many people thought so, but anyone who keeps a caged bird near cobras runs the risk of attracting the snakes for an easy meal. Nevertheless, few anthropologists would deny that curses can have a profound psychological impact. Some people have actually died because of their strong beliefs in the effectiveness of curses placed on them.

There was no written curse found in the tomb. One passage from the hieroglyphs reads, "It is I who hinder the sand from choking the secret chamber. I am for the protection of the deceased."[35] Thomas Hoving, one of the leading experts on the King Tut excavations, has pointed out that a creative newspaper writer embellished the hieroglyphs by adding, "I will kill all those who cross this threshold into the sacred precincts of the Royal King who lives forever." The story of the curse was further perpetuated by both an imaginative French Egyptologist and by Sir Arthur Conan Doyle. Carter did not believe in it. Yet the mummy's-curse story continues to have an impact. In 1979 a guard who was protecting the traveling King Tut exhibit in San Francisco had a stroke and attempted to sue the city on grounds of being struck down by the curse.

Curses aside, Howard Carter and Lord Carnarvon found themselves caught in the very real political turmoil associated with the winds of change in Egypt.[36] Nationalism was on the rise, and work by the two Englishmen was symbolic of continued British colonialism. The previously lax antiquities laws were being reconsidered, and new proposals would prevent the excavators from keeping any of the finds, rather than the 50 percent cut that was anticipated originally. Carter reacted stubbornly to the bureaucratic changes and thereby provoked further animosity. Then, when Lord Carnarvon granted exclusive press rights to the *London Times*, other newspapers, including those of the local Egyptian press, were deemed second rate in their coverage of the sensational finds. This produced a backlash on the part of jealous newswriters.

Tensions peaked when the sarcophagus was opened. This was certainly a high point of the work, and world attention was focused on the exciting moment of discovery in the Valley of the Kings. In what would seem to be a reasonable request, Carter wanted the excavators' wives to have an initial, private viewing. Much to his anger and surprise, the request was refused. He fired off a stormy reply stating that he would be closing the tomb following a visit by the press and would thereafter not continue the work. The wheels had been set in motion for a nasty scene. Initially the *London Times* and a number of leading Egyptologists strongly supported Carter, but he was opposed by others, including the Egyptian press. Soon the Egyptian government took over, cut off Carter's padlocks, and staged a reopening of the tomb: "an immense and triumphant political rally."[37] A court case followed, during which unintentional insults were uttered by a lawyer supporting Carter. News of this hit the press and caused a riot in Cairo. Subsequently, the Egyptians tried to find someone else to take over the project, but none of the foreign Egyptologists would step into this tumultuous scene, and there were, at that time, no Egyptians who were qualified or willing to do the work.

Howard Carter was a complex person in whom courage, patience, and an explosive temper were combined in an unusual mixture. He was not one to back down. He once confronted some thieves in the middle of the night in the rock-cut tomb of Queen Hatshupset. The tomb was located in a precarious position on the side of a cliff, where it could be reached only by rope from the top of the cliff. He cut the thieves' rope and entered alone, using his own rope. In a tense moment, he persuaded the surprised bandits to leave. In this case, confrontation worked; in the Tutankhamen project, it did not. Afterward Carter wrote, "We are all of us human. No man is wise at all times . . . It is not for me to affix the blame for what occurred, nor yet to bear responsibility for a dispute in which at one moment the interests of archaeology in Egypt seemed menaced."[38] As we have seen, it was not the only time the ambitions of archaeologists clashed with emerging nationalism and professional rivalries (see Chapter 1).

In the case of King Tut, more rational forces eventually prevailed. There were some official reconciliations, and, after nearly a year had passed, Carter was allowed to resume work in the tomb. There were no more serious problems as a more complacent Howard Carter carried the work to completion. The law eventually required that all of the artifacts remain in Egypt. Almost all of them are now in Cairo, but a small number are also found scattered in the collections of several museums elsewhere, possibly the result of private deals carried out by Carter and Lord Carnarvon. Finally, the mummy itself was returned to its tomb, where it is resting, it is hoped, for eternity.

4

LOST CITIES

The Frontier of Ruins

The dawn of archaeological discovery was punctuated with unusual and adventurous stories, especially in the nineteenth century, when the ruins of lost cities were being uncovered in such unlikely places as deserts and tropical forests. Pioneer explorer-scholars risked their lives and reputations following legends and other clues that led them on quests that rivaled the King Tut adventure. The discoveries of lost cities also had a profound impact on the public and often generated heated debates of major proportions. There were intriguing questions about who had lived at some of these sites and what had happened to them. I will illustrate some of these problems, as well as others, with four striking examples: Troy, Pompeii/Herculaneum, Zimbabwe, and Machu Picchu.

TROY: FROM MYTH INTO HISTORY

In the eighth century B.C., the Greek poet Homer created a landmark in Western literature. In the *Iliad* he describes heroic events of some 500 years earlier, when the Greeks laid seige to Troy in an effort to recapture the beautiful Helen. Scholars for centuries considered Homer's work a masterpiece of mythology and poetry; few would have thought the legend of Troy was real. There was some speculation that if Troy had existed, it would probably have been located at Bounarbashi, in western Turkey, but few scholars thought seriously of finding it, much less of excavating and documenting the site. Such skepticism will remind you of Eugène Dubois, who was discouraged from going to the Far East to search for the "missing link" of his time, and of Louis Leakey, who was discouraged by his mentors from researching human origins in East Africa. In a similar vein, Howard Carter and Lord Carnarvon were told that they would not find King Tut's tomb in the Valley of the Kings. To this elite, persevering group of pioneers add Heinrich Schliemann, the discoverer of Troy, who, like the others, successfully bucked the mainstream of scholarship.

Schliemann was profoundly influenced by an inspirational childhood experience that drove him toward the ultimate discovery of Troy. In 1829, in a quiet German town, Schliemann's father gave him a copy of *Jerrer's Universal History* as a Christmas present. Schliemann, who was seven years old at the time, relates that he was fascinated by "an engraving representing Troy in flames with its huge walls and the Scaen gate . . ."[1] His father explained that the picture was imaginative but agreed that the huge walls may well have existed. After some lively discussion, father and son both concluded that young Heinrich would, in fact, "one day excavate Troy."

But Schliemann's father, a minister, was also unscrupulous; because of his numerous affairs and financial debacles, the younger Schliemann led a most impoverished and harsh early life. As an adolescent, he worked extremely long hours in a grocery store, eking out a living. He relates that he would have worked in the store indefinitely had he not one day lifted a barrel that was much too heavy, causing him to spit blood. He quit his job for health reasons and found work as a cabin boy on a ship bound for South America. That was a near disaster. The boat foundered in a storm, but young Schliemann luckily escaped in a lifeboat, which eventually washed up on the Dutch coast. He was left penniless, without a coat for the winter, and utterly destitute. Conditions were so bad that the youth "feigned illness and was taken to the hospital."

The winds of fortune slowly began to change in his favor when he was hired as an office boy. In his spare time, mainly at night in his room, Schliemann taught himself languages by reciting passages aloud, over and over again. In this way, he learned to speak a variety of languages, such as Portuguese, Russian, Arabic, and Greek. Not infrequently, these late-night mumblings annoyed other tenants, who complained bitterly about the strange noises and finally forced him to move. Nevertheless, Schliemann was finally able to put his natural skills as a linguist, especially his knowledge of Russian, to good use, by becoming an agent for his company in Russia. There he developed his considerable talents as a businessman. He was given free rein by his company and eventually amassed a fortune by exploiting shortages, selling goods at substantial profits, and subsequently reinvesting the money. Schliemann did this with great success during the Crimean War and the Civil War in America. His scruples, however, were bent easily. All indications hint that he was a gunrunner and made enormous personal profits through this illicit business.[2]

Schliemann retired at age forty-six in order to pursue his childhood dream of finding Troy. He confides, "I loved money indeed, but solely as the means of realizing this great idea of my life."[3] Others have maintained that it was really the love of money that, in fact, motivated him to search for the site. He was after Trojan gold.

After spending some time traveling around the world, Schliemann began his quest in earnest. He was aware of the reasoning of those mid-nineteenth-century scholars who, while skeptical of finding the real city, postulated that legendary Troy would have been in the vicinity of Bounarbashi. The city was in the general region described by Homer: near the Aegean Sea and the Dardanelles, the strait connecting the Aegean-Mediterranean basin to the Black Sea. Furthermore, some natural springs there were believed to be the same ones described in the *Iliad*. And so, in 1868, Schliemann arrived in western Turkey, filled with anticipation. He was at last in the land of his childhood fantasies.

While searching for Troy, Schliemann in some ways anticipated some of the present-day approaches in archaeology aimed at problem solving and the testing of hypotheses. Advocates of problem-oriented archaeology believe that research objectives should contain a hypothesis, which can be either confirmed, rejected, or modified on the basis of excavations and analysis. Schliemann practiced this technique about a century before it became an integral part of archaeology. He began by using the *Iliad* as a definitive source for testing Bounarbashi as the site of ancient Troy. The *Iliad* described two springs at Troy, one with cold water and the other warm. Schliemann found not two, but thirty-four springs at Bounarbashi. In addition, he recorded the temperature of all of them and found that they all were 62.6 degrees Fahrenheit. Moreover, he calculated from the *Iliad* that Troy was no more than three miles from the Hellespont (mouth of the Dardanelles). Because Bounarbashi was eight miles from this point, he reasoned it was simply too far away to suit the description provided by Homer. Next, Schliemann conducted a series of test excavations in the area situated between the springs and the adjacent high ground, which could not have been the locale for the site. He sank hundreds of shallow pits to bedrock and found "only pure virgin soil."[4] Schliemann was one of the first archaeologists to employ large numbers of test pits to solve a problem.

Schliemann's subsequent efforts, however, were more encouraging.

> Bounarbashi having thus given negative results, I next carefully examined all the heights to the right and left of the Trojan Plain, but my researches bore no fruits until I came to the site of the city called by Strabo New Ilium, which is at a distance of only three miles from the Hellespont and perfectly answers in this, as well as in all other respects, to the topographical requirements of the *Iliad*.

The northwest corner of the site was marked by the hill known as Hissarlik. It was obviously formed by an accumulation of archaeological deposits. The hill was owned partly by Barker Webb, who had excavated two small trenches in it. Schliemann, along with several others who were involved in the Troy debate (notably Frank Calvert, the U.S. vice consul to the Dardanelles), were convinced that Hissarlik was, indeed, the site of Troy. Schliemann planned to follow up on Webb's initial probes, believing that more extensive excavations would settle the issue. While Schliemann was not the first to propose that Hissarlik was Troy, it was his work that was most influential.

Naturally Schliemann was eager to excavate the site, but he states that "circumstances obliged me to remain nearly the whole of 1869 in the United States." Evidently, the pragmatic Schliemann enjoyed a double benefit from his sojourn in America.[5] First, "Henry" Schliemann became a U.S. citizen and was therefore able to obtain an excavation permit from the Turkish authorities more easily than he could have as a German or Russian. Second, he desperately wanted to end his troublesome marriage to a Russian woman, and living in the United States enabled him to arrange for a divorce with fewer problems than he would have encountered in Europe. He took up residence in Indiana, where divorces were relatively easy to obtain, and began making arrangements to find a new wife before the divorce was concluded. The middle-aged Schliemann picked out Sophia, a sixteen-year-old girl from Athens, from a series of photographs of prospective brides sent by the archbishop of Athens.

In his autobiography, Schliemann cast himself as an honest hero, yet recent investigations by David Traill and William Calder reveal another side to his personality. There is reason to believe that Schliemann obtained U.S. citizenship by fraud. The residency requirement was five years, and the facts argue that he did not live in the country that long. Traill shows that Schliemann also must have obtained his divorce in a similar manner, because there are indications that he bribed witnesses to testify that he had lived in Indiana for the required length of time. Calder, for his part, states that Schliemann could not have written his dissertation in Greek as he claimed. In addition, Schliemann's description of a lengthy meeting with U.S. President Millard Fillmore was evidently fabricated, as was his "personal" view of the famous San Francisco fire, which he probably plagiarized from a California newspaper. Finally, Schliemann claims to have left California because of a deathly fever, but Traill thinks this was probably a cover-up for some financial cheating that caused him to close his California bank suddenly and leave.

Schliemann returned to Hissarlik, but the major excavations did not commence until 1871, when he at last obtained the necessary permit from the Turkish government. At that time Hissarlik was a substantial mound just over fifty feet thick, built up of successive layers of occupation debris. The principal ruins cover a time span extending from approximately 3000 B.C. (Troy I) to the Roman period at about A.D. 300 (Troy IX). A quick view of Hissarlik at present reveals that much of the site has been excavated, and it is not as large as one might expect, given the great literary significance of the *Iliad*. A casual walk around the perimeter of the site takes only about twenty minutes. From the highest point, the narrow Dardanelles Strait, gateway to the Sea of Marmara, appears as a faint blue ribbon in the distance. It doesn't take much imagination to envision Bronze Age ships entering the strategic waterway from the Aegean Sea. With the Mycenaean Greeks to the west and the Hittites not far to the east, Hissarlik was well situated with respect to trade routes. At present, the visitor to Hissarlik will see mainly walls amidst the cut-away areas and rubble piles created by Schliemann. There are also remnants of houses, a tower, and various other buildings, as well as a small Roman theater. A closer inspection of the ground surface reveals scattered potsherds and eroded pockets of refuse consisting of shells and bones. Unfortunately, the potential importance of this economic and ecological data was not recognized by the pioneering Schliemann, whose destructive techniques were primarily aimed at uncovering the Homeric city.

Schliemann believed initially that the Homeric level at Hissarlik was at the bottom of the site, because preliminary digging suggested that the upper layers were too recent. His excavation strategy was grandiose: He planned to dig a north-south trench, one hundred feet wide at the top, that would cut the site in half. He employed a large number of local laborers; frequently as many as 150 people were excavating. With this many diggers, it would have been next to impossible to maintain close supervision of the fieldwork. Schliemann was aided by "three overseers and an engineer to make the maps and plans."[6] They used shovels, picks, baskets, and wheelbarrows, as well as horse-drawn carts, to remove the debris and "screw-jacks, chains and windlasses" to deal with the heavy material. Schliemann's excavation methods were very destructive, but this is partly a reflection on the pioneering state of archaeology at the time. Schliemann writes, "As it was my object to excavate Troy, which I expected to find in one of the lower cities, I was forced to demolish many interesting ruins in the upper strata." Schliemann used huge iron levers to undermine some of the oldest deposits. This proved to be a risky procedure, as two of his workmen were nearly killed when a mass of debris caved in on them.

Schliemann uncovered evidence of seven cities at Hissarlik. Which, if any, was really Troy? Schliemann became increasingly convinced that the second, the "burnt city," was the remains of the Troy described by Homer. The evidence of fire seemed to match Homer's account of the fall of Troy following the classic incident with the wooden horse. It is ironic that Schliemann, who used good scientific judgment in disproving that Bounarbashi was Troy, did just the opposite in trying to demonstrate that Hissarlik was the site of Troy and in ascertaining which level was the Homeric city. He haphazardly labeled various parts of the site after the Trojan city with no basis for doing this other than his all-too-vivid imagination. A clear example of this is seen in his description of an unearthed tower.

> There is not a more sublime situation in the area of Troy than this, and I therefore presume that it is the Great Tower of Ilium which Andromache ascended because she heard that the Trojans were hard pressed and the power of the Achaeans was great.[7]

He also "discovers" the Scaen gate, Priam's palace, and, last but not least, Priam's treasure. All of these are described by Homer, and they served as evidence to reinforce Schliemann's circular reasoning that he had, in fact, found Troy. It is clear that Schliemann eagerly sought artifacts and architectural evidence that would confirm conclusions already reached and that he did not have a complete understanding of the stratigraphy. The sad fact is that the burned city is now known to date to around 2500–2200 B.C., far too old to have been the Homeric level.

Follow-up work carried out by Wilhelm Dörpfeld, Schliemann's student, and Carl Blegen has revealed a more complex stratigraphy, with numerous subdivisions not distinguished by Schliemann. According to Blegen, who excavated in the 1930s, the occupation level known as Troy VIIa is the most likely candidate for the Homeric city. It was burned and pillaged at around 1250 B.C., a date far more consistent with estimates for the age of Troy. More recently, Michael Wood has marshaled evidence that Troy VI is the most reasonable choice.[8] Nevertheless, there is by no means complete agreement that Hissarlik is, in fact, the site of Troy. The linkage between the site and Troy is still rooted largely in circumstantial evidence. As far as I am aware, there are no positive relationships between Hissarlik and any of the artifacts, events, and individuals described in the *Iliad*. It was simply the best choice for the site via the process of elimination.

Schliemann had originally eliminated Bounarbashi as the site of Troy by using geographical data described in Homer and assuming that the distance from the site to the Hellespont, or Dardanelles, was the same in ancient times as it was in the nineteenth century. He had no way of knowing that, about a century after he began digging at Hissarlik, geologists would determine that the ancient topography was quite different. John C. Kraft, of the University of Delaware, and his Turkish colleagues drilled into the sediments at various localities ranging from Hissarlik to the Dardanelles and also along the nearby Scamander River. The Scamander flows into an estuary of the Dardanelles about five kilometers to the north of the city's present site. The drill samples revealed that during the initial occupation of Hissarlik (Troy I, radiocarbon-dated to about 4,500 years ago), the sea level was about two meters higher than at present and must have encroached upon the edge of the site. In fact, the site must have had water on three sides of it. This was also true during the time of Troy II, which was Schliemann's prime candidate for the Homeric city. Even during the time of Troy VI–VII (about 3,250 years ago), which is closest to the periods accepted by recent authorities for the Homeric city, the site was still situated very near to a substantial bay, because the delta of the Scamander River was then located to the south of Hissarlik. Since the city was still well protected by the surrounding waters, Kraft and his associates reason that the Greeks probably would have been based farther to the south and would have moved across the plain rather than attack via the naturally protected estuary.

Until Schliemann's work at Troy, archaeologists had not recovered significant amounts of gold in their excavations. Schliemann was one of the first archaeologists to be associated with the discovery of a "treasure" and, therefore, attracted much public attention. According to Schliemann's account, the discovery occurred near the end of the field season of 1873, which he thought would be his last at Troy. He informs us that he was excavating a wall when he noticed an unusual copper artifact that appeared to have the glitter of gold coming from behind it. He reacted quickly by calling for a work break "in order to withdraw the treasure from the greed of my workmen and to save it for archaeology."[9] After the workmen left, Schliemann jumped into the trench and proceeded to cut out the treasure as quickly as possible with his knife. This was a dangerous operation, since the treasure was embedded beneath an overhanging wall at a depth of about twenty-eight feet. Despite the threat of a cave-in, he hacked feverishly at the deposits and dug the treasure out. The priceless artifacts of gold and silver were taken secretly out of the site by his wife, Sophia, who hid them in her shawl.

The highlight of the treasure was a large silver vase loaded with nearly 9,000 gold artifacts, most of which were small rings. Other notable finds of gold included half a dozen bracelets, a bottle, and several cups. In addition, there were silver knife blades, as well as various other items of gold, silver, and copper. Schliemann called it "Priam's treasure." He figured that because the large concentration of gold and silver artifacts was found in "a rectangular mass or packed into one another, it seems to be certain that they were placed on the city wall in a wooden chest, such as those mentioned by Homer as being in the palace of King Priam." This interpretation was supported by the nearby find of a copper key. (There was, in fact, no wooden chest.) Priam's treasure was the most valuable find of its day and was not surpassed until the discovery of the tomb of Tutankhamen.

Recent evidence reveals that there are strong reasons to doubt that Schliemann's account of the discovery of the treasure is true. David Traill, in a penetrating analysis, shows that there are major inconsistencies in the earliest reports of the discovery. It seems that the original location of the treasure varies considerably in the different reports issued by Schliemann. Furthermore, it is almost certain that Sophia, who Schliemann said secretly removed the treasure, was not even at the site when the treasure was allegedly found. Traill believes that Priam's treasure was really an accumulation of small finds that were presented collectively as a single treasure after the fact. Whether or not this was done as a calculated effort to gain publicity is uncertain. It is known that Schliemann was advised by a high-ranking U.S. diplomat to "pocket" any small items of gold that he found. Perhaps he did this and then later on claimed that they belonged to a single treasure, romantically linking it with King Priam of Troy.

No one is certain how Schliemann smuggled the treasure out of Turkey to Greece, but recent evidence cited by Donald Easton shows that he sent six baskets and a bag to his associate Frank Calvert, who lived near his residence there. In a letter to Calvert, who apparently had no idea of what was in the containers, he said that he was being watched closely. He was convinced his house was going to be searched and urged Calvert to lock the containers up "and not allow by any means the Turks to touch them."[10]

After Schliemann returned to Greece, the discovery of Priam's treasure was publicized widely. The incensed Turkish authorities wanted the treasure returned, and they collaborated with the Greeks in an attempt to recover it. Meanwhile, according to Leo Deuel, who wrote Schliemann's memoirs, Sophia secretly divided the treasure among her relatives in Greece, who reburied the items in barns and other obscure places. Thus when Schliemann's property was ransacked, nothing was recovered. Apparently threats made by Schliemann to sell the treasure were carefully orchestrated to drive the Greeks and the Turks toward a quick settlement. Finally, the dispute culminated in a court case, which resulted in the wealthy Schliemann paying a nominal fine. (In fact, he paid much more than he was asked.) This case was one of the first regarding the disposition of major archaeological treasures, setting the stage for other confrontations such as those regarding the finds of Tutankhamen, Sutton Hoo, and Chichén Itzá (see Chapter 5). "Priam's treasure" was never returned to Turkey, and its whereabouts, like the remains of Peking man, remains a mystery. It is reported that the gold was stored in Berlin during World War II and possibly fell into Russian hands when the Red Army swept through the city.[11]

In 1874, following the episode with the treasure, Schliemann devoted his attention to the ancient site of Mycenae in the Peloponnesus of southern Greece, another famous landmark in the Homeric world. Here, according to a Greek source from the second century A.D., was the legendary tomb of King Agamemnon, who led the Greek forces in the siege against Troy. Schliemann, in characteristic fashion, first interpreted this source in a fundamentally different way than most other scholars, then tried to prove he was right by digging a large number of test pits in the area he thought contained the tombs. Eventually he found what he believed might have been a tombstone. Two years later, with the help of a large labor force, he began an extensive program of excavation in the selected area. As luck would have it, he uncovered several tombs that were richly laden. The most spectacular find was an individual, the flesh of whose face was "wonderfully preserved under its ponderous gold mask . . ."[12] There was a gold leaf on the forehead and another on one of the eyes, as well as a gold breast cover and a long gold shoulder belt with the remnant of a double-edged bronze sword. Schliemann was convinced that he had found the tomb of Agamemnon, thus further confirming the accuracy of the Homeric story. Modern research has rejected this specific linkage between the tombs of Mycenae and Agamemnon, but the treasures rank among the greatest ever found.[13]

In final analysis, the most valuable contribution of the work at Troy was not the missing treasure; it was the gradual transformation of a legendary world into one that had some basis in reality. The work was one of the cornerstones in the foundation of classical archaeology. Schliemann, through his excavations at Hissarlik, Mycenae, and also at Tiryns (in Greece), became recognized as the "father" of Greek archaeology.

POMPEII

The continent of Africa has been moving slowly and imperceptibly toward Europe. For eons, continental plates carrying the two land masses have been grinding together. One of the results has been a chain of volcanoes, acting periodically as geological pressure valves, near the Bay of Naples on the west coast of Italy. One of these volcanoes, Vesuvius, owes much of its fame to the devastating eruption of late August, A.D. 79, which buried the two Roman cities of

Pompeii and Herculaneum. Pompeii, the most notable of the victims, was a port city of perhaps 20,000 people and well known for its wines.

Among all the archaeological sites in the world, Pompeii, in particular, would have to be ranked as one of the most significant. Because of the sudden and rapid covering of the city by volcanic ash, the ruins seem to have been frozen in time. Not only are the conditions of preservation extraordinary, but, incredibly, there is even a vivid eyewitness account of the eruption, which buried Pompeii nearly two thousand years ago. Pliny the Younger, a Roman, wrote a report of the events to the noted historian Tacitus, in which the former described the death of his uncle, Pliny the Elder, at the time of the eruption. Pliny the Elder was a well-known naturalist and a Roman naval commander in charge of the fleet at Misenum, about twenty miles from Vesuvius. The initial eruption, clearly visible at Misenum, appeared as a cloud in the shape of a pine tree. "Projected into the air like an immense tree-trunk, as it were, it opened out into branches."[14] Pliny the Elder's keen sense of curiosity got the better of him, and he decided to have a closer view by approaching the scene by sea. While he was preparing to go, he received an urgent letter from a friend's wife pleading to be rescued from the impending doom of the eruption. Pliny tried his best to reach her but had to stop short of his goal. His nephew provides a lucid description of the events: "Already ashes were falling on the boat, hotter and more thickly in proportion as it drew nearer; and also pumice-stones, black, ashen flints shattered by the fire." The pilot of the boat urged Pliny to return; but Pliny replied, "Fortune favors the brave," and he headed for Stabiae, which he believed was relatively safe. Once there, he tried to reassure people who were attempting to flee, but the danger increased as volcanic debris continued falling on the house he was visiting. "Houses, shaken by frequent and prolonged tremors, and as if torn from their foundations tilted to the right, to the left, then resumed their original positions." Alarmed, Pliny fled with the others, all holding towels and pillows over their heads "as protection against the falling stones. Elsewhere the dawn had come but here it was night, the blackest and thickest of nights, though counteracted by numerous torches and lights of every kind." They reached the beach, where the exhausted Pliny the Elder was overcome by the fumes.

"Leaning on two young slaves, he rose and immediately fell down dead."

Pliny's nephew, while still at Misenum, wrote another letter describing some of his own experiences during the disaster. He was fleeing with his mother amidst a panic-stricken mob.

> The sea appeared to have shrunk into itself, as if pushed back by the tremors of the earth. At all events, the banks had widened, and many sea-creatures were beached on the earth. In the other direction gaped a horrible black cloud torn by sudden bursts of fire in snakelike flashes, revealing elongated flames similar to lightning but larger. And now came the ashes, though as yet sparsely. I turned round. Ominous behind us, a thick smoke spreading over the earth like a flood followed us. We were enveloped in night, not a moonless night or one dimmed by a cloud, but the darkness of a sealed room without lights. Only the shrill cries of women, the wailing of children, the shouting of men were to be heard. . . . Many lifted up their hands to the gods, but a great number believed that there were no more gods and that this night was the world's last, eternal one.

From this description, we see that the devastation and panic were great even in areas that were some distance from the volcano. Luckily, Pliny the Younger escaped.

Historical records indicate that Vesuvius has erupted frequently. For example, in the winter of A.D. 1631 there was another major eruption of Vesuvius, during which mudflows and lava destroyed many villages, killing thousands of people.[15] Despite this threat, people continued to live in the area, and, as a result, many tragic events occurred that mirror Pliny's ancient description. For instance, in the eruption of 1759 many people prayed to their special saints. One wealthy man refused to take anything out of his doomed villa since it was protected by Saint Januarius. As a last gesture of his convictions, he threw the key into the hot lava.[16] Vesuvius has continued to erupt with destructive force. There were five major eruptions in the previous century and three in this century. The most recent one, in 1944, resulted in the devastation of San Sebastiano, where the presence of Allied troops resulted in the rescue of many.

Geologists with a thorough knowledge of recent volcanic eruptions have analyzed the deposits exposed by archaeologists at the buried sites of Pompeii and Herculaneum. Michael Sheridan of Arizona State University and Italian associates have shown how the sequence in the eruption of Vesuvius was complicated when the volcanic magma, or molten rock, mixed with ground water. The impact of the eruption on Pompeii and Herculaneum differed significantly. The deposits at Pompeii are about four and a half meters thick. On August 24, A.D. 79, there was an eruption of pumice (small pieces of spongy-textured volcanic glass). The following day the city was hit by a combination of surge deposits, which move rapidly over the ground, and more air-laid pumice. The surge deposits contain gas, ash, and other volcanic debris. The first of the surges included superheated dry steam while the last surge was marked by wet steam. Pliny's graphic description of the day being like the "blackest and thickest of nights" is completely consistent with the thick deposits of pumice and ash that must have blown many miles into the sky and showered on the area for hours like a macabre snowstorm. The recent eruption of Mount St. Helens was a minor event compared to what happened in A.D. 79.

At Herculaneum the deposits are much thicker, measuring about 20 meters. Herculaneum was upwind from the eruption but was closer to the center of volcanic activity. Herculaneum was hit by a surge flow followed by a thick accumulation of pyroclastic deposits, then another surge and more of the pyroclastics. The last ten meters or so were marked by what is known as lahar, or volcanic mudflows. Mudflows are caused by mixtures of ash and hot water. These mudflows deeply buried Herculaneum and made the eventual excavation of the site much more difficult than was the case for Pompeii.

The number of people killed at Pompeii is difficult to estimate. There may have been thousands. On the other hand, many may have escaped in the fashion described by Pliny. According to Martin Prinz, early researchers thought that most of the victims were asphyxiated by sulfur fumes or were buried by the collapsing roofs of houses. It now looks, however, as if people were caught in a surge of hot volcanic ash, though asphyxiation was likely a factor as well. Prinz notes that some of the victims were coming back to the city, perhaps to reclaim valuables or to loot during a lull in the volcanic eruption.

At Herculaneum, the situation was different. The eruption could be seen clearly, and the great rain of pumice that struck Pompeii did not hit Herculaneum. While Pompeii first felt the wrath of Vesuvius on the night of August 24, Herculaneum, which was upwind, was spared until the next morning. Therefore, most authorities believe that many of the people had adequate warning and safely fled the city. Relatively few bodies were found originally at Herculaneum, in contrast to the larger number of victims at Pompeii. Recent work along the old beach area at Herculaneum, however, has significantly changed this picture.

After the disaster, both Herculaneum and Pompeii had vanished completely, covered by nearly sixty feet of deposits. Here and there, some of the taller buildings were visible, but as the years passed even these vestiges succumbed to the decay and dust of time. Plants began to grow, and soon all lingering traces of the cities vanished. Pompeii and Herculaneum, once thriving cities of the Roman Empire, became faded memories, mere marks on Roman maps. Pompeii itself was buried beneath an area that became known as Civita, while Herculaneum was underneath the town of Resina. The rediscovery of these cities is a complex story involving the familiar appearance of luck, a good deal of bungling, and even murder.

One of the first encounters with the Pompeii ruins occurred in 1594, when a certain Italian count decided to divert water to his villa. The workmen actually dug directly across Pompeii, where they encountered ruins and found an inscription that contained the name of the site. But this was strictly a construction project, and no one seemed to pay much attention to the finds. The significance of the name Pompeii was apparently not recognized, because the inscription was confused with the name of Pompey the Great (a famous Roman general who lived during the time of Julius Caesar).[17]

During the following century, various scholars debated about the location of Pompeii. One astute German scholar argued correctly that it was beneath Civita, but, as in the case of Troy, there was much opposition to his views. The key event leading to the discovery happened quite by accident in 1709, when Naples was under the rule of the Austrian Hapsburgs. According to various accounts, a man was either digging a well for a monastery at Resina or enlarging a spring on his land when he struck substantial amounts of valuable marble, which he promptly sold.[18] A high-ranking Austrian cavalry officer, Prince d'Elboeuf, got wind of the marble find and went to investigate the area. He wanted marble for the construction of his villa and was also interested in the possibility of finding sculptures. Prince d'Elboeuf, correctly reasoning that further digging might uncover some valuable finds, arranged to buy the field adjacent to where the marble was recovered. Little did he know that he had bought ancient Herculaneum.

In those days, there was no attempt to dig scientifically; the main interest was simply to collect art objects for display. Sites were essentially "mined" for artifacts. When Prince d'Elboeuf tunneled into the deposits, he found more marble and three Roman statues. He described the statues as "vestal virgins" and wanted to ship them to Eugene of Savoy, in Austria, who was greatly interested in ancient art. Since this was illegal without permission from the pope, the prince smuggled the artifacts out of Italy, just as Schliemann would do later at Troy. Rumors began to circulate about his clandestine activities, and political pressures mounted, forcing him to stop digging. Thus was Herculaneum rediscovered, but the correct historical identity of the site was still unknown. The prevailing opinion was that the prince had found a temple of Hercules. As far as I am aware, no one realized that he had found Herculaneum because most scholars thought it was located elsewhere.

Following the period of Austrian rule, Naples fell under the control of Spain, and Charles III became the king of the two Sicilies. As luck would have it, King Charles moved into the house that used to belong to d'Elboeuf, where he found some of the artifacts that the prince had excavated. King Charles's interest in the site was heightened further when he married an Austrian whose father had purchased the three excavated statues of the "vestal virgins." The king and queen wondered whether more of the striking art objects awaited discovery deep beneath the earth at Resina. There was only one way to find out. The tunneling begun by d'Elboeuf was resumed with vigor in the fall of 1738. The deposits, about sixty feet deep, were blasted out and removed ruthlessly by picks; the king's supervisor at the site, an engineer by the name of Alcubierre, had little patience for anyone who wanted to do things in a systematic, less destructive way. Within a few months, some remarkable finds were encountered, including remains of bronze horses and a number of marble statues. Interest began to peak when the workers uncovered a stairway. As the work proceeded, it was clear that the steps were part of a substantial Roman theater. Great excitement ensued when an inscription was found that identified the building as the theater of Herculaneum. After being buried by the eruption of Vesuvius for more than 1,600 years, Herculaneum was finally identified.

The king and queen began to amass a substantial collection for their private museum. They endorsed the destructive tunneling technique of excavation, however, instead of attempting to uncover buildings. Admittedly, delicate uncovering would have been difficult because of the extreme hardness and massive thicknesses of the hardened mudflow. Nevertheless, Herculaneum began to resemble a giant series of rabbit holes rather than an archaeological site. The tunnels were cold and damp, and foul gases were encountered. It was a dangerous and destructive treasure-seeking operation. Artwork was stripped off the walls of buildings, and objects were taken out of their context. When certain valuable items began to disappear, the convict laborers were threatened with flogging and execution.

A glimmer of hope in the work flickered when Karl Weber, a Swiss architect, came on the scene. He was interested in documenting the finds, but his ideas ran against the grain of his boss, Alcubierre, and there was much conflict between them. One of Weber's key finds was made in 1750, when workmen encountered an enormous villa containing a great wealth of bronze statues and a library with a large quantity of papyrus scrolls. This was one of the first finds of ancient documents and, as such, attracted much attention among scholars. Unfortunately, the papyri were heavily carbonized, and, at the time, no one knew how to open them without destroying them. More recent attempts have been successful, and it has now been determined that much of the writing on the scrolls is philosophical in nature.[19] The large "Villa of Papyri" was one of the major discoveries at

Herculaneum, but the workers encountered poisonous gases and the tunnels leading to the villa had to be closed.

While Herculaneum was being "mined," there was renewed interest in locating its legendary sister city, Pompeii. Unlike other scholars, an Italian professor, A. G. Martorelli, believed strongly that the hill at Civita was indeed the location of Pompeii, and he was supposedly able to persuade the king to investigate the site.[20] Joseph Diess maintains that it was really Alcubierre who got the king to dig there because the treasures of Herculaneum were decreasing. The work commenced in the spring of 1748 with a crew that featured a number of convicts. Just by chance, the diggers excavated directly into a major area of Pompeii, where they uncovered houses, but they failed to recognize the importance of the finds. Not long afterward, the diggers found a human skeleton associated with silver and gold. This was the first of the actual victims of Vesuvius to be discovered, but no one knew that the site was, in fact, Pompeii. Finally, in the summer of 1763, the base of a statue was uncovered that contained an inscription mentioning Pompeians.[21] Thereafter, there was a major interest in the site, which, because of the relatively shallow deposits, could be excavated rather than tunneled.

One of the major figures in the history of the early discoveries at Herculaneum and Pompeii was Johann Joachim Winckelmann. Having been fascinated by archaeology as a child, Winckelmann came to be seen as one of the founders of German archaeology and as a major figure in art history. He was greatly interested in the work at Herculaneum but experienced considerable difficulty in gaining access to the site and the artifacts that he wished to study. He was not allowed to draw or even to see some of the finds. This was a classic case of an inquisitive scholar butting heads with treasure-seekers and collectors.

Nonetheless, Winckelmann was instrumental in spreading the news of the discoveries to scholars elsewhere in Europe through his writings. He also "blew the whistle" on the excavators because of their shoddy techniques and the resultant destruction. Winckelmann met with a tragic end in 1769. While waiting for a ship in Trieste, he unknowingly befriended a robber and showed him some gifts that he had received from Queen Maria Theresa. Later on, when Winckelmann was busy writing at his inn, the rogue silently entered the room, choked him with a rope, and stabbed him many times. Winckelmann struggled to get help, but apparently people panicked at the sight of him. He soon died from the wounds, and the killer escaped.

The early work surrounding Pompeii and Herculaneum was a major attraction to distinguished visitors and royalty, just as many important excavations are today.[22] Moreover, the visitors were often guaranteed the thrill of experiencing an important "discovery." Certain objects or skeletons were simply reburied, then uncovered again when the visitors came. Another interesting tidbit is that Alexandre Dumas, author of *The Three Musketeers* and *The Count of Monte Cristo*, briefly headed the work at Pompeii. This came about as a result of his backing the Italian patriot Giuseppe Garibaldi, who fought against the Austrians. The Frenchman's work was short-lived, however, amidst the rising Italian national interests.

A major change in the work at Pompeii took place in 1860, when Guiseppe Fiorelli was made the official director of the excavations. Although Fiorelli had a checkered background, which included a stint in prison for political reasons, he was a professor of archaeology at the University of Naples and had a sound understanding of how to excavate sites. This signaled a new era of scientific work, much in the same way that Boucher de Perthes' findings had ushered in a modern viewpoint toward Stone Age archaeology the year before. Fiorelli was much more systematic than previous workers. He excavated individual areas in specific sections of Pompeii. In addition, he is credited with being one of the first excavators who did not strip the beautiful frescoes off the walls for display in museums.

One of his major innovations centered on the treatment of the victims who were buried by the eruption of Vesuvius. Careful excavation of some of their skeletons revealed that the volcanic ash had originally hardened around the bodies, which eventually decomposed, leaving only the bones. The negative impressions of the bodies remained, however, much in the same way as the 3.7-million-year-old footprints in East Africa had been hardened in ash. Fiorelli found that filling each cavity with plaster would provide a mold of the bodies, which would reveal the exact position of the victims and even their facial expressions at the moment of death. Examples of the casts are on display at Pompeii, and a visit to the Roman bath

provides a vivid testimony to the tragic fate of the victim
trapped there. Perhaps as much as any other aspect of Po
plaster casts of the bodies have given the site its fame.

Many other archaeological sites have yielded strikin
skeletons. Shang tombs were loaded with sacrificial victims,
are numerous cases of well-preserved mummies. But Pompeii is unique in its preservation of the details of a mass disaster. Many people were caught in the act of fleeing, unsuccessfully trying to reach the sea, which, according to Pliny the Elder, was extremely turbulent. People in all walks of life were trapped. For example, several priests died trying to flee the Temple of Isis, while about sixty gladiators were found trapped in their barracks. Two of the victims were shackled and had no chance at all. There was a group of slaves found seeking shelter in one building. Women were found with jewelry and money scattered nearby. There were also some victims with pillows covering their heads, as in the eyewitness description of Pliny. In one case, a person made a heroic effort to escape from a building; he had hacked his way through several walls but collapsed with his ax in hand.[23] In another situation, a group of people was found in a cellar. These victims included two boys who were hugging each other, no doubt in terror. One large group of people tried to wait out the disaster by provisioning themselves with food, including a goat. This desperate strategy also failed. A dog was found chained inside a house. Another dog was trapped in a room with a person. Researchers feel that this dog had actually eaten the corpse of the person, since there were gnawing marks on the bones.

At Herculaneum, many more people were killed than earlier researchers had guessed. In 1982, archaeologists found large numbers of skeletons along the ancient beach area, evidence that these people were trying to escape when they were caught by the fiery volcanic eruption.[24] One group of adults and children seem to have been members of the same family trying to escape together. Several rooms along the beach contained the skeletons of large numbers of people desperately trying to get away. One of the unique finds in this area is the carbonized remains of a Roman boat. A person found nearby may well have had an oar in his hand. All in all, the emerging details imply a situation of great panic.

In the post-Fiorelli years, archaeological research has continued th varying degrees of intensity at Pompeii, exposing many details about the nature of a Roman town. A walk through the restored parts of Pompeii is almost like walking through an extant, or recently abandoned, town. At first, it is difficult to imagine that the city was last inhabited about 1,900 years ago. But a view of the grooves cut by ancient chariots in the cobblestone streets quickly brings one back to reality. One wanders past government buildings where the local Roman bureaucrats and legal officials worked, inns where visitors from various parts of the Empire stayed and indulged in the area's fine wines, bakeries, and small streetside restaurants. There are also theaters, temples, and a large amphitheater where gladiators fought both each other and wild animals. One of the streets goes through the cemetery, where elaborate tombs can be seen. The tombs contain cremations, but, ironically, some victims fleeing the wrath of Vesuvius were found seeking shelter in one of them. The lead pipes that brought water to the city are still evident, and the public baths, an important feature of Roman life, are incredibly well preserved. The restored houses are of exceptional interest, built around an open courtyard with their roofs supported by columns. Rainwater was collected in an open pool in each house, walls were richly painted, and there were gardens in the courtyard area.

The artwork preserved at Pompeii is exceptional and is certainly one of the major highlights of the city. There are mosaics and paintings on a wide variety of themes ranging from mythology and history to everyday life and sex. Regarding the latter, the house of the Vetti Brothers, successful wine merchants, had a special room that features pictures of people copulating and a statue with a very large erection. Elsewhere in Pompeii there is much more on the theme of sex, including various paintings and statues depicting sexual acts between mythological figures, humans, and animals.

Another highlight of Pompeii is the "handwriting on the walls," the graffiti. The amount of writing is so prolific that even the citizens of Pompeii made fun of it. One wrote: "Wall, I am amazed that you haven't collapsed long ago, you are condemned to carry so much idle chatter."[25] The graffiti was an important means of communication on subjects ranging from politics to sex. In the political realm, the wall served the purpose of boosting particular candidates, much as lawn signs do today. For example, one candidate was reputed to be "an economy watch-dog on the treasury." Another writer chides people to vote for his candidate: "If anyone refuses to vote for Quintius, let him be carried through the town on a donkey!"

While the graffiti may seem lighthearted, a more somber note on Roman life is provided by advertisements for the "games" in the amphitheater.

> Twenty pairs of gladiators offered for as long as they live by Lucretius Satrius Valens, priest of Nero, and ten pairs given by his son, will compete against one another in Pompeii on the fourth of April. There will also be a fight between men and wild beasts.

This was a thumbs up—thumbs down proposition, and each gladiator's life was held in the balance. The audiences took the games quite seriously, and on one occasion a major riot resulting in deaths broke out between spectators from rival cities. It is no wonder that a major slave revolt took place under the leadership of Spartacus, a gladiator who used the slopes of Vesuvius as a base of operations.

Inn walls contain still other fascinating comments on life at Pompeii. One customer, troubled by the poor quality of the wine, condemned the innkeeper: "You sell us this watery liquid and drink pure wine yourself." Another noted, "You can get a drink here for a single copper; if you hand over two coppers, you drink better; if you give four coppers, you drink Falernian." The taverns were not only for drinking. In one of them someone wrote, "Here stretched Euplia with very strong men who were knocked out." Inevitably, graffiti can become quite base, and Pompeii's were no exception: "Passer, don't urinate upon my bones, I pray, nor defecate, if you'd be yet more kind. See the thick piles of (stinging) nettle—turn away. Here it's not safe to squat with bare behind." The lupanars, or brothels, also contain much spicy graffiti describing the virtues and vices of both the customers and the women.

Pompeii also has a treasure story, though not as dramatic as the one for Troy. Egon C. Corti wrote about an important villa discovered in 1894 at Boscoreale, on the outskirts of Pompeii. Excavations revealed that the villa had belonged to a very successful wine merchant. The following year, when one of the diggers had penetrated the tight confines of a wine vat, he found hundreds of gold coins in a leather sack, a gold necklace, and a large number of silver vessels, as well as a human skeleton. Instead of proclaiming the news, the clever digger surfaced from the treasure-laden wine vat announcing that he had encountered poisonous gases. Work was discontinued immediately in the area. The workman, whose name was Michele, then secretly informed the man who owned the property, and together they plotted to steal the treasure and smuggle it out of the country. That night they sneaked into the site and removed the items. Soon after the deed was done, Michele went to a bar, got drunk, and boasted about his trickery. By the time the news circulated, it was too late to do anything about it, for the treasure reached France and had been sold for a fortune. Many of the items were subsequently presented to the Louvre in Paris.

As with Troy, the treasure of Pompeii consists not of gold looted from the site, but instead preservation of a moment in time coupled with rich artwork and unprecedented details about life and death in an ancient town.

ZIMBABWE: THE DARK CONTINENT MYTH

Until recently Africa's past, other than Egypt's, was seen as being, at best, uneventful in terms of archaeological finds. With the exception of human-origins research, few, if any, books on this subject even mention Africa south of the Sahara. Geoffrey Bibby, in his classic book *The Testimony of the Spade,* states that "the African is comparatively rootless, with no feeling of history behind him."[26] The great moments in archaeology were believed to have occurred in Europe, the ancient Near East, or in Middle and South America. Africa was viewed as a rather stagnant area, where people had changed little since the Stone Age. Accounts of early explorers and travelers frequently gave the impression that the continent was filled with wild animals and wild, uncivilized peoples. This viewpoint was, of course, highly supportive of the colonial regimes, which imposed alien systems of rule and beliefs on the local African peoples. It also served to justify the slave trade, which had already cut deeply into the very fabric of many African societies. Written records that described precolonial Africa were largely unavailable.

Archaeologists and historians, frequently working with oral history, have begun to correct this erroneous view. Take, for instance, the belated impact of the discovery of massive stone walls in East Central Africa in 1871. One hundred and nine years later, the name for these ruins would be applied to a newly independent African country in what was formerly Rhodesia. As far as I am aware, Zimbabwe is the only country in the world that takes its name from a major archaeological site. This strongly indicates that the African is far from rootless, despite the efforts of others to make him appear so.

The Great Zimbabwe ruins are located on approximately one hundred acres of the central plateau of Zimbabwe, about twenty-nine kilometers from the town of Nyanda. Originally dubbed the acropolis, the Zimbabwe hill ruin is accented by massive stone walls that link together large boulders. In the valley below are found stone-walled enclosures, the most famous of which is The Great Enclosure or elliptical building, the largest prehistoric stone structure found in Africa south of the Sahara. It is about 800 feet long, and its walls extend to a maximum height of thirty-two feet.[27] The walls, made of granite slabs, are about seventeen feet thick at the base and taper to between four and eleven feet thick at the top. Portions of the top have been decorated with an elaborate chevron pattern. Two entrances to the enclosure lead to other stone walls, traces of huts, and a conical-shaped stone tower.

The amazing story of Zimbabwe begins with the biblical account of Solomon, a fabulous king credited with great wisdom and tremendous wealth. According to the Book of Kings, Solomon's wealth came from the land of Ophir via the Queen of Sheba.

> King Solomon built a fleet . . . on the shore of the Red Sea, in the land of Edom. And Hiram sent with the fleet his servants, seamen who were familiar with the sea, together with the servants of Solomon; and they went to Ophir, and brought from there gold . . . and they brought it to King Solomon. [1 Kings 9:26–28]
>
> Now when the queen of Sheba heard of the fame

> of Solomon . . . she came to test him with hard questions. She came to Jerusalem with a very great retinue, with camels bearing spices, and very much gold, and precious stones . . . [1 Kings 10:1–3]

During the mid-nineteenth century, many people were convinced that Ophir was located in some unknown part of southeast Africa. The roots of this belief can be traced back to the tenth century A.D., when Arab traders sailing with the monsoon winds told of great wealth in the region known as Sofala, in what is now Mozambique. "One of the wonders of the land of Sofala is that there are found under the soil, nuggets of gold in great number," wrote Ibn al-Wardi, an Arab who lived from 1290 to 1349.[28] The Arab stories were embellished further by the Portuguese explorers who sailed along the east coast of Africa. During the voyage of Vasco da Gama in 1502, one crew member became certain that one of the towns they visited along the East African coast was, in fact, the Ophir of the Bible. In the next century, English poet John Milton (1608–1674) mentions the legend in his famous epic *Paradise Lost*: "And Sofala, thought Ophir to the realm of Congo, and Angola farthest south" (XI 396–401). Finally, in 1885, not long after Zimbabwe was discovered, the gold of Ophir was enshrined in fiction by H. Rider Haggard when he wrote *King Solomon's Mines*:

> "Ay," said Evans, "but I will spin you a queerer yarn than that"; and he went on to tell me how he had found in the far interior a ruined city, which he believed to be the Ophir of the Bible, and, by the way, other more learned men have said the same long since poor Evan's time.[29]

The legend of Ophir and the ruins of Zimbabwe were to become linked through the efforts of Carl Mauch, son of a poor carpenter, who grew up in a small village near Stuttgart, Germany. According to the research of E. E. Burke, Carl Mauch was inspired by the gift of an atlas in 1847, when he was ten years old. Young Carl was intrigued by the huge blank areas in the continent of Africa and wondered what might be found there. Africa represented one of the last frontiers for European exploration. During the next twenty-five years, Heinrich Barth's trip across the Sahara, David Livingstone's journey across central Africa, and John Speke's discovery of the Lake Victoria source of the Nile would fascinate Europeans. The profound influence of the atlas on Mauch is similar to that of *Jerrer's Universal History* on Schliemann. Unlike Schliemann and others, however, Mauch did not have formal university training, nor do we get the impression that he was brilliant as a self-taught scholar.

By the time Mauch was fifteen years old, he was convinced that his future would lead him eventually on a journey of exploration through the vast interior of southern Africa. To achieve his goal, he studied natural history, geology, and languages and read the latest explorer's reports. Because he was not considered an expert and had no official backing for his plans, he needed to find a practical way of getting to Africa. When he was twenty-seven, Mauch went to London, where he studied briefly at the British Museum, an important research center of scientific specimens collected from around the world. Then he joined the crew of a German ship bound for the port of Durban on the east coast of South Africa. It must have been an exciting moment for Mauch as he landed in Africa on the threshold of the unknown and realized that his childhood dreams might come true.

In 1865 Durban had been established only for about thirty years. The Limpopo River was seen as the northern frontier, and few Europeans had penetrated beyond it. Mauch, with his geological background, believed that gold fields or, perhaps, even diamonds might be found in this area. There were also vague rumors of stone ruins to the north of the Limpopo. The Reverend Adam Merensky, a missionary based in northern South Africa, even stated in a South African newspaper that these were, in fact, the ruins of the Biblical Ophir of King Solomon's time. It is suspected that he was either influenced by reading Milton's comments about Ophir in *Paradise Lost* or perhaps knew of the Portuguese accounts. In any case, Merensky did try to find the ruins but aborted his mission because of rumors of a smallpox epidemic in the regions to the north.

Carl Mauch met Merensky and was, no doubt, influenced strongly by his ideas. The lure of gold fields and Ophir and, especially, curiosity about the unknown spurred on Mauch's attempts to travel north of the Limpopo. He did some preliminary exploring with an American elephant hunter, Henry Hartley, and managed to locate an important gold field. Then, in 1871, when a joint expedition with Reverend Merensky did not prove feasible, Mauch started alone on a search for the ruins of Ophir. He headed for the base of an Italian adventurer known as Albasini, who lived past the frontier. This was the last European outpost. Then, as he prepared to leave Albasini's farm in late July, Mauch wrote grandly in his journal.

> In the sight of the re-united Fatherland, standing in fore-front of all nations, and with the image of the Kaiser, crowned with victory, may now the most valuable and important, the hitherto most mysterious part of Africa be tackled, the old Monomotapa or Ophir! May God help me![30]

One could easily imagine music and the beat of drums rolling through Mauch's thoughts as he embarked on his journey into the unknown.

Mauch traveled with up to forty African porters, including a gunbearer and interpreters. He recorded observations about the geology and botany of the landscape, plotted his latitude and longitude, and recorded temperatures. Mauch was interested in the people he encountered, but his notes about their customs and behavior are often colored with the typical prejudices of the times. He had little patience with their version of hospitality—goats roasted in his honor, much conversation, and drinking of the local brew. This was time-consuming, and Mauch was in a hurry. Yet it was not all roast goats and beer for Mauch; there were times when he was extremely hungry and thirsty.

He had been traveling for about one month when a crisis developed among his crew, which had been reduced to about ten porters. These remaining men vigorously demanded payment before they would go any farther. Mauch knew they would abandon him if they were paid in advance, so he tried to humor them along with promises. Thinking they had been deceived, the Africans left and took some of his goods with them, perhaps as payment. Thus Mauch was totally deserted in the bush without his interpreters or help of any kind. He had little food left and believed that he would be robbed or murdered. On August 27, he wrote in his journal, "I had everything to fear here, not only the loss of my goods, but the loss of my life, either through poisoned food or by arrow." He felt like a trapped animal pondering which way to go and seeing risks at almost every point. There was only one hope. He wrote that he attempted to find and pay a local African to lead him to Adam Render, a mysterious German elephant hunter who lived in the bush, "a white man who, unfortunately, belongs to the German Nation and who has sunk to the state of a Kaffir by marrying two Kaffir women."

Much to his surprise, seven men arrived at his camp the following morning to help him out of his plight. Led by an amazing one-legged man who hopped the entire way, the group traveled about half a day before camping again. The following day, August 29, Mauch scribbled a note to be delivered by a messenger to Render, who was thought to be living in the area. Miraculously, Render appeared in his camp that same evening.

The next day they left for Render's home, which was at Chief Pika's village, about three hours away. During the walk, the Africans began to tell Mauch about an ancient group of white people who had lived in the area before they had entered the country. These early settlers had left behind iron tools and furnaces as relics. This is, of course, just what Mauch wanted to hear, and I suspect that he must have asked them leading questions that made them tell him what he wanted to know. While at Render's home, he heard more stories that fired his wildest dreams. The chief told him about "the whites who formerly lived here and the ruins of their structures which were probably to be found in the vicinity." He was especially intrigued by the story of a magic pot with four legs that was filled with a yellow substance (gold?). The pot could move, and one man who had made the mistake of reaching into it lost his hand when the pot clamped shut.

The magic mountain (the pot was located on a mountain that was held in awe because the grass could never be burned off the top) and pot were held in great esteem. Mauch decided to go to the mountain and search for the mysterious pot. After eating a hearty breakfast of roast goat and rice, he left the village in the company of the chief's sons and several other assistants. The mountain, which he skeptically named "Spook Mountain," was only three miles away. During his approach, he noticed pits in the ground, which he thought were traces of the ancient mines of the early white inhabitants of the area. Mauch was initially disappointed. Like the pot of gold at the end of the rainbow, the mystery pot on top of "Spook Mountain" could not be found. He gazed at the sweeping view from the mountaintop and asked about the stone ruins. He was elated to learn they were only eight miles away, associated with a hill called Zimbabye or Zimbaoe.

Mauch returned to Render's place filled with anticipation. On September 4 he left to see the ruins and achieve the most important goal of his journey. It had been more than a month since he left Albasini's outpost, and his total journey had led him about 145 miles north of the Limpopo River. Even though he was very close to his goal, he had to exercise the utmost caution in going to the ruins. They were in the territory of a chief who was a political rival of the chief who supported Render. A trip to the ruins could easily arouse suspicion and promote hostility. Mauch thought it prudent to claim he was on a hunting trip.

He spent the night at the compound of an old man who lived about halfway between Render's place and the ruins, then proceeded on by a devious route so as to avoid contacting the rival chief's people. After walking for about two and a half hours, he encountered the first traces of the Zimbabwe ruins. He found granite walls estimated to be up to twenty feet high, choked with stinging nettle plants. He located a strange conical-shaped tower that was also constructed from granite slabs. Subsequently, one of the local inhabitants of the area summoned him to meet the chief. Surprisingly, this chief proved to be very friendly and granted him permission to return to his territory. Mauch was, oddly enough, rather unemotional about his initial discovery of the ruins. He writes in his journal merely that "the lights were extinguished on the day which had been rich in discoveries."

Exploring the ruins was no picnic. Mauch's subsequent investigations at Zimbabwe were hampered by his own impatience and by local suspicions about his real purpose for visiting the ruins. Much of his investigation was done on the sly to avoid contact with people, which might increase the wariness of the competing chiefs. Mauch reported that tensions had reached the point where at least one person had been killed and cornfields had been cut down. His last visit to the ruins with Render in March 1872 nearly resulted in bloodshed. He carried a loaded revolver and took advantage of the high grass for protection while quickly doing an overall sketch plan of the site.

Mauch concluded that Zimbabwe was built by the Queen of Sheba as an imitation of King Solomon's temple and palace. He had certainly been influenced by Reverend Merensky's views about Ophir and local African stories of an ancient white population. During his last visit to the site, he had taken a sample of wood from a cross beam over the entrance to one of the buildings. On the basis of the consistency, color, and odor of the wood, Mauch decided it was cedar and, therefore, one of the biblical cedars of Lebanon. Solomon, he noted, had made extensive use of cedar in building his palaces. Surely only the seafaring Phoenicians could have brought the wood to Zimbabwe. His journal entry of 6 March 1872 concludes with the statement that the Queen of Sheba was, in fact, the Queen of Zimbabwe. Furthermore, the elusive magic pot may be "an Ark of the Covenant."

Mauch had a very fertile imagination and carried his conclusions even further. Reports of periodic ritual sacrifices of cattle on a mountaintop near the ruins fascinated him. If Zimbabwe mimicked Solomon's temple, then these rituals were handed down from Solomon's time. Mauch was convinced that an ancient form of Judaism had been transferred to Zimbabwe, where it had survived for nearly 3,000 years before being interrupted by the recent invasions of the Matebele and Zulu. Mauch even believed that one of the area chiefs known as Bebereke was a direct descendant of a high priest whom Solomon had sent with the Queen of Sheba. He did not propose, however, that he had found King Solomon's mines.

Five days after the discovery of Zimbabwe, Mauch wrote a letter to Dr. A. Petermann, one of the leading geographers in Germany, describing the discovery. He had met Petermann in Germany and had received encouragement from him. Petermann published the letter along with two others in the March 1872 issue of *Geographischen Mittheilungen*. This was the first formal account of Zimbabwe in Europe. News of the site appeared in England in 1873, when the *London Illustrated News* reported that "strange stories have been told of late about the Ophir of Solomon having been discovered . . . in the interior of Sofala."[31] The article was very skeptical regarding the link with Ophir.

Mauch does not say very much in his journal about Adam Render, but it is clear that he looked down on Render and grew increasingly weary of him. When Mauch planned to leave, Render asked to go along so that Mauch could use his influence to find a position for him in Europe. After an abortive start, they left the Zimbabwe area in May 1872, embarking on a journey that would take them more than 400 miles to the northeast. Their destination was the east coast near the mouth of the Zambezi River, at that time in Portuguese territory. This was a tortuous trip for Mauch, who suffered greatly with a tropical fever along the way. After traveling for about a month, Mauch was desperate.

> There was no thought on my part of getting up and climbing around in the strangely rocky and broken country; I was entitled to fear truly that here I might—but no!—I do not want to put it down on paper! Enough! I was in deplorable shape.[32]

Despite illness and other hardships of travel, Mauch and Render reached the Zambezi River and were in Senna, an outpost in what is now Mozambique, by the middle of July. From there, Mauch went by boat to the port of Quelimane at the mouth of the Zambezi. He proposed to continue his exploration in the Portuguese area known as Zambezia, but the Portuguese governor-general was not interested. At this point, Mauch gave up and decided that his only option was to return to Europe. A small French schooner sailed from Quelimane in October 1872, with Carl Mauch as a passenger. His adventure in Africa had ended.

In comparison to the adventures of Livingstone and other notable explorers, Carl Mauch's travels received little attention in Europe. When he returned to Germany, he expected to be employed by a university or museum but, ironically, lacked the necessary academic qualifications. He ended up working in a cement factory, a rather heavy ending for an explorer. Mauch, who had walked with sure feet over hundreds of miles of African footpaths, died at age thirty-eight after falling out a window.

Carl Mauch was not an archaeologist. He did not excavate at Zimbabwe and, as we have seen, was hampered in his study of the ruins because of adverse local political conditions. Some of his observations about the site were good, while others were in error.[33] Nonetheless, Mauch followed his dreams and discovered the Zimbabwe ruins, and his gravestone in Germany credits him with this important accomplishment.

The first major digging at Zimbabwe was done in 1891 by Theodore Bent, an Englishman. He was sponsored by the British South Africa company and the British Association of Science. Bent gave credit to Mauch for discovering the site but said that the connection of Zimbabwe with Solomon and Sheba was so unbelievable "that the subject of Zimbabwe ruins was in abeyance for nearly twenty years after Mauch's visit and was rather accredited as a traveler's tale . . ."[34]

Bent and his wife, along with a surveyor, outfitted themselves in Kimberly, South Africa, where they bought "Two wagons, thirty-six oxen and heaps of tinned provisions . . ." Bent reports that it took them about three months of "trekking" to reach Zimbabwe and about a week to build a wagon track and travel the last fourteen miles from what was then Fort Victoria to Zimbabwe. Bent hired thirty Africans to help in clearing the ruins of tangled vegetation and in digging. He paid them one blanket per month, which was the going rate for labor at the time. Bent spent about two months at the site, working from 8:00 A.M. until sundown. We don't know much about the details of his excavations because he did not write field notes. He recovered many intriguing artifacts, most notably several soapstone birds, which were carved on the tops of columns. Bent thought that these carvings were very similar to certain birds found in ancient Assyrian sites, where the birds were believed to "represent the female element in creation." Thus he saw a link between Zimbabwe and the ancient Middle East.

Bent felt that the ruins of Zimbabwe and other sites could not have been built by Africans.

As a feature in the country they are most remarkable—
ancient, massive, mysterious, standing out in startling
contrast to the primitive huts of the barbarians who
dwell around them and the wilderness of nature.

He concluded that Zimbabwe was built by "a northern race coming from Arabia . . . a race closely akin to the Phoenician and the Egyptian, strongly commercial and eventually developing into the more civilized races of the ancient world."

Another early investigator at Zimbabwe was Richard N. Hall, who excavated the site from 1902 to 1904. His work was very destructive. He stripped away vast areas of deposits with little regard to their contents. Hall dedicated his book *Great Zimbabwe* to his predecessor, Bent. Like Bent, he thought that Zimbabwe was built by ancient Middle Easterners, perhaps Sabeo-Arabians. Hall, working with a crew of as many as forty Africans, recovered numerous gold artifacts such as beads, crucibles, and bars. He also found two more of the famous Zimbabwe soapstone birds and numerous small soapstone phalli, along with ivory beads, iron implements, pottery, and numerous other objects.

In retrospect, is is not difficult to understand how the first workers—Mauch, Bent, Hall, and others—reached their conclusion about the exotic origins of Zimbabwe. The main reason was that such an explanation could be used to support the prevalent racial stereotype that belittled the creative abilities of Africans. In addition, next to nothing was known about the prehistory of Africa at the turn of the century, and it was commonplace for archaeologists of that period to make sweeping comparisons and generalizations on the basis of very tenuous evidence. Furthermore, early investigators were quick to note that the Africans who lived near the ruins at the time of their discovery did not build in stone and recounted traditions of alien people having done this.

Later, the interpretation of the Zimbabwe ruins became politically important for the British colony of Southern Rhodesia. It became clearly advantageous for the white Rhodesian government to help justify its rule over a black African majority by supporting the theory that Zimbabwe was not built by Africans. The implication of this position was that the Africans did not have the organizational skills and leadership qualities necessary to build and govern sites as large and as complex as Zimbabwe. The curator of the ruins theorized about their construction.

> It is also almost impossible to think that the mentality of the Bantu would be capable of such conception. It is more than likely that the Bantu people were used as slaves, beasts of burden to carry from some distances the thousands of tons of granite blocks necessary to erect such colossal buildings.[35]

A 1938 Rhodesian government poster actually depicts an African bowing in front of the ruins before the ghost of the Queen of Sheba.[36]

There have been some recent attempts to prove that Zimbabwe was built by peoples from southern Arabia rather than by Africans.[37] The question of who built Zimbabwe became so heated and emotional that the official government archaeologist for Rhodesia resigned in 1970 because of government pressure: He supported the unacceptable view that Zimbabwe was built by Africans.

Setting aside the political and racist overtones, there is overwhelming archaeological evidence that Zimbabwe was built and governed by Bantu-speaking black Africans. This point of view was first argued by David Randall-McIver in 1905 and has been supported heavily by the research of numerous other archaeologists. An important key to this argument is chronology. People such as Mauch, Bent, and Hall did not know Zimbabwe's age. They probably would not have dreamed that a technique would be invented enabling scientists to date the wooden lintels found at the site. There are now numerous radiocarbon dates available for Zimbabwe and related ruins. These dates demonstrate that the first stone walls at Zimbabwe were built in approximately A.D. 1250 and that Zimbabwe was at its zenith at about A.D. 1380. The radiocarbon dates are supported independently by the recovery of a bronze coin at Zimbabwe, which was minted at the East African coastal town of Kilwa in A.D. 1330. Other imported trade items, including beads and porcelain, also confirm the above dates. Thus Zimbabwe could have been built neither by Solomon, who reigned at about 1000 B.C., nor the seafaring Phoenicians (ca. 1000 B.C.), nor the southern Arabian Sabean peoples, who predate Zimbabwe by about 700 years. These exotic peoples lived during earlier times, and there is no archaeological evidence for their presence in the interior of East Africa.

Instead of finding traces of exotic peoples, archaeologists working at many sites in eastern and southern Africa have unearthed a long general background sequence to Zimbabwe that is associated with the development of traditional African Iron Age cultures. The African Iron Age has, in turn, been linked by linguistic studies and archaeology to the Bantu speakers.

The Bantu language family includes numerous African languages related in the same general sense that German and English are historically akin to each other. Bantu speakers are the most numerous people inhabiting Africa south of the Sahara Desert. Their ancestral homeland was probably the Cameroon grasslands in West Africa; at least that is what the linguistic data implies. These people were early Iron Age farmers who kept some domestic livestock and lived in small villages. They made iron implements, such as hoes and axes, and engaged in small-scale trade. Gradually the population grew, and the societies became more complex. By the late Iron Age (about A.D. 1200–1400), they were organized into a number of kingdoms or states, some of which were involved with extensive international trade networks. The latest research shows that Bantu speakers had spread into East Africa by the advent of the Christian era.

By about A.D. 1000 change was also sweeping through parts of southern Africa. Archaeologist James Denbow has found some remarkable clues to the growth of social complexity by studying aerial photos of a region along the eastern edge of Botswana, not far from where other Zimbabwe-style ruins are found. The photos show circular patterns on numerous hilltops that contrast with surrounding vegetation. Excavations of the mysterious circles revealed great thicknesses (up to three feet) of a glassy, slaglike material, which turned out to be cow dung altered by intense burning. Some of these cattle enclosures were evidently in use about 300 years before Zimbabwe. Further study of the aerial photos reveals that there was a hierarchy of settlement types, ranging from small camps to sizable centers, where large herds of cattle were kept. Among many traditional pastoralists in Africa today, large herd size is a sign of a person's prestige, and high-status individuals can amass herds consisting of hundreds of animals. Cattle may well have been an economic and social basis for the growth of societies like Zimbabwe.

Researchers now believe that Zimbabwe was an important center in a widespread trade network linking the interior of southeast Africa to the east coast Swahili towns. One of the most notable of these towns was Kilwa, which reached its height at the same time as Zimbabwe. Africans were mining gold in the greater Zimbabwe area beginning about A.D. 1200, and gold was found at Kilwa. In addition, elephants were hunted for their ivory tusks long before European hunters like Adam Render entered the area. Rhinoceroses were also hunted for their horns, for in the Far East they were believed to have aphrodisiac powers when they were powdered and eaten. All of these valuable commodities were traded to the coastal towns in exchange for beads, porcelain, and cloth brought by the southern Arabian ships called dhows, which sailed with the monsoon winds. Similar boats can still be seen in the old harbor at Mombasa, in Kenya, and some of them are reputed to contain smuggled ivory and rhino horns.

Zimbabwe may have been a center of trade and a regional capital, but it did not stand alone. At least 150 ruin sites of a generally similar nature have been found on the granite-rich plateau of what is now the nation of Zimbabwe. Ruin sites such as Inyanga, Dhlo-Dhlo, and Khami show that Late Iron Age cultures were socially and politically complex, and some could be considered states, or kingdoms. The rulers and their cadre of supporters were skilled in organizing the labor for large-scale building projects, which, in turn, enhanced their own status. One estimate, that about 400 people could have constructed the elliptical building at Zimbabwe during a four-year period, is based on the assumption that each person transported twelve blocks of granite per day and worked for fifty days a year.[38] At its height, there could have been 10,000 people living in and around Zimbabwe.

The architecture at Zimbabwe is completely in keeping with African traditions, in particular those of the Bantu-speaking Shona people, who have inhabited the area for centuries. The circular enclosures are expressions of traditional African concepts, seen in the construction of both houses and cattle corrals. The use of stone for building walls and covering graves is also fairly widespread in Africa, though such use was not observed at the time of European discovery of Zimbabwe. The so-called acropolis at Zimbabwe is situated on top of a hill, as are the royal residence areas of the Shona rulers; they wanted to be closer to their god, who lived in the sky. The soapstone birds, found in what was probably the king's royal residence on the hilltop, may represent the spiritual messengers of individual Zimbabwe kings, just as eagles are seen as the Shona king's personal messengers to their god.[39] Even the word *zimbabwe* is similar to the Shona words meaning "houses of stone" or "venerated houses."[40] The common people, or peasant farmers, of Zimbabwe evidently lived, as many do today, in typical African-style huts constructed of daga, a mixture of dried mud and sticks, and covered by thatched roofs. Traces of daga houses were recovered at Zimbabwe.

Zimbabwe was a ruin choked by vegetation when Carl Mauch first visited it. The site was abandoned at approximately A.D. 1450, more than 400 years prior to Mauch's visit. Anthropologists believe that people left Great Zimbabwe because of an upset in the fragile balance between the needs of the society and its adaptation to the environment. First of all, farming was almost certainly done by the slash-and-burn method, in which forests are cleared for cultivation by cutting trees and burning over the areas. In the first years of their use, the resultant fields can support reasonably large numbers of people; but the fertility of the soil is gradually depleted by this method, and people are forced to move to new areas. This problem may have been aggravated because Zimbabwe, as a center of trade and religion, attracted more people than the dwindling food supply could support. Similarly, suitable grazing areas for the large herds of cattle probably became increasingly scarce.

An additional problem was energy. At Zimbabwe, firewood was used for cooking, firing pottery, and, especially, smelting iron. Fire was probably also used in cracking the granite blocks used for construction of the walls. Whereas even today, transporting firewood for many miles is a regular part of village life. Resources may have been strained by supporting the heavily concentrated population centered around Zimbabwe.

When Zimbabwe was abandoned, Shona political power shifted

to the site of Khami, where fresh resources were available. Another related Shona political development led to the rise of the Mwene-Mutapa Empire, which was in existence when the Portuguese explorers began to penetrate the coast. In fact, the advent of the Portuguese, with their lust for gold, disrupted the long-standing trade networks. The Europeans never found the fabled richness of Sofala or the legendary Ophir. The Shona themselves were eventually defeated by the Nguni, who invaded the area in the 1800s. As trees and vines began to grow over its crumbling walls, Zimbabwe became a memory.

MACHU PICCHU: MOUNTAIN STRONGHOLD OF THE INCAS

Diffusionist Theories

In the formative days of archaeology, the discovery of "lost cities" and other elaborate sites evoked much mystery and almost endless speculation. Zimbabwe was an example of this in Africa. Yet nowhere, perhaps, has this speculation been so rampant as in the New World. Sites like the prehistoric Indian mounds of the Midwest were once considered to have been relics of the "lost Tribes of Israel" or other wandering groups of exotic peoples. Similarly, "diffusionists" maintain that certain civilizations in the New World resulted from trans-oceanic contact with peoples such as the Egyptians or Bronze Age Chinese. They assert that there are too many striking similarities between certain "totally independent" inventions to have occurred otherwise.

A good example of the diffusionist argument is seen in Peru. Both the Incas and the Egyptians believed in a form of divine kingship in which their respective rulers were direct descendants of the sun-god. Both cultures mummified their rulers and allowed them to marry their sisters.[41] Diffusionists feel such similarities could not be due to chance. Others argue that it is perfectly reasonable to find solar-based religions among peoples who depend on intensive farming. Nor is mummification that rare a practice in societies needing to demonstrate that the king continues to exist spiritually after death.

We have already seen such tendencies among the Scythian burials at Pazyryk, in Siberia. There is also a serious time gap in the diffusionist argument in this case. The Incas flourished in A.D. 1450, while the Egyptian culture peaked about 3,000 years earlier. Finally, the most difficult problem with the diffusionist view is that no Egyptian, Chinese, or other equally alien artifacts have ever been found in any of the sites associated with New World civilizations. Instead, excavations have revealed a step-by-step process of cultural development that bear witness to these cultures' regional beginnings.

The Enigmatic Nazca Line Drawings

Going further afield, one speculative theory involves crossing entire galaxies rather than oceans. The extraterrestrial-contact theory is light-years away from being science, even though its proponents assure us otherwise. Once again, a classic example is seen in Peru, where Erich von Däniken has argued that the mysterious, prehistoric Nazca line drawings may have been an airfield.[42] He asks, "What is wrong with the idea that the lines were laid out to say to the 'gods': Land here! Everything has been prepared as you ordered."

The drawings, found in a barren desert on the southern coast of Peru, were made by picking up the stones that litter the ground surface, thereby exposing the underlying desert soil. The drawings include lines that go on for miles, as well as some enormous pictures of animals (nearly the length of a football field) that are best seen from the air. In fact, the Nazca lines were first noticed from airplanes and were believed initially to be traces of ancient irrigation works. Although they are considerably earlier than the Inca, local people called the lines Inca roads. According to Maria Reiche, a mathematician who has spent many years studying the drawings, the lines are of a variety of types, such as zigzags, triangles, and those resembling whips. The most numerous of the large animals are birds. Some of the notable pictures include a killer whale, a giant condor, a monkey, and a spider.

Despite skepticism by von Däniken, there is evidence that the lines were made by Nazca Indians, one of the notable pre-Inca cultural groups who lived in the area between 200 B.C. and A.D. 600.

There is even a radiocarbon date of roughly A.D. 520 attributed to one of the wooden stakes believed to have been used to lay out the lines. It is certain, however, that they were made over an extensive period during the Nazca occupation of the area rather than at one specific time. Recent evidence suggests that the animal drawings may be earlier than the extensive lines. There are close links between the remarkably well-executed Nazca pottery and the ground drawings. For example, William H. Isbell, an expert on the archaeology of Peru, has brought attention to a killer whale effigy pot that is unmistakably similar in details to the giant line drawing of the same kind of whale. The spider also appears as a decoration on Nazca pottery, and there are close similarities between one of the drawings and mouth masks found on Nazca burials.

At first glance, it seems amazing that the huge drawings could have been made by peoples who had simple technologies and even lacked writing, but experiments conducted by Joe Nickell have shown that producing the line drawings does not require elaborate surveying techniques. Nickell created a 440-foot condor similar to the one at Nazca by using a cross, stakes, and strings. Anthony F. Aveni, an astronomer, has also shown that some of the drawings could have been produced by relatively few people, with no surveying techniques, and in a short space of time.

There is much debate about why the Nazca drawings were made. Probably there were many reasons. Paul Kosok, who is credited with discovering the giant symbols in 1939, provides one intriguing explanation. During his pioneering work, he tells us how he and his wife, with "minds whirling with endless questions about these strange and fantastic remains," watched a magnificent sunset from a newly discovered drawing.[43] Just by chance, they noticed that the sun "was setting almost exactly over the end of one of the long single lines!" It was a remarkable coincidence that they made this observation on the day of the winter solstice, which is the shortest day of the year. To Kosok, this was the "key to the riddle!" The ancient Nazca people were using some of the lines to keep track of the solstice, possibly for agricultural and ceremonial reasons. Reiche, who has carried on with the astronomical approach to the Nazca problem, has found a number of other alignments with solstices and suspects there may also be relationships to moon sets and moon rises. On the other hand, Gerald S. Hawkins, an astronomer, did not find significant astronomical correlations when he analyzed the data with a computer utilizing the approach he followed at Stonehenge in England (see Chapter 6).

Another interpretation is provided by Isbell, who views the Nazca drawings as the expression of large-scale group work efforts that are intertwined with the ceremonial and economic sides of Nazca life. The archaeological record is replete with examples of large earthworks, temple mounds, and other other ceremonial structures. While these structures reflect the ability of political leaders to organize labor projects, they often serve a religious purpose and may also symbolize group identity. When the Nazca lines are considered in this broad context they can be seen as a unique expression of the same general relationships. Recently, Anthony Aveni has done a detailed study of the problem. He believes that the lines (not the animals) are footpaths. Aveni found a significant correlation between the orientation of the lines and the direction and location of water in the Nazca area. The management of water and the seasonal prediction of its availability must have been crucial to the Nazca farmers. Aveni suggests that the lines may be a prototype of a very complex system used later on by the Incas. The Inca system incorporated astronomical and ecological factors and also mapped religious pilgrimage routes. Of course a simple explanation for the animals, which is entirely speculative, is that they may simply have been Nazca representations of gods that they believed lived in the sky. The various interpretations we have seen make one thing certain: The Nazca lines do not represent an airport destined for use by aliens. It is very clear that the growth of Peruvian civilization was the result of indigenous factors.

The Appearance of the Incas

There is a long and complex history of development in Peru and adjacent areas that leads to the growth of the first two pre-Incan empires in about the seventh century A.D. Many spectacular archaeological sites are associated with these empires, especially at Tiahuanaco (Tiwanaku), in Bolivia, where large-scale ruins are seen above the tree line at 4,000 meters. This is the highest ancient civilization known to archaeologists. Following the first empires was a period featuring regionalized states. These states were based economically on corn, potatoes, beans, and a number of other indigenous crops, all of which were first cultivated thousands of years earlier. The ancient Peruvians had also domesticated native members of the Camelidae family (llamas and alpacas) as well as guinea pigs.

The Incas are first detected as a relatively small group in the central Andes in the early part of the thirteenth century. In about 1440, they underwent a dramatic expansion under the rule of an emperor known as Pachacuti, who was appropriately called "the earth shaker." Legend has it that the besieged Pachacuti defeated the powerful forces of the Chanca by miraculously transforming stones in the fields into soldiers. Under his son, Topa Inca, much of western South America was brought under Incan control. At its zenith, the Incan realm covered 2,500 miles from north to south, about the distance separating New York City from San Francisco. The eastern boundary of the Incas' land was the edge of the Amazon rainforest, and they ruled an estimated 6 million people. The secret of their remarkable success was evidently a combination of organizational skills, military conquest (often via threat rather than open warfare), and religious indoctrination. In addition Quechua, the language of the Incas, was imposed as a second language on other populations. This language is still spoken in Peru.

The highlights of Incan political organization are well known. Control was rooted in an ingenious decimal system in which the entire population was divided into units ranging from tens to thousands. Each unit had an administrative leader who was, in turn, responsible to increasingly more powerful authorities who oversaw larger combinations of political groupings. In this fashion the hierarchy of control extended from individual family groups to provincial governors, who ruled each of the four quarters of the empire. The governors were responsible to the emperor, who was descended from the sun-god. The boundaries dividing the four quarters met in the capital city of Cuzco.

The Incan empire was linked together by an estimated 20,000 miles of roads, which were used for foot travel. (The Incas, along with other American Indian civilizations, lacked wheeled vehicles.)

The roads featured specially built way stations at regular intervals, suspension bridges, and steps cut out of solid rock. Relay runners are reported to have been able to cover about 240 kilometers (149 miles) in a day, and the often-quoted example is that the emperor, who resided in the highland capital at Cuzco, was brought fresh fish from the Pacific Ocean.

One of the surprising events in the history of the New World was that this very powerful Incan Empire was crushed by a small group of Spaniards. This was possible partly because when Francisco Pizarro, the Spanish explorer, arrived in 1532, the region was rent by civil war. Following the death of the emperor in 1527, two brothers, Atahuallpa and Huascar, were competing for control of the empire. When Pizarro arrived at the city of Caramalca with fewer than 200 troops, Atahuallpa, not suspecting treachery, was carried into the town plaza on his royal litter to meet the Spaniards. There were thousands of Incas in the vicinity. Pizarro's spokesman, a chaplain, dutifully explained that the Spaniards represented a powerful empire across the sea whose mission was to Christianize the Incas. As if this wasn't enough, the chaplain demanded that the Incas become subservient to Spain. Naturally, the Incan leader was irate and refused to comply.

> I will be no man's tributary. I am greater than any prince upon earth. Your emperor may be a great prince; I do not doubt it, when I see that he has sent his subjects so far across the waters; and I am willing to hold him as a brother.[44]

At a prearranged signal, the Spanish troops opened fire and charged on horseback. The surprised Incas, unfamiliar with either firearms or charging horsemen, panicked, and the Spaniards massacred several thousand of them in the square. The Spaniards' mounts may have caused much of the Incan panic, as horses had become extinct in America late in the Ice Age. Horses were unknown to the Indians until they were obtained from the Spaniards in the American Southwest. In any case, there were no Spanish casualties, and Pizarro easily captured the Incan leader. After receiving an enormous amount of

View of Olduvai Gorge.

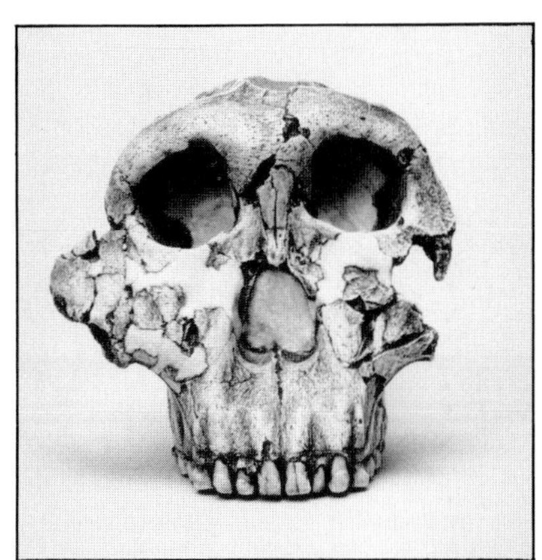

Zinjanthropus skull from Olduvai (*Australopithecus boisei*).

View of Lothagam.

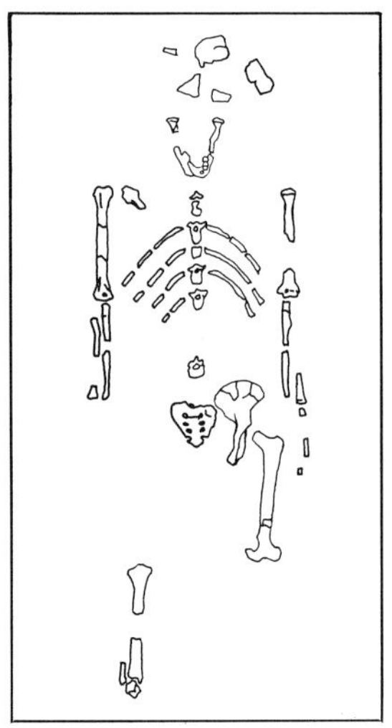

Lucy (*Australopithecus afarensis*).

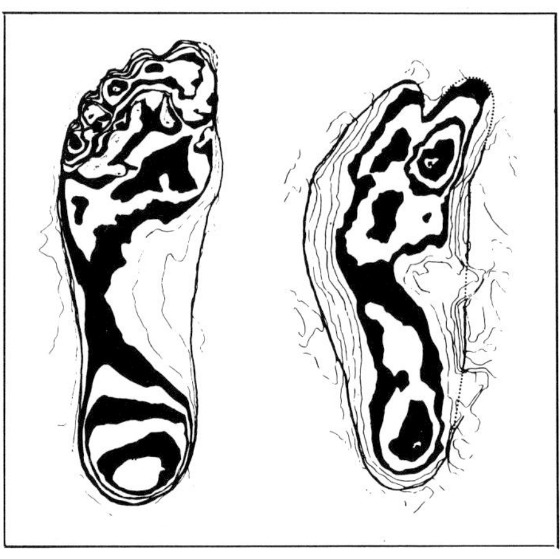

Comparison of Laetoli footprint contour patterns (right) with modern human female (left). Scale = 1:1, contours = 2 mm. intervals.

Les Trois Frères cave. (Arrow indicates location of sorcerer.)
Inset: Sorcerer of Les Trois Frères, as depicted by Abbé Brueil.

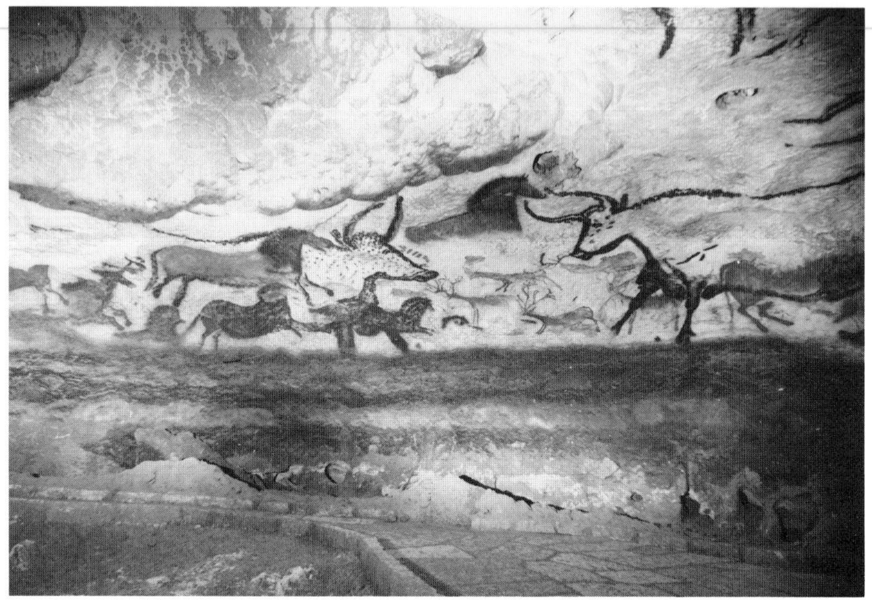

Lascaux Cave, Hall of the Bulls, showing wild cattle, horse, and cervids.

Lascaux, dead man scene.

Rock art from Africa: Tsodilo hills, Botswana, showing cattle, humans, and elands (lower animal).

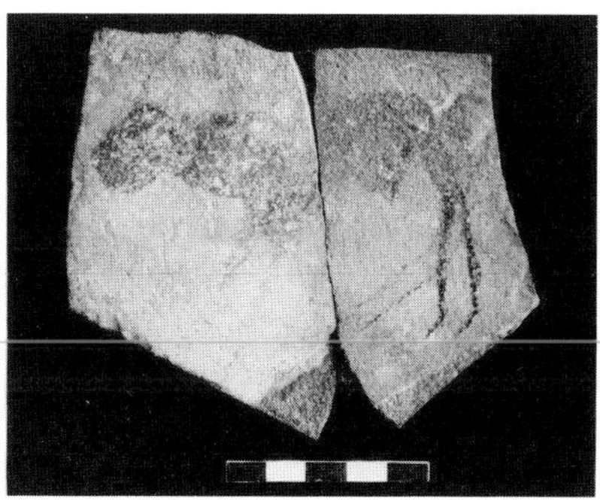

The oldest art in Africa: Painted slabs from Apollo 11 Cave, Namibia.

South African rock art, Kamberg.

The Sutton Hoo ship.

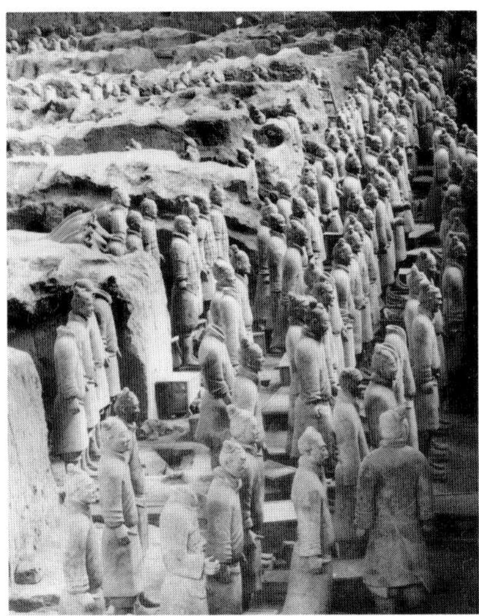

Buried life-size army of Qin-Shi-Huang.

Outer gold shrine of Tutankhamen's tomb. The innermost shrine contained the gold coffin and mummy of Tutankhamen.

Throne from Tutankhamen's tomb.

Gold coffin containing mummy of Tutankhamen.

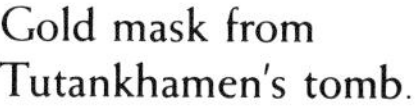

Gold mask from Tutankhamen's tomb.

View of Hissarlik (Troy).

View of Pompeii.

Great Zimbabwe hill ruin.

Great Zimbabwe: great enclosure.

View of Machu Picchu.

Machu Picchu.

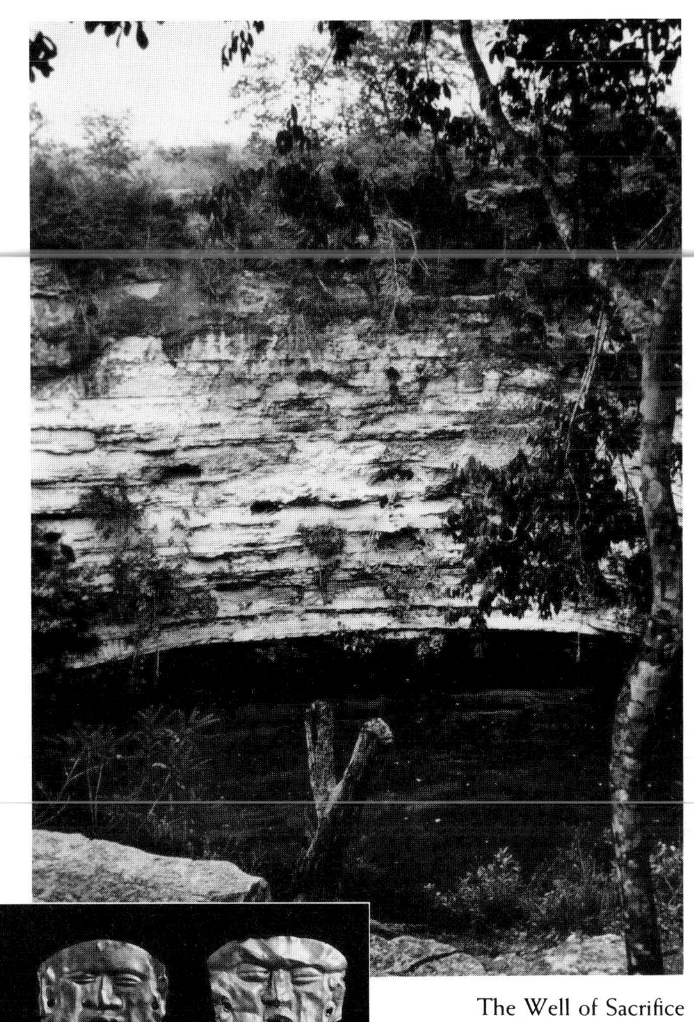

The Well of Sacrifice at Chichén Itzá.

Gold faces from the Well of Sacrifice, Chichén Itzá.

Heavily encrusted cannon from the *Mary Rose*—the gun that identified the ship.

The *Mary Rose* in a new home.

View of Stonehenge showing sarsen circle and trilithons.

Stonehenge showing the heelstone centrally framed.

The Rosetta Stone.

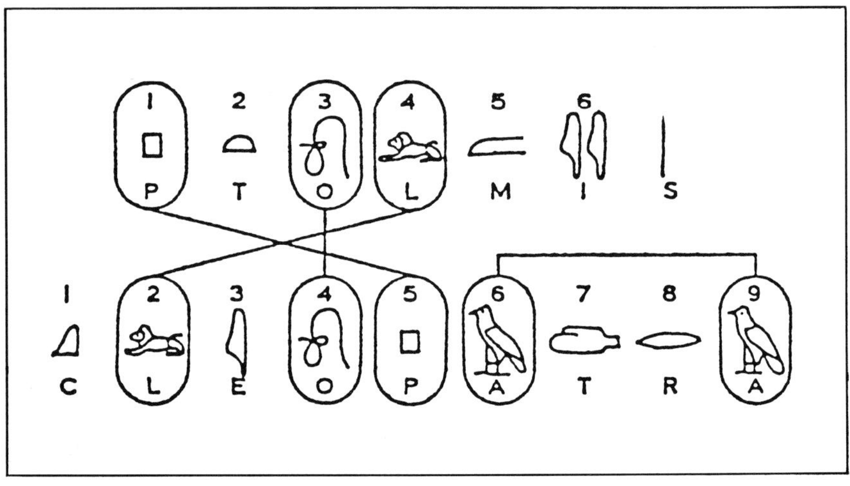

Comparison of Ptolemy and Cleopatra as used by Champollion in deciphering Egyptian hieroglyphics.

Dead Sea cave at Qumran (behind man), where scrolls were first found.

The Isaiah Scroll.

Stelae of King Hammurabi containing the law code.

Clay tablet with the Gilgamesh epic.

gold and silver from the Incas for their leader's ransom, the Spaniards "tried" and executed Atahuallpa, who had, through a plot, already arranged to have his brother drowned. This left the empire without an emperor, and the Spanish moved in. The Incas fought a guerrilla war, but the Spanish conquistadors eventually prevailed and gained control over the empire. The Spaniards, obsessed with finding gold, tortured Indians to death and raped the Incan chosen women, who lived in convents and were dedicated to serving the sun-god. Spanish priests melted down and destroyed many priceless works of Incan art in an effort to stamp out pagan beliefs. At the same time, the Incas were decimated by European diseases, such as smallpox and measles, to which they had no resistance.

The Lost City

The realm of the Incas was vast, and the mountains contained many naturally protected, inaccessible places far removed from direct Spanish influence. Probably about a century before the advent of the Spanish, the Incas started to build a remarkable city on a remote mountain spine overshadowed by a peak known today as Machu Picchu.[45] The Incan city was hidden completely and protected by surrounding mountains, thick forests, and a river with treacherous rapids.

When the conquistadors had firmly established themselves at Cuzco, they heard rumors about an alleged Incan stronghold, which they viewed as a symbol of Incan resistance. The Spanish priests called this infamous place the "University of Idolatry." An expeditionary force of 1,000 troops was sent out in 1637 to destroy the place, but they failed to find it. There are reasons to believe that a small group of them may have reached Machu Picchu, in one way or another, but they never returned. Support for this idea is provided by the discovery of horse bones at the site by archaeologists.

Through the years, the "lost city of the Incas" began to assume legendary qualities, much like the Sofala-Ophir-Zimbabwe story. Driven by the lure of the unknown and gold, explorers searched for it as well as other Peruvian ruins. No one could find the site, though in the late 1800s a Frenchman was told about ruins near a mountain called "Matcho-Picchu." He located the mountain on a map but was unable to find the actual site.

Machu Picchu awaited Hiram Bingham, a remarkable man who was to have a distinguished career. A graduate of Yale with a degree in history, Bingham not only found Machu Picchu, but he also taught history at several universities and eventually became governor of Connecticut. Unlike Schliemann, Bingham did not originally plan to search for a site. He went to Peru in 1911, the same year Olduvai Gorge was discovered, for the purpose of retracing the route of Simón Bolívar, who had marched across the Andes to fight against the Spanish. Bingham was drawn slowly into the search for Incan ruins after a local government official invited him to look for a site whose name meant "the cradle of gold." The opportunity interested him, though he was not seeking treasure. Explorations for this site led him into the mountains high above a tributary of the Amazon, where he said, "Nowhere had I ever witnessed such beauty and grandeur as was here displayed."[46] He was captivated by the snow-capped peaks, sheer canyon walls, and forests. Bingham did find some ruins, but, naturally, the "cradle of gold" eluded him. This initial trip sparked an interest in further exploration, and he began to set his sights on the lost city of the Incas.

Bingham returned to the United States and spoke at a Yale Club dinner, where he announced his plans to return to Peru. He organized a Yale expedition, which included an engineer, naturalist, geologist, and several other specialists. In a way, his party foreshadowed some of the present-day multidisciplinary efforts in archaeological research.

Bingham's team left Cuzco in July 1911. Their first efforts resulted in finding Vitcos (though it may not have been the real Vitcos), an Incan base used to mount guerrilla raids against the Spanish. In this initial venture, Bingham used notes from a Spanish religious order as a guide to find the site. The notes described the setting as being marked by a white stone and a spring. Bingham's use of these notes recalls Schliemann's use of the *Iliad* to search for Troy and Hans Reck's efforts in using crude pictures and a sketch map in the quest for Olduvai.

Following the adventure with Vitcos, Bingham's party planned to search for the legendary lost city of the Incas. In this case there was no sound documentary evidence, yet the city was rumored to be near a place inhabited by hostile Indians who were armed with poisoned arrows. Furthermore, the Indians were said to be controlled by a man who had an unsavory reputation and who simply did not like strangers. Accompanied by Indian porters, the party of explorers crossed over the rugged mountains, where they followed steep, mist-shrouded trails and descended into pockets of thick jungle. When they reached the area in question, they were relieved to find that the local villain was, surprisingly, very helpful. He arranged for nearby Indians to guide Bingham's group to various ruins hidden in the jungle. The ruins were, however, all too small to be the site in question.

The search narrowed when Bingham's party pitched camp along the Grand Canyon of the Urabamba River. Although not far from Cuzco, this was wilderness area, highlighted by the churning rapids of the Urabamba, steep gorges, dense jungle, and towering mountains. Penetration of the area had recently been made possible by the construction of a road. One day, when no one felt like climbing into the mountains, an old Indian named Arteaga walked into Bingham's camp. The Indian, speaking through an interpreter, claimed that there were some extensive ruins in the nearby mountains. One of these mountains was Machu Picchu. Bingham was not about to let this opportunity pass, even though it could be a wild-goose chase; he agreed to pay Arteaga a Peruvian silver dollar to act as his guide.

Bingham left camp accompanied only by Arteaga and an interpreter. Their first task was to cross the treacherous Urabamba rapids on a makeshift log bridge. With great care, Bingham inched his way slowly over the churning river. One slip would have been fatal. Next came a steep climb up the jungle-choked mountainside that led them out of the river valley. The heat and humidity sapped Bingham's energy. He knew that the thick vegetation was the natural habitat of two of the deadliest snakes known, the fer-de-lance and bushmaster. (The latter is akin to a rattlesnake, and sometimes grows to a length of eleven feet.) Slowly and steadily, Bingham followed Arteaga on a climb that eventually rose 2,000 feet above the river valley. In a clearing, they encountered a small group of Indians. Arteaga conferred with them, while Bingham walked ahead, guided by a boy. As they progressed, Bingham began to see agricultural terraces built on the steep mountainside and all but obscured by the overgrown vegetation. Ahead was the precipitous peak of Machu Picchu.

> Surprise followed surprise in bewildering succession [he wrote].[47] Suddenly we found ourselves standing in front of the ruins of two of the finest and most interesting structures in ancient America. Made of beautiful white granite, the walls contained blocks of Cyclopean size, larger than a man. The sight held me spellbound. [Later he added] Would anyone believe what I had found?

Others who would follow him would echo his sentiments by calling the site the "eighth wonder of the world."

Following the discovery of Machu Picchu, the elated Bingham organized a joint Yale University–National Geographic Society expedition in 1912. The work was difficult because the group had to build a bridge over the Urabamba rapids, clear trails through the snake-infested undergrowth, and hand-carry all supplies to the site. Exploration of the steep terrain was especially hazardous, and one member of the expedition was nearly killed in a precipitous fall. Much of the initial work centered on clearing the site of large trees and dense undergrowth. This massive work effort was carried out by a large crew of Indians.

Naturally the prospect of excavating the site was exciting. Bingham hoped to discover the age of the site and why it was built. In addition, the team hoped that the city, which was spared Spanish looting, might yield some remarkable new artifacts. The digging, however, met with mixed success. Some of the excavations carried out near promising-looking buildings yielded surprisingly little, while work in burial caves produced many finds, including skeletons, pottery, animal bones, bronze knives, chisels, and mirrors.

Unlike Troy, there was no gold recovered, but then Machu Picchu is not famous because of its artifactual finds. It is, instead, significant because of its being a "city" built into the spine of a mountain. It is this remarkable blending of architecture and unusual setting that has captivated the interest of both scholars and the public. Machu Picchu is set between two towering peaks, concentrated in an area 700 by 300 meters (2,280 by 984 feet). It was built from locally available granite, which was quarried at the site and cut into blocks. The work was most likely done by Incan laborers, who were periodically required to donate their time to state projects. The engineering feats are exceptional. It has been noted that the huge granite blocks are cut so precisely and fitted together so tightly that a razor blade cannot pass between them. The blocks were placed at a carefully planned incline in order to protect the buildings from earthquakes, which, notably, have destroyed modern buildings while leaving the Incan city unscathed. The buildings were constructed using bronze and stone tools as well as levers. Angles were measured with strings, and plumbs were used to achieve vertical lines.

Manuel Chávez of the University of Cuzco describes Machu Picchu as being divided into urban and agricultural sectors. The site is divided by a series of eight "streets." Numerous long stairways are evident, some of which have steps cut out of solid rock. There are fourteen groups of houses, with a grand total of 216 rooms. The site also features temples, tombs, prisons, a series of irrigation tanks, castlelike towers, and various other buildings, as well as a city wall with a main gate. One of the hallmarks of Machu Picchu is the temple of three windows. Bingham felt that these windows symbolized the three caves that figure prominently in Incan-origin myths. The top of the site is dominated by a large granite altar with a projection at its top. Altars such as this were known to the Incas as "Inti-huanta," which means "hitching post of the sun."[48] The importance of the sun in Incan religion is also seen in a prominent tower that may well have been used to observe the June solstice. In addition, recent work has revealed that a unique cave with a carefully constructed stone window was probably a sighting device for the December solstice.[49] This is in keeping with information provided by the Inca historian Garcilaso de la Vega, El Inca. In 1609 he described how the Inca monitored the winter and summer solstices in the Cuzco area. Garcilasco, the son of an Inca princess and a Spanish captain, tells us that the Inca used towers as observatories. He also noted that they kept track of the equinoxes and held a number of very important festivals dedicated to the sun. The Inca regarded the sun as the sustainer of life.

Speculation about the purpose of this remarkable site continues to excite scholars. Was it essentially a military fortress built to help protect the empire from periodic attacks by hostile Indians? Located at an elevation of nearly 2,450 meters (8,038 feet), the site is nearly impregnable. It overlooks sheer cliffs and is protected on three sides by the rapids of the Urabamba, which thunder 450 meters (1,486 feet) below. Bingham surmised that even a small group of defenders could have held Machu Picchu against any attacking force. The natural defenses are enhanced by the clever way in which the Incas made one of the paths leading to the site. It crosses a narrow ledge overlooking a sheer cliff. Over the chasm, the Incas constructed a log footbridge that, when removed, rendered the narrow path impassable. Additional protection was provided by "signal posts" situated on the mountain high above the city. Bingham remarks that one of them was built over a sheer 3,000-foot drop. In spite of these observations, the theory of Machu Picchu as a military construct has been criticized. Clearly, the Incas had little to fear from the jungle tribes because of their sophisticated political and military organization. The Incas did build forts, but they are quite different from Machu Picchu in their architecture.

Could the site have been a religious center that became a safe spiritual retreat from the Spaniards? There are religious buildings, to be sure, but the primacy of religion, like the military explanation, can be overstressed. An interesting example of this occurred when Bingham's expedition excavated a large number of graves believed to contain "Virgins of the Sun." This theory was dealt a blow when analysis of the skeletons revealed that many of the so-called virgins were males. Bingham also believed that Machu Picchu was the place where the Incas originated, the legendary kingdom of Tampu-tocco, about 1,000 years before the Spanish arrived. Whereas it must have been appealing to relate such a spectacular site to legends, Bingham's theory about Tampu-tocco is not correct, for neither the city nor the Incas are that old. As was previously discussed, the Inca underwent a remarkable expansion in the fifteenth century. A large area was conquered and there were extensive building projects carried out under the system where people contributed their labor as a form of tax. Machu Picchu was built during this time. Inca architecture such as the styles of windows and doorways as well as techniques of terracing are all well known and are clearly evident at Machu Picchu.

There is compelling evidence that Machu Picchu was, for the most part, a city of the elite. This is not to deny that it also had important religious and military functions. John Rowe, a leading Peruvianist archaeologist, has found many striking similarities between the layout of Machu Picchu and that of the former Incan capital of Cuzco before it was destroyed and rebuilt during the Spanish conquest. Because of this, he feels that Machu Picchu, like Cuzco, was occupied by the upper echelon of the Incan social hierarchy.

Despite the fact that Machu Picchu is now on the main tourist route, the area continues to surprise archaeologists with new discoveries. In 1982, a team of Peruvian archaeologists was exploring the dense jungle adjacent to the old Incan road leading to the site when one of them suddenly disappeared.[50] He had dropped through the vegetation into a jungle-covered passageway, which connects a completely hidden group of stone ruins with a huge agricultural terrace wall. The site is reported to contain some of the largest terraces known, with walls up to twenty feet high. At least thirty new Incan tombs were found and appear to be intact. It is clear that much more work awaits archaeologists near the fascinating site of Machu Picchu.

5

THE WET FRONTIER

Underwater Archaeology

I once did a study of an abandoned fisherman's camp along the shore of Lake Turkana in East Africa. The settlement had been abandoned for only eighteen months, yet none of the dome-shaped huts of thatched palm leaves that had originally dotted the sandy lake edge was left standing. In fact, the only evidence of the huts' existence were some clumps of palm leaves projecting a few inches above the sand, along with discarded fish bones scattered around the bases of several palm trees that had been used as dumps. I was not surprised to find that some of the bones were already covered by several inches of loose sand, which had been driven by the strong winds that blow off the lake and had accumulated around the bases of the trees.

Here was an archaeological site in the making. Virtually nothing in the way of wood or cloth was evident at the site because everything of value had been packed up and taken to the next camp. Probably nothing would be left after a century or two—unless the fish bones survived. By contrast, our inventory of an inhabited Turkana nomad's camp showed that about 90 percent of the items were made of wood, gourds, or animal skin. All of this material is perishable and normally does not appear in the archaeological record. In terms of use, the most important of the belongings inventoried were containers for food and beverages. Almost none of them would survive, with the exception of a plastic bottle obtained from my camp.

The above study, along with other archaeological studies of contemporary settlements (termed *ethnoarchaeology*), underscores clearly why wet sites are so important to archaeologists. Under the right conditions, wet or waterlogged deposits provide remarkably good preservation of wood, leather, and other materials that normally do not survive. The wet deposits seal the finds from air and decomposition brought about by bacteria, thus providing information that would otherwise be only speculation by archaeologists. In this chapter, we will explore the murky bottoms of Alpine lakes, several limestone wells, a fjord being drained, and an English shipwreck as well as a waterlogged site on land. We will see that the quest to explore the underwater frontier, like that in other areas, is punctuated with adventure and examples of unusual perserverance.

Perhaps more than any other area in archaeology, underwater research has been made possible because of technological advances. Pioneer explorers dived without any equipment at all or used primitive gear. The critical breakthrough came in 1943, when Jacques Cousteau and Emile Gagnon developed a workable Aqualung. Their invention, rooted in earlier efforts, increased dramatically the depths at, and operating time in, which divers could work safely. Archaeologists scoffed at the first efforts to do underwater archaeology with the newly developed equipment. They saw this work as little more than adventuresome treasure hunting, for the divers who were doing the work were not trained in archaeology and made little effort to record the context of the finds. In 1960 George Bass, an American archaeologist, turned the tables by learning to dive and demonstrating to skeptical colleagues that dry-land archaeological techniques could be adapted to underwater environments, especially shipwrecks. He blazed a new trail in archaeology by demonstrating on a Bronze Age shipwreck at Cape Gelidonya, Turkey, that one could effectively map, excavate, and recover artifacts from beneath the sea. Most recently he has directed excavations of a 3,000-year-old Bronze Age ship found by sponge divers off the coast of Turkey.

Shipwrecks have often been seen as miniature time capsules, in which events from particular periods were frozen, awaiting archaeological discovery. Unfortunately, a growing interest in diving also contributed to the romantic image of unspoiled shipwrecks lying on the ocean bottom, filled with treasure. In point of fact, relatively few ships have gone down with vast amounts of treasure compared to those that have been destroyed in the hopes of finding treasure. Archaeological finds in the sea are protected by rules established by the United Nations as well as by the laws of individual nations. In the United States, where conflict between treasure salvagers and archaeologists has been a long-standing problem, an act protecting abandoned shipwrecks was passed by Congress in 1988. This act gives individual states control over wrecks found within three miles of the coast. Under the new law, these sites can no longer be looted.

THE LAKE DWELLINGS

One of archaeology's first encounters with wet sites, excluding shipwreck finds, occurred in the middle of the last century when some unusually cold weather retarded the melting of snow in the Swiss Alps, thus greatly decreasing the volume of water in the rivers that fed the Alpine lakes. In the winters of 1853 and 1854, the lake levels receded to their lowest marks in recorded history, and farmers began to reclaim fertile land at the edge of the retreating water. Along the shore of Lake Zurich, near Ober Meilen, some workers were using mud from the lake edge to repair holes in a wall when their shovels began to strike cut logs, pieces of deer antler, and other artifacts. These logs had served as posts and building material for houses. Further search revealed that the log field extended out into the lake. As in the discoveries of both Lascaux and the first Neandertal, a local schoolteacher appeared on the scene, recognized the importance of the find, and notified the Antiquarian Society of Zurich, which was headed by Dr. Ferdinand Keller. Keller subsequently devoted much of his life to the study of lake dwellers. The lake dwellers lived in small villages and practiced a mixture of farming, livestock herding, and hunting.

Following the historically significant discovery at Ober Meilen, similar sites were found at other Alpine lakes. The preservation was remarkable and included large numbers of normally perishable finds such as seeds, leaves, pieces of cloth, wooden tools, and some stone implements that were still fastened to their handles. Collectors began to scan the lake bottoms from small fishing boats; they pulled up artifacts with long tongs and used specially rigged, rakelike tools to scrape through the mud, which was, in turn, brought up and sifted for relics. These nineteenth-century methods were crude and destructive, so very little could be learned about the context of the finds.

In addition, no one knew exactly how old the sites were. The pioneer Keller suggested that the oldest sites "had their origins in that dark time when, at least in these districts, the use of metal was yet unknown."[1] Keller remarked that the earliest lake dwellers were pastoralists who kept "the dog, the cow, the sheep, the goat and the horse." A more specific estimate was suggested by Dr. Oswald Heer, a botanist who examined the plant remains in the 1860s. Interestingly, Heer used the Bible as a point of historical reference, noting that the cereals, beans, and lentils found at the Swiss sites thrived in Bible lands during Old Testament times, which he believed to be about 1100 B.C. He therefore concluded that the lake dwellings most likely dated to between 2000 and 1000 B.C. It is now generally accepted that the sites are either Neolithic or Bronze Age. Radiocarbon-dating suggests the year 3000 B.C. for the Neolithic settlements, while the Bronze Age sites are, in fact, very close to Heer's estimate.

One of the most interesting of the nineteenth-century discoveries was the site of Robenhausen, located near Zurich at the edge of a small lake known as Pffafikon. Robenhausen was discovered in 1858 by Jacob Messikomer, a self-educated farmer who had developed a passion for the new field of archaeology. When Messikomer learned that some local peat cutters had found artifacts at Robenhausen, he began many years of work at the site, slowly draining small areas of the waterlogged peat with a hand pump. In a synthesis of the newly discovered lake sites, Keller estimated that Robenhausen more than likely contained at least 100,000 logs of oak, beach, and pine, some of which were about ten feet long. Messikomer also recovered some complete wooden bows, a flint arrowhead still attached to the shaft of the arrow with cord and mastic, a twelve-foot dugout canoe, wooden knives, and a wide range of other finds. The wet peat deposits also preserved fish netting, balls of string, woven cloth, and seeds. The carbonized grains of wheat and barley were among the first found in an ancient settlement in Europe, and there were also pieces of bread, charred apples, pears, nuts and berries, fish scales, and dung from domesticated livestock.

Dr. Heer studied the plant remains of Robenhausen, asking some of the same kinds of questions that are currently being posed by researchers in archaeobotany. For instance, he compared the harvest seasons of the various fruits and nuts, considered the other data, and reasoned that the lake dwellings were more than likely inhabited on a year-round basis. He also compared the ancient plants with their modern counterparts to evaluate how much change had occurred in these plants through the centuries. Heer judged that the wild plants and fruits eaten by the lake dwellers were identical to their modern forms but that the cereals were quite different and must have been subjected to considerable selective breeding through the years. He concluded that the wheat and barley were of Mediterranean origin, reaching Switzerland as the result of "scattered rays" of diffusion.[2] These observations were generally correct.

The discoveries in the Alps demonstrated that another frontier in archaeology was being penetrated that rivaled some of the other important breakthroughs of the nineteenth century. Each of the discoveries posed significant questions, especially about the interpretations of the sites. In the case of the lake dwellings, the views of the pioneer worker Keller came to dominate the field, much as the theories of the Abbé Breuil held sway over the early period of cave-art studies in the first part of the present century. Keller felt that because there were a large number of sites found at many of the Alpine lakes and because most of the logs were found either underwater, embedded in the lake bottom, or in places that were covered recently by water, the ancient villagers must have lived out on the lakes, ingeniously building their houses on platforms supported by stilts or piles driven into the bottom of the lakes. He believed that the settlements were connected to the shore by means of a pierlike walkway and that, as the finds at Robenhausen demonstrated, the people also used canoes. The various artifacts found on the lake bottom were either discarded as trash, fell through the cracks of the platforms, or resulted from the ultimate abandonment of the settlements. Since cow dung was found at the bottom of the lakes, it was assumed that the lake dwellers corralled their cattle out on the platforms. The motive for such a lifestyle appeared to be defense.

Keller supported his interpretation with what today's archaeologists call ethnographic analogies, the comparison of known human behavior with the archaeological record. He noted that both the famous early physician Hippocrates and the historian Herodotus describe ancient historical cases of pile dwellings. He also used contemporary travelers' accounts from areas as far afield as New Guinea and Africa. For example, a British officer's account of lake dwellers in Africa seemed to provide a fascinating analogy for Keller's interpretation, so much so that he used the officer's illustrations as a model in his own book. These reports gave Keller's interpretation increased credibility, and it survived unchallenged for decades. Nevertheless, unlike Lewis-Williams' careful comparison of South African rock paintings with known San customs, Keller found no direct, historical linkages between reported lake dwellers and the Swiss sites. Inconsistencies of this nature, however, were generally ignored by nineteenth-century pioneers in archaeology; only those examples supporting an interpretation were used as evidence.

Keller did consider another hypothesis—that the settlements were built on the shores and were abandoned when the lake levels rose and covered the villages, but he rejected this idea as an alternative that was "virtually set at rest."[3] He simply did not think this was a reasonable explanation for the deeply submerged logs and other finds. Nevertheless, it was this rejected theory that eventually proved to be correct.

That the houses were built on the beaches rather than on platforms as envisioned by Keller is clearly revealed at Lake Paladru, near Grenoble, France. The first sites at Paladru were noticed in 1866, when Ernest Chantres dredged up cultural remains from Grand Roseaux, at the north edge of the lake.[4] At that time, there was even a local Atlantis-type legend about an ancient city that had sunk beneath the lake after God punished the inhabitants for persecuting some monks. Chantres' reconstruction of the site followed the interpretations of Keller by concluding that the settlement was out in the lake and was connected to the shore via footbridges.

Chantres and, no doubt, Keller would have marveled at the

ingenious underwater project that took place a little over a century later at the site of Baigneurs located at the opposite end of Lake Paladru. In 1972, Aimé Bocquet and his research team began to piece together an unusually detailed site reconstruction. The archaeological layers were buried beneath sterile (artifact-free) sediments that lay submerged beneath about nine feet of water. This sterile layer was removed by an air lift, which is essentially an underwater suction hose. (Such devices are now commonly employed in excavating shipwrecks.) The team also used a special kind of pressure hose that forces away the cloudy water from the excavation area. As in most underwater projects, much of the excavation was done by hand. The sense of touch enables underwater archaeologists to recover very delicate finds, which sometimes must be raised in containers of wet sand and kept wet until proper preservation techniques can be applied. At Baigneurs many perishable finds were recovered, including balls of thread, basketry, pieces of moss used for chinking the spaces in house walls, ax handles, and some stone knives still set in their handles. Probably most of these finds would have been missed or destroyed by the old dredging techniques used by early workers.

During Keller's time, the most serious problem hampering the understanding of the Alpine sites was that there was no way to map or otherwise document the context of the finds because of the crude techniques that were first used. In contrast, a modern underwater team is able to map the site precisely by using a grid placed over the submerged habitation area. All logs, bones, and artifacts are plotted accurately and the data recorded on plastic sheets. The various mapping sheets are then pieced together in the laboratory.

At Paladru, the mapping efforts were further enhanced by coloring the exposed logs so that they could be photographed from the air. The pattern that emerged from this work revealed a palisaded community consisting of a few log houses situated on the shore of the lake. The palisade formed an arc around the houses and ended at the lake edge. (Quite possibly, early investigators would have interpreted palisades like this one as supports for platforms and houses on the lake.) Interestingly, the underwater researchers were able to determine that the houses were rectangular by following discarded nut shells along the edges of the walls. Artifacts, along with animal bones and plant remains, indicate that the Neolithic peoples of Baigneurs herded livestock, farmed grains, hunted, and collected wild foods.

The Baigneurs settlement has been radiocarbon-dated to 2900 B.C.[5] Paleoclimatic studies have confirmed that prolonged cold spells in the past inhibited thawing and lowered the lake levels even more dramatically than did the weather of the mid-nineteenth century. The ancient houses were evidently built on the lake shores when the water levels were low. A study of the tree rings in the logs indicates that the village survived for no longer than thirty years.[6] Apparently a fire destroyed the first houses, and the people left. Climatic conditions changed, and the local forests began to thin out. Then the lake level rose and covered the abandoned village with several feet of water. About thirty years later the water receded, and people returned to the shore and built a new community on top of the silt layer that had buried the old settlement. Subsequent rises in the lakes again covered the structures with the sediments that preserved them.

Thus the modern excavations have allowed for a much more accurate reconstruction of these kinds of sites and contrast greatly with the archaeological assumptions of the nineteenth century. Such changing interpretations in archaeology are not that uncommon, and they are signs of a healthy science in which old ideas are discredited or modified substantially as more sophisticated techniques are developed. In hindsight, it is easy to discredit the ideas of early workers who lacked modern perspective, yet their discoveries and theories paved the way for future work.

CHICHÉN ITZÁ: THE MAYAN WELL OF SACRIFICE

Near the mid-nineteenth century, just before Ferdinand Keller began studying the Swiss lake sites, John Lloyd Stephens, U.S. ambassador to Central America, and Frederick Catherwood, an English architect, rediscovered the magnificent ruins of the lost Mayan civilization, choked in jungle vegetation. News of their incredible finds captured the imagination of one particularly adventurous student named Edward H. Thompson, who resolved to follow in their footsteps.

While researching Mayan lore, Thompson came across a then

recently recovered document written by the bishop of Yucatan in 1566. In it was a vivid description of the Well of Sacrifice at the site of Chichén Itzá, in the northern Yucatán Peninsula of southern Mexico. The bishop wrote that the Mayas had thrown people into the well alive to appease the gods and that "they also threw into it many other things they prized, and so if this country had possessed gold it would be this Well that would have the greater part of it, so great is the devotion that the Indians show for it."[7] Thompson was captivated by this description, and, in his own words, it became "an obsession."[8] Chichén Itzá was a known site, which John Lloyd Stephens had already visited. He had described the well as "an immense circular hole, with cragged perpendicular sides."[9] There was only one way to find out what lay at the bottom of the well, and that was to explore it. Thompson took the diplomatic route to Central America. In 1885 he was appointed U.S. consul to Yucatán, a post which made possible his intended archaeological explorations.

Thompson was a strong advocate of "going native" in his explorations. He wrote, "I was physically well endowed, fortunately possessed of a rugged physique, so I decided that the best and surest way to lay the foundation for future success was to live among the Mayans as much as possible, make them my friends, study their legends . . . and master their language."[10] During his excursions he explored several ancient Mayan wells, called *chultunes*, some of which were decorated with artwork. On one occasion, his Indian assistants lowered him into one of these dimly lit pits with a hunting knife between his teeth and one hand on the rope. When he reached the bottom of the pit, he immediately heard the buzzing of a very large rattlesnake, coiled to strike. Thompson was trapped. Slowly, he backed against the wall of the well, as the snake's jaws "dripped saliva and a strong odor like musk" permeated the well. Thompson pushed against the wall and, with a great amount of strain, cracked off a rocklike piece of mortar. Somehow he managed to reach behind himself, grab the mortar and hurl it at the snake. Luckily, he hit it and stunned it. Quick follow-up throws killed the rattler, and he escaped from the well.

Unperturbed, Thompson arranged to visit Chichén Itzá in the northern Yucatán peninsula of Mexico. Originally a Mayan town founded in A.D. 530, not long after the fall of the Roman Empire, it was one of many important Mayan sites. Most experts believe that the site was conquered by the Toltecs or related northern peoples in A.D. 1201. Indeed, the architecture displays a fusion of native Mayan and Toltec influences. The site was finally abandoned in the fifteenth century. In addition to the Well of Sacrifice, the site is well known for its Temple of the Warriors, its remarkable *castillo* (castle) with its steep flight of steps, a large number of roofless colonnades, an observatory, and a spectacular ball court. The game played there was widespread in Mesoamerica. The goal was to knock the rubber ball, without the aid of feet or hands, through a stone ring. The game was very rough, and the losers were sometimes killed. The winners were allowed to chase the spectators after the game and claim the clothes of the ones they caught.

Chichén Itzá did not disappoint Thompson. In fact he arranged to buy the site and lived there so that he could carry out his research. While exploring one of the pyramids, he managed to open a blocked passage and followed it to a deep and dark pit. Once again, he descended into it on a rope with a knife between his teeth. This time there was no rattlesnake, but he and his workers lost track of time. When they emerged, it was nearly midnight, and the families of Thompson's workers were wailing, convinced that their men had been swallowed by "the Great Serpent!"

The Well of Sacrifice itself was a steep-sided limestone pit fed by underground waters. Such natural wells are called *cenotes*. They are similar to caves except that they are large sinkholes formed in limestone deposits rather than tunnel-like systems extending horizontally beneath the earth. To the ancient inhabitants of Chichén Itzá, the cenote must have been a formidable sight, one which was naturally and divinely appropriate for their rituals. It measured about 200 feet across and dropped steeply to the water, which was about thirty-five feet deep and covered a great thickness of sediments. The dark color of the water varied with the sunlight, giving the well an eerie appearance at times. Occasionally, snakes and large frogs would slip through the water.

Thompson pondered how to explore the well. Some of his friends argued strongly against his plans, saying, "If you want to commit suicide, why not seek a less shocking way of doing it?" Not to be deterred, Thompson took deep-sea-diving lessons in Boston and rigged up a dredge with cables and a "thirty foot swinging boom." However, since the well was so large, he did not know where to start. To find the "fertile zone" for the dredging operations, Thompson tied ropes to logs that each weighed about as much as a person, heaved them into the well, and judged the distances from the edge where the victims might have landed. The dredging went on for a long period without any success, and Thompson became "nervous by day and sleepless at night." Then one day he noticed some suspicious-looking lumps in the dredging bucket. He burned one of them, and the fumes demonstrated that the lumps were a form of incense used in Mayan religious rituals. Thereafter, the dredging produced many priceless artifacts, and the well became one of the most treasure-laden archaeological discoveries in the New World.

It became apparent that Bishop de Landa's sixteenth-century account of the Well of Sacrifice was, for the most part, correct. Besides a plethora of bones, the well contained copper bells, jewelry, exquisite works of gold and jade, pieces of basketry, textiles, rubber, wood, and a variety of other finds. There were wooden spear-throwers, carved sticks, benches, and a stone sacrificial knife with a carved handle, such as those most likely used to tear the hearts out of sacrificial victims. Many of the artifacts had been broken intentionally before they were thrown into the well, possibly to "kill" the objects when sacrificing them to the gods. The Indians had coated the wooden artifacts with resin, which helped preserve them. Thompson kept them moist after removing them from the well and added preservatives.[11]

The skeletons found were assumed to be those of the sacrificial virgins. A 1936 *National Geographic* article includes an artist's reconstruction of the terrifying sacrificial scene, showing the women being thrown into the well.[12] Later analysis of the more complete skeletons revealed, however, that there were not only women in the well but also men, children, and even dogs, turkeys, deer, and other animals.

When the dredging failed to produce any significant new finds, the intrepid Thompson set up his diving operation. He employed two experienced Greek divers and trained the Mayas to run the pump. Thompson says that after he slipped into the water, it changed to a "purplish black," thick with "gruel"-like sediments.[13] Unable to see, he and the Greek divers groped about in the darkness of the well and managed to find more artifacts and skeletons. He survived one close call when he forgot to adjust the air valves properly and rose too suddenly. Thompson's pioneering efforts in underwater archaeology made for a courageous, if somewhat foolhardy, adventure. From a modern archaeological perspective, we know that the dredging was certain to destroy much of the original context of the finds at the bottom of the well, as was the case with the Swiss lakes, but more sophisticated methods did not exist at that time.

In an effort to protect the remains, Thompson shipped them to the Peabody Museum at Harvard University. This was his undoing. The word got out that a substantial amount of treasure, including much gold, had been recovered from the well, and by the time the news reached the Mexican government, the value of the treasure had been blown out of proportion. The Mexicans were incensed and accused Thompson of stealing the artifacts. He was forced to flee the country on a jury-rigged schooner without the aid of proper navigation instruments. Luckily, he made it to Cuba after nearly two weeks at sea. Thompson was eventually vindicated, albeit posthumously, when the Mexican government found that he had not violated any laws. In 1960 the museum returned many of the artifacts to Mexico.

That was also the year of renewed efforts at the Well of Sacrifice. The National Geographic Society and the Water Sports Club of Mexico combined efforts, with the benefit of an airlift pump and scuba gear. This expedition recovered thousands of artifacts, but the work was discontinued because the powerful airlift, which sucked artifacts out of the murky bottom, was deemed too destructive.

Yet another project was carried out in 1967. The researchers' efforts to pump all the water out of the well failed after lowering the water level only fifteen feet. Chemically treating the murky water, described as being in a condition "worse than in a New York sewer," cleared it enough, however, to allow the workers to use scuba gear and exercise greater control over the excavations.[14] They were also able to modify the airlift so that it was much less destructive. The divers recovered a great many artifacts, including wooden stools and buckets, textiles, worked jade, bells, and stone projectile points. The human bones found indicate that many more children than adults had been sacrificed.

In summary, the Well of Sacrifice was an important ritual center for generations of Mayans. Many artifacts, such as the jade and obsidian objects, came from distant sources via the widespread Mayan trade networks. The gold and copper originated far to the north. Although found in a disturbed context, the artifacts can be compared stylistically to specimens recovered from other sites that have been dated. This cross-dating suggests that the well was used, off and on, between A.D. 800 and 1539.[15] The practice of human sacrifice was an ancient religious custom in Mesoamerica, and early evidence of it may go back to when peoples were beginning to farm. Sacrificial burials of children in the Tehuacan Valley, south of Mexico City, for example, date from 6500 to 4800 B.C. At the more recent end of this time span are the Aztec sacrifices, in which the victims were spread-eagled and their hearts torn out to appease their gods. In spite of this grisly aspect of their culture, the Mesoamericans made remarkable achievements in domesticating crops, developing writing and calendars, creating unique architectural styles, and perfecting a wide range of artistically pleasing crafts.

LITTLE SALT SPRING: THE OLDEST ARCHAEOLOGICAL SITE IN FLORIDA

One of the most debated issues in American archaeology concerns the question of when the ancestors of the Indians (the Paleoindians) first settled in the New World. It is clear that they entered North America by way of the Bering Strait land bridge, which connected Alaska to the eastern tip of Siberia during late Ice Age times, when world sea levels were lowered. Recent findings in the Meadowcroft rock shelter southwest of Pittsburgh suggests that the ancestral native Americans were settled as far south as western Pennsylvania by at least 19,000 years ago. Finally, new data from a waterlogged peat bog in Chile shows that they had reached southern South America 13,000 years ago. There are many other sites, especially in the western United States, which date between 11,000 and 12,000 years ago.

An interesting and potentially important Paleoindian site was discovered accidentally in 1959 when William Royal, a retired Air Force colonel, was scuba diving in a shallow pond known as Little

Salt Spring, near Sarasota on the southwest coast of Florida. The surprised colonel found that the gently sloping pond bottom opened suddenly into a sinkhole, or cenote, more than 300 feet deep. Further investigation revealed old-looking bones on the sinkhole's sloping edge. While professional archaeologists were skeptical of these amateur finds, Royal continued to collect and exhibit bones from Little Salt Spring. According to the *Miami Herald*, he even built a fireplace with some of the fossils and dressed bones up in scuba gear for amusement.[16] Eventually, Royal got a crippling case of the bends from diving in the cenote. For many years Royal was seen as perpetuating a hoax regarding his finds at Little Salt Spring.

Finally, in the 1970s, a team of underwater archaeologists, geologists, and paleontologists began to explore the spring and an adjacent slough, which contained peat deposits. The scientists determined that the water level in the cenote was substantially lower in late Ice Age times, roughly around 13,000 years ago, because much of the world's fresh water was contained in the ice sheets far to the north. At that time, the southern Florida climate was much drier. The springs in the area of the sinkhole must have made it an oasis in the arid landscape. The Paleoindian peoples who frequented the area camped and hunted along the edge of the freshwater sinkhole, and some of their artifacts and animal bones were deposited on nearby dry slopes and ledges. When the glaciers began to melt and climates changed, heralding the close of the Ice Age, the water in the cenote rose, covering up all traces of those ancient Indians.

The research team made some unprecedented discoveries. While excavating a two-meter-wide trench on a ledge ninety feet underwater, archaeologists found the shell of an extinct giant tortoise that had a sharpened wooden stake driven into it. The stake was radiocarbon-dated as being about 12,030 years old and was probably used either to kill the animal or to assist in cooking it over a fire on the ledge.[17] The tortoise, and perhaps its hunter, may have fallen into the cenote; on the other hand, it is possible that the Indians lowered themselves down onto the ledge in order to catch and kill animals that had fallen into the natural trap. Whatever the case, the tortoise and the stake provided the earliest well-dated traces of human occupation of the southern United States. There were bones of other animals on the ledge, too, including those of various turtles, a diamondback rattlesnake, ground sloth, mastodon, and other species. An extraordinary wooden artifact found there is believed to be a boomerang. As the archaeologists worked higher up along the slope of Little Salt Spring, they found ancient wooden stakes, hearths, food refuse, and artifacts of wood and stone that had been driven into the pond's bottom. The wooden tools are the oldest known in North America. The stakes were dated as being about 9,572 years old; a mortar, about 9,080 years old.

The nearby slough, with its wet peat deposits, is in some ways even more interesting than the spring. Here the archaeologists found a very large cemetery, which dates to what is called the Archaic period in North American archaeology. This period follows the Paleoindian, and at Little Salt Spring the dates suggest an age of 6,000 to 7,000 years. The preservation conditions in the cemetery are exceptional. Wooden, shell, and bone artifacts were placed in the graves, and the bodies were placed on branches of myrtle and wrapped partially with grass. One of the skulls found contained "a substantial portion of a brain with still discernible convolutions and cellular processes."[18] This is one of the oldest known examples of a human brain.

THE SKUDELEV FINDS: VIKING SHIPS EMERGE FROM A DANISH FJORD

Each year at low tide, the rock pile, with its projecting timbers, was visible at Skudelev, in the narrow, shallow channel of Roskilde Fjord. Local fishermen would find pieces of wood from Margrethe's ship among the rocks and would recall the legend: Long ago, Queen Margrethe of Denmark had ordered the ship filled with rocks and sunk in the channel to prevent enemy ships from attacking the town of Roskilde, at the south end of the fjord. The ship had been there since the late Middle Ages. This local folk tradition accounted for the ancient timbers, but archaeology would show it was not correct.

Following the invention of the Aqualung there was considerable interest in investigating this legendary site. Several divers visited the scene of Margrethe's wreck, and in 1956 a piece of the ship was brought to the Danish Museum. Much to everyone's surprise, the ship turned out to be much older than Queen Margrethe herself. In fact, it was judged to be a Viking ship. At that time, almost all archaeological evidence of Viking ships was from ship-burial sites on land, in particular the Oseberg and Gokstaad ships in Norway. These were rather like the Sutton Hoo find, which predated them by a few hundred years. These buried Viking ships were used to inter royalty and were not necessarily typical Viking vessels. People wondered how the Skudelev ship would compare.

Aware of the new potentials of underwater archaeology, the Danish Museum decided to excavate the site. The Skudelev project was headed by Olaf Olsen and Ole Crumlin-Pederson, who started by learning to dive. The work began in 1957 in water that was only a meter deep but cold, with low visibility and a strong current. Underwater archaeology was still a novelty; previous efforts by amateurs did not take into account the context of the finds and were seen as little more than treasure hunting. Olsen and Crumlin-Pederson had to devise many of their own methods. They stretched a long steel wire between concrete blocks for taking measurements and mapping the finds. Excavations were carried out largely by hand and by a firehose used to blow the sediments away. Gradually the rocks were removed, and the wood from the sunken ship was exposed and removed carefully.

As the work progressed, it became clear that the site was much more complex than was believed originally. There was not one but at least four ships buried in the channel. Work on the third ship was "the unsurpassed high point of the underwater excavation" to the Danish excavators, who wrote, "To lie in that ship in the underwater silence and uncover one magnificent piece of timber after another was a unique experience. The oak wood was hard and strong, so well preserved in many places that axe marks could be seen in the finely hewn timber."[19] Nevertheless, it became increasingly apparent that the excavation methods were not suited to the task at hand. Only the larger pieces of wood could be removed safely; much of the rest was too fragile and would be destroyed if brought to the surface.

The unique and imaginative solution to this problem was to build a dam completely around the site and drain it—in other words, to create an island in the fjord. This was certainly an expensive and elaborate proposition, considering the fact that the dam might not be able to withstand winter ice and storms, meaning that the ship remains would have to be recorded and removed in a single season. Luckily, several wealthy Danish foundations came to the rescue of the Skudelev ships, and in 1962, an engineering firm carried out the task of building the dam at a relatively low cost. Most of the water was piped out slowly, creating an artificial island in the fjord that covered about 1,600 square meters (17,216 square feet). Enough water remained to keep the ancient wood wet during the excavation.

After lowering the water level came the slippery job of removing the seaweed and the eels that had made their home in the rocks. Next a series of small boardwalks were built out over the wrecks so that the excavators could lie down carefully on the walkways and work without putting any weight on the thin pieces of wood. A sprinkler system was installed at the site in order to keep the remains wet. The tangled mass of stones and wrecked ships was mapped, photographed, and removed carefully, piece by piece. The Viking ships, like most ships found underwater, were not complete. Yet the estimated 50,000 pieces recovered were labeled, sprayed with water, and put into large airtight plastic sacks to keep them wet and prevent deterioration.

An enormous puzzle was in the making for the boat-building specialist in the lab, and there were other problems as well. First, it was difficult to preserve the wood so that the ships could be reconstructed accurately. Secondly, the Danish Museum simply did not have the facilities to exhibit the ships. (A new museum with special atmospheric conditions was eventually built to house them at Roskilde, along the edge of the fjord.)

The Skudelev ships provide much detailed information about Viking shipbuilding. They were made from a variety of woods, especially oak, and their builders used axes mostly. The ships were "clinker built," which means that the planks overlap each other. The caulking, which was still preserved, consisted of animal hair and wood tar. Some of this material has been radiocarbon-dated, which indicates that the Skudelev ships were probably built between A.D. 950 and 1050.[20]

Skudelev produced more information on Viking ships than any other site. Altogether, five ships were recovered, all different in detail. There were two trading ships, a fishing boat, and two warships. One of the warships, not well preserved, was a classic longship, estimated to have been about twenty-nine meters (ninety-five feet) long. At first, the excavators had believed this ship was actually two vessels because of the difficulty in correctly reading the evidence underwater. It is estimated that the Skudelev longship probably had between twenty and twenty-five oars. Like other Viking ships, it was also sail-powered. Agile on the open seas, the sleek Viking warships were also able to enter shallow rivers for surprise attacks.

The Vikings were engaged in widespread trading, which extended from the Middle East to Canada, yet no Viking trading ships had ever been found before Skudelev. According to Olsen and Crumlin-Pederson, the largest of the trading ships, measuring about seventeen meters (fifty-six feet) in length, was originally a sturdy vessel designed for major ocean voyages. They note that similar vessels were probably used by Leif Ericsson, the first European to visit North America. (Leif was the son of Eric the Red, who was noted for establishing settlements in Greenland.) Viking artifacts excavated at L'anse aux Meadows, in Newfoundland, date to around A.D. 1000. This was part of the larger area of North America known as Vinland in Viking literature. It is thought that opposition from the Indians, known as Skraelings to the Vikings, combined with the vast sailing distance caused the Vikings to abandon their plans to settle in the New World.

Unfortunately, the excavations did not reveal any clues about why or when the ships were sunk at Skudelev. They were evidently cleared of artifacts first, for, in contrast to the burial ships, next to nothing was found on these ships. It is known that there was considerable raiding in the area, especially by Vikings from Norway, and that Roskilde was an important and prosperous town. Perhaps the ships were sunk to protect the town after all, but not by Queen Margrethe.

THE *MARY ROSE*

In midsummer, 1545, a French fleet with more than 200 ships was poised for attack near the Isle of Wight, off England's south coast. The English fleet was outnumbered by more than three to one. As the wind picked up, Henry VIII watched from shore as his flagship, the *Mary Rose*, named after his sister Mary, set sail to meet the enemy with a crew of 700 led by Sir George Carew. It weighed about 600 tons, had four decks, and was heavily armed. The *Mary Rose* was the first English ship to be fitted with heavy cannon. Previously, most fighting at sea was done by a combination of archers and the use of light arms, but now it would be possible to sink ships at a distance. The ship was overloaded, however, carrying several hundred more people than usual, the heavy guns, and other gear.

Suddenly, the *Mary Rose* began to heel. Admiral Carew's uncle, commanding another English ship, passed within shouting distance and tried to find out what was wrong. Carew replied, "I have the sort of knaves I cannot rule."[21] Then, in the sight of Henry VIII and others on the shore, the *Mary Rose* capsized. The open gunports, which may have been positioned too low, filled with water; the ship sank suddenly, drowning almost the entire crew. The screams of the trapped men could be heard briefly before the ship disappeared beneath the waves. The French forces were elated and, of course, claimed to have sunk the ship. Following this unexpected turn of events, a major battle did not really develop; instead, the French conducted a series of raids on the Isle of Wight. As it turned out, the British were in a sound defensive position despite the fact that their ships were greatly outnumbered. The invading fleet withdrew and returned to France.

Not long after these tragic events, there was an attempt to salvage the *Mary Rose* by securing two ships to it with cables and exploiting the rising tide to lift the sunken ship. The attempt failed, and the *Mary Rose* was eventually lost to the swirling currents and tides and covered by sediments.

The ship rested, undisturbed by humans, in her watery grave for nearly 300 years until some fishermen caught their lines on some protruding debris. In 1836, they notified the Deane brothers, who had developed a diving business by inventing and using a primitive diving helmet into which air was pumped from a boat. Working at depths approaching seventy feet, they recovered guns, bows, and some other artifacts. They knew they had found the site of the *Mary Rose*, but very little of the ship was actually exposed above the sediments. In the hope of salvaging more artifacts, they used powerful explosives and blew a large hole in the boat. Relatively little was recovered, and the quest for further artifacts was abandoned. A few years later, it was alleged that a demolition team blew up what was left of the wreck of the *Mary Rose*. The site was subsequently forgotten, and whatever might have been left of the ship was lost with the site itself.

Over a century later, Alexander McKee, a British journalist and historian, set his sights on finding the *Mary Rose*. McKee was not a treasure seeker. He was a member of the British Sub Aqua Club, an amateur diving society, and believed that the *Mary Rose* was, in some ways, a kind of missing link in a historical sense. As McKee pointed out, there was a fundamental gap in the record between the Viking ships and those built in the 1700s. The *Mary Rose* was especially significant because of the major changes that took place in the sixteenth century in the development of warships, both in construction and in the use of heavy cannon. McKee believed that finding the ship might shed new light on a critical period in naval history and on life during the Tudor period in England. Discovery of the ship would also be of major national interest because of its association with Henry VII, who had brought about many historical changes in England.

Few people believed that McKee or anyone else would ever find the *Mary Rose*. After all, it was assumed that the ship had been blown up. Furthermore experts, citing experience with Mediterranean shipwrecks, argued that very little could have survived anyway because of poor preservation conditions in English waters.[22] A final problem was that the waters of The Solent, the channel between the Isle of Wight and the south coast of England where the ship went down, had low visibility, were rough, and constituted a major shipping lane. Nevertheless, Alexander McKee began planning his quest for the *Mary Rose*. He wrote, "Even in the local sub-aqua club I was regarded as something of an impractical visionary."[23] Later on, one of his volunteer helpers admitted that he was once "convinced Mac was a crank and the idea of a Tudor warship was just a figment of his vivid imagination."

In 1965, McKee began a low-key exploration of The Solent with a small contingent of volunteer divers, trying to locate any shipwrecks. There was initially some competition with a rival group from the University of London, and the two groups decided to divide the underwater "turf" into two zones: McKee was convinced that the ship would be found at a depth of less than sixty feet, while his rivals believed it would be below this depth. McKee felt he had a reasonable idea of where to search, but his divers found no evidence of the ship. He soon reasoned that its remains were most likely buried due to the scouring effect of the currents. Moreover, he was aware that Harold Edgerton of the Massachusetts Institute of Technology had invented some new techniques for using sonar to penetrate the sea bottom and detect anomalies there. The technique had great potential for underwater archaeology, and so McKee decided to try it in his quest for the *Mary Rose*. In October 1967, as his ship passed over what he thought was the most likely search area, the side-scanning sonar device picked up an anomaly consistent with the size of the *Mary Rose*. The elated McKee wrote, "Optimistically I thought we had 85 per cent proof already." Yet proving it was another matter. In addition, there was no law at the time to protect the promising site from looters. Following the results of the sonar, the *Mary Rose* Committee was formed and, under existing law, arranged to lease the site area for one pound a year.

The next task was to actually locate the elusive wreck. Working with long probes, the divers finally touched debris buried deeply in the sand. One of the divers describes the thrilling moment of this discovery: "In our excitement we had forgotten all the rules of diving, and I believe Mac nearly lost his mask and mouthpiece during our speed tour to our probe." But these probe contacts, while very exciting, were not proof that the ship was the *Mary Rose*. Stronger evidence was needed. It came in the form of a heavily encrusted cannon discovered by McKee himself in 1970. It appeared to be similar to those recovered by the Deanes more than a hundred years earlier, before the location of the ship was lost. It was later found to be loaded, as would have been the case in the *Mary Rose*. Once the gun was raised, McKee radioed the news to colleagues on the shore. In what must have been a triumphant moment, he writes, "After so many years of being denigrated behind my back as a mad chaser of wild geese, it was with great satisfaction that I saw that message go off."

The discovery of the gun stimulated a great deal of public interest and eventually helped to pave the way for large-scale funding, which was essential to excavate the site properly. The *Mary Rose* project included everyone from volunteer divers to some of the wealthiest British industries, all combined to give their support. Even royal interest was kindled in King Henry VIII's flagship. Lord Mountbatten was a bastion of support, and Prince Charles, who had studied archaeology at Cambridge, became the president of the *Mary Rose* Trust, formed in 1979. Prince Charles even made numerous dives to visit the excavations. He wrote the foreword to archaeologist Margaret Rule's 1982 book *The Mary Rose* and made cogent remarks about the ship's significance to British history.

With the necessary funding and equipment, the excavations proceeded under the astute direction of Rule. The base of operations for the divers was a large ship that had been used in the raising of the *Wasa*, a Swedish warship that sank in 1628. First, the interior of the surviving section of the *Mary Rose*, estimated by Rule to have included slightly less than half of the shell, was excavated carefully. The structure was incompletely preserved because of the action of currents, sediments, and destructive undersea organisms. The deeply buried portions of the ship were exposed by removing the sediments with airlifts. As is standard for land excavations, the site was mapped and the finds were plotted on the map, an essential procedure allowing archaeologists to place the artifacts in their original context and to reconstruct the original nature of the site.

The thousands of artifacts recovered have enhanced our knowledge of Tudor culture and lifestyles and is providing a wealth of new information on a critical period in shipbuilding and armament. Wood, leather, seeds, and other normally perishable objects were found, and the preservation was aided by the pitch that was used in the ship. Chemical analysis has shown that the pitch came from pine tar most likely imported from Russia.[24]

One of the more interesting finds was a chest discovered in an area identified as the surgeon's cabin. The chest contained razors, syringes, and other medical equipment. The diver who opened the chest underwater reported that it contained "clay pigeons." This seemed bizarre to Margaret Rule, who subsequently went down to have a look for herself.[25] She found a medicine chest filled with sealed wooden "pigeon-shaped" jars. The sixteenth-century medicine from the jars is being analyzed and compared with historical sources. They appear to have been resin-based ointments, probably used for treating wounds and various ship-board ailments.

Even though the *Mary Rose* dates to a well-known historical period, there were many artifacts found on the ship that modern people had never seen before. For instance, archery was of major importance during the Tudor period but, surprisingly, almost no archery gear has survived. The *Mary Rose* has changed this by providing a very large number of the famous longbows, as well as arrows and wrist guards. Margaret Rule notes that one chest contained 1,238 arrows. She feels that it will now be possible to re-create the famous English longbow and conduct tests of its strength and accuracy. Numerous guns have also been recovered, along with gun carriages and stores of shot. Leather shoes and other items of clothing, barrels, leather book covers, musical instruments, games such as backgammon and chess, food, and a wide variety of other Tudor artifacts were found. Many of these have had to be handled with utmost care when removed from the protective environment of the sea bottom. Even the bronze artifacts will eventually deteriorate with what is known as bronze disease if not treated properly. The preservation experts working on the *Mary Rose* have used a variety of chemicals and freeze-drying techniques to preserve the finds.

The ship itself yielded wooden sail-rigging parts, the ship's bell engraved with its year of manufacture, and the oldest actual specimen of a mariner's compass. Researchers are studying the nature of the planking, the gunports, the brick galley (which had collapsed, contributing to the sinking of the ship), the size of the officers' quarters, and other aspects of the ship's construction.

Inevitably, skeletons of the people, manning their battle stations or attempting to escape, were found. There were four decks in the ship and most of the men were not on the uppermost deck when the ship pitched over. Two archers were doomed after falling on the steps in a desperate attempt to escape. People were trapped in the sick bay, where they had absolutely no chance to get away; they were kept far removed from the scene of action so that their moans and screams would not have a negative impact on the crew.[26] Study of the skeletons has provided new information about the health conditions of Tudor seamen. In recent years, physical anthropologists have made major breakthroughs in methods of studying human bones, with the objective of gleaning detailed information about past diseases, nutritional stress, and other aspects of diet. Other than poor dental conditions, the crew of the *Mary Rose* was generally healthy.

The great dream of McKee and others on the project was to raise the ship itself following the excavations and return her to the shore, where she could eventually be exhibited in a museum. The overall plan was to use a specially built lifting frame, coupled with a protective cradle for holding the ship. The lifting of the *Mary Rose* took place in October 1982 in front of hundreds of newspaper reporters and with full international television coverage. Things were upbeat until one of the legs on the lifting frames developed problems. The operation was suspended while a crew of engineers worked feverishly through the night repairing the leg. The next day, the *Mary Rose* was lifted. When she came to the surface after more than 400 years, Alexander McKee was elated to note that the ship's hull was still watertight and had to be pumped out. Prince Charles was to be the first one to step out on the emergent *Mary Rose*, but just then, the frame collapsed and miraculously stopped just short of demolishing the ship. In fact, the frame was held by a single bolt until a skillful crane operator managed to bring the *Mary Rose* successfully to shore amidst fireworks and a massive celebration.

Once ashore, the ship needed a proper home, as did the Viking ships at Skudelev. A specially designed museum was constructed at Portsmouth, where the ship was built. This museum features a spraying system to keep the ship wet and ensure its preservation. The *Mary Rose* is perhaps as much a marvel today as it was in the time of Henry VIII. A final comment is that the unfortunate victims of the *Mary Rose* disaster have been buried with an appropriate religious ceremony based on Tudor practices as re-created through historical research.

GWISHO HOT SPRINGS

A southern-African waterlogged site is found at the Gwisho Hot Springs, situated near the Kafue River in Central Zambia. Gwisho is a Late Stone Age site, radiocarbon-dated to between 3000 and 1500 B.C.[27] The Late Stone Age in Africa has much in common with the European Mesolithic. It marks the last period of "pure" hunting and foraging for wild foods. As we have seen, Late Stone Age peoples are renowned for their beautiful rock paintings, especially in southern Africa, where the sites are linked to the ancestors of the San (Bushmen). For the most part, these Late Stone Age hunters are known archaeologically by the stone tools they made, which frequently include numerous small geometrically shaped pieces called microliths. The Gwisho Hot Springs site, in which the unique wet conditions preserved much more than the usual stones and bones, is the only one of its kind in Africa.

The hot springs were formed originally by faulting. This produced a series of vents, which issue forth nearly boiling water at various places spread over a square mile. The spring vents have shifted about, and through time the hot water has forced its way up at different places. Late Stone Age peoples camped in the area beginning about 3000 B.C., which is roughly about the time the first Pharaoh established his rule in Egypt, far to the north. The Gwisho people lived in the area intermittently for about 1,500 years. The shifting hot-spring deposits eventually penetrated and covered the lower levels of the camp sites with water, preserving much of the organic material. When archaeologists appeared on the scene, the sites appeared as a series of low mounds.

The Gwisho site was located by J. Desmond Clark in the 1950s, and the waterlogged spring deposits were eventually excavated by Brian Fagan and Francis Van Noten in the early 1960s. Their excavations revealed more than two meters of deposits, which they exposed by lowering the water table substantially with a pump. The excavators uncovered the remnants of a shelter consisting of grass, posts, and a semicircle of stones. There was also a V-shaped arrangement of posts, which may have been an animal trap. Wooden tools, which are rarely found on most sites, were numerous. They were highlighted by arrowheads, link shafts (a part which connects the arrowhead to the shaft), and digging sticks. Interestingly, the arrow parts, which also include bone points, are similar to those used recently by the San of neighboring Botswana.

More than 10,000 plant remains were recovered from the waterlogged deposits. Richard Lee, a noted expert on the San, visited Gwisho while the excavations were in progress. With him came one of his San informants who could recognize and identify the ancient plants and tell the archaeologists how these plants are used in San society today. This is one of the few prehistoric archaeological sites known where this kind of direct bridge between past and present has been used. They found, for instance, that the San drink the liquid from the ivory palm seed and eat the roots and fruit of the bauhinia shrub, both prevalent at the site. They use gourds for containers and eat the fruit of the baobob. One of the trees at Gwisho yields pods that are used to make poison. If it was used in this way by the ancient campers, it is among the oldest traces of poison use known.

Nearly 200,000 bone fragments were uncovered at the spring site. The small proportion of those that could be identified belonged to buffalo, antelope, zebra, rhino, hippo, and elephant as well as other animals. Fagan calculated the approximate number of fauna at the site, considered the body weight of each species, and, finally, estimated the amount of usable meat. By estimating as well the number of inhabitants at the site and the period of occupation, he figured that each person may have had more than a pound of meat a day, supplemented by an abundance of plant foods. This is better than many of us do at the supermarket today.

FLOTATION TECHNIQUES

This chapter has progressed from a variety of underwater sites to a waterlogged site on land. It is fitting to carry this transition from water to land a step further with a brief account of how the usual dry sites can often be made to yield organic remains, some not even visible to the naked eye, through the application of water and certain chemicals. Such methodology in the field and in the laboratory, has had a fundamental impact on findings in archaeology.

The fundamental breakthrough in the development of flotation methods happened about the same time that the techniques of underwater archaeology were being refined. In 1960 Stuart Struever, an American archaeologist, excavated an ashy pit in a prehistoric Indian site in the midwestern United States. Following the advice of a colleague in botany, he immersed material from the pit in water to see if any small plant fragments might float to the surface. He says,

"To our surprise, we screened from the surface a few charred seeds whose presence had been masked in the fill."[28] Struever then went on to pioneer the new recovery technique that is known as flotation. Following the lead of a geologist, he added a zinc-chloride solution to the flotation process and found that this quickly separated extremely small bone fragments from plants. Then he proved to colleagues at prehistoric Indian sites in the Illinois valley that he could recover thousands of seeds and small fishbones through flotation from soils that already had been dry-screened by archaeologists. Amazingly, standard excavation techniques, which employ screens to sieve the soil, fail to retrieve about 90 percent of the plant materials. Small seeds and other plant fragments either pass through the screens or are seen only rarely in the soils, which are ordinarily discarded.

One early use of the flotation method in 1963 illustrates the importance of this technique in archaeological interpretation. At that time, a group of archaeologists was investigating the origins of farming and the development of early villages on the Deh Luran plain of southwestern Iran, just below the hill ranges where the wild ancestors of wheat and barley thrive. A test pit at one of the key sites, Tepe Ali Kosh, led the investigators to believe that "no concentrated deposits of plant material could be expected."[29] Indeed, one of the paramount problems in researching the origins of farming was that few sites in the Near East appeared to contain plant remains. Hans Helbaek, a Danish expert on the domestication of plants, sought to remedy this situation by trying a basic water-flotation method. He notes "that when called in on the excavation I made up my mind to transfer to the field, for the first time, the laboratory technique for segregating plant remains from mineral samples by means of buoyancy." This was no easy task, since the scarce water had to be trucked into the site.

The results were a great success. Samples of carbonized plant materials were recovered both from ashy areas, where meals had been spilled on ancient house floors, and in other areas. From this refuse, Helbaek's flotation methods recovered about 45,000 plant fragments. The number of finds was unprecedented for the area and provided major new information on the development of early farming communities. There were numerous species of cultivated plants, mostly wheat and barley, and a wide variety of wild grasses, legumes, and other plants.

Helbaek was able to estimate the average grain weights and quantify the relative importance of various plants, wild and domestic, through time. For example, between 7500 and 6750 B.C., the first villagers collected an abundance of edible wild plants (about 94 percent legumes). Only 3.4 percent of the plants were domesticated, including emmer wheat and two-hulled barley. From other information, we know that they also kept goats and sheep and hunted wild game. All evidence suggests that these earliest Tepe Ali Kosh inhabitants brought their domesticates from the nearby mountains, where it is reasoned that the first steps in the domestication of wheat and barley, along with sheep and goats, occurred. By the next phase, dated to between 6750 and 6000 B.C., the ratio of wheat and barley rose to 40 percent of the plants, while the wild plants declined in significance. Later, other detailed changes in plant usage occurred, including the advent of a new hybrid strain of barley that was adapted to irrigation techniques. This detailed study of plant remains, coupled with studies of fauna, helped to confirm that the advent of food production and the village way of life was a gradual process, not a sudden revolution.

In the United States we have learned more about when Indians started to practice plant cultivation by floating bulk samples from key sites. Such samples indicate that Midwest Indians domesticated indigenous plants by about 3000 B.C. Squash, derived from Mexico, was cultivated even earlier. At the deeply stratified Koster site in Illinois, domesticated squash-rind fragments were recovered "in three of the 239 flotation samples" at a depth of nearly four meters.[30] The squash has been dated to about 5000 B.C. by the technique of accelerator radiocarbon-dating, which allows for the dating of extremely small samples. Other sites, such as those along the Green River in Kentucky and in southwest Missouri, indicate a younger age for squash cultivation, about 2300 B.C.[31]

The flotation process is now used at digs throughout the world and has even undergone various refinements, such as pumping air into the water to aid in the separation and recovery of organic materials. Before the process was used, large bone fragments were the most visible traces of evidence at most sites. But now flotation has corrected the flawed concept that the food of ancient peoples was obtained predominantly by hunting.

6

THE SKY FRONTIER

Archaeoastronomy

Archaeologists who work in remote areas sometimes have unusual experiences that, quite by accident, can add insights to the archaeological record. This happened to me in East Africa when a "star with a tail like smoke" was sighted by local herdsmen. It was pointing down toward Lothagam Hill, where I was working. As I watched the comet in the middle of the night with the Turkana nomads, huddled in their togalike cloaks, I felt as if I had been transposed back to biblical times. The Turkana pondered the meaning of the comet, fearing that it was a bad omen. They remembered that the last one was followed by a tragic famine. The men went on to lament the fact that their diviners were not as powerful as they used to be, which meant that it would be more difficult to cope with this particular bad omen. Fortunately, nothing unusual happened in the immediate area during the following months that I spent there.

Ironically, about seven years later in nearby Uganda, I had a similar experience. Mixed with the night calls of the hyena and lion, we could hear singing in a nearby Pokot village and found that the chants were prompted by another comet visible in the early morning sky. The people were greatly disturbed about the sign, for the last one had, again, been associated with a disastrous drought and famine. We attended a large ceremony held in an effort to ward off the threatened disaster, during which we were all "protected" by having the contents of an ox's stomach smeared on our chests. There was much celebration as well, with dancing, singing, and feasting, until we, the outsiders, were thoroughly exhausted. In the years since, these comets, as well as other unusual astronomical events, have been remembered by those nonliterate pastoralists and have become part of their oral traditions. Stories are told and incidents remembered by reference to a particular comet or eclipse.

Having seen how important astronomical events can be to a society, it is not difficult to imagine how prehistoric peoples sometimes went a step further and reinforced their oral accounts of sky events by building monuments to mark them. Study of such ancient monuments of an astronomical nature is called archaeoastronomy. While it is often controversial, this discipline is not to be confused with the farfetched theories that prehistoric monuments were the result of contact with astronauts from outer space. Students of archaeoastronomy generally search for correlations between the placement of prehistoric monuments and various astronomical data such as the position of the sunrise at specific times of the year, eclipses, and the like. Predictably, scholars interested in archaeoastronomy are usually either astronomers or archaeologists; not surprisingly, some of the controversy involves concerns from scientists of one discipline that those of the other are trespassing on their turf without adequate understanding. Other debates occur over just how sophisticated the prehistoric astronomers could have been.

STONEHENGE

Stonehenge is a classic example of a site believed to have archaeoastronomical significance. No one can deny how impressive it is, standing starkly by itself at the edge of Salisbury Plain in southwestern England. Stonehenge is a megalithic site, which literally means, "large stones." Such megaliths are very widespread in Britain and elsewhere in Europe, with some quite spectacular ones in the Brittany area of northwest France. These sites are quite varied, ranging from stone circles to other types of alignments. Until recently, many scholars believed that the megaliths were an expression of religious ideas spread by "missionaries" who brought their teachings from the Mediterranean basin via the Atlantic coast. This made sense because it looked as if there were prototypes in the basin area. In addition, there was an implicit assumption that northwestern Europe was a cultural backwater compared to the basin. This perspective has been changed substantially, however, insofar as it applies to the megaliths. It now seems clear that they were invented independently in several areas and that some of the earliest ones were, in fact, in northwestern Europe.[1]

Stonehenge was built over an extensive period beginning around 2900 B.C., if not slightly earlier. In fact, one of the earliest radiocarbon dates, obtained from a piece of antler excavated in the main enclosure ditch, is approximately 3180 B.C.[2] Neolithic farmers and herders initiated the building of Stonehenge, and the work was carried on into Bronze Age times. The latest period of construction seems to date to about 1100 B.C.[3] Overall, an incredible amount of effort and planning went into the construction of the site. At first it may have been a relatively modest project, although one that had great social and ritual significance to the peoples of the area. As the site became increasingly significant, however, the work effort and political organization increased.

The earliest period, known as Stonehenge I, is marked by the shaping of the earthwork and ditch that enclose the site. It was also during this time that a circle of fifty-six holes was laid out precisely between the outer earthworks and the immense ring of standing stones. These mysterious holes are called Aubrey holes, named after John Aubrey, who discovered them more than 300 years ago. They are two and a half feet deep and contain evidence of human cremations. Stonehenge I is also associated with the placement of the heelstone, which stands as an isolated landmark at the site. The name *heelstone* appears to have been derived from John Aubrey's comments made in the seventeenth century that one of the prominent stones had a heel-like depression in it. The famous heelstone figures significantly in the astronomical interpretations of the site. It is a large tilted boulder of sarsen sandstone approximately twenty feet long.

It has not been deliberately shaped, in contrast to other sarsens erected later on.

Stonehenge II is marked by the introduction of the bluestones, smaller stones each weighing about four tons. Their source of origin has been traced to a locality in Wales about 240 miles away. Most likely, they were transported via land and sea. The movement of these stones over such a long distance, partially by boat, provides a silent testimony of the remarkable organizational skills and dedication of the people.

The most impressive parts of Stonehenge, the outer sarsen circle and the trilithons (two upright stones capped by a lintel), are the highlights of Stonehenge III (2000 B.C.). The sarsen sandstone has its origin about twenty miles from the site. The large pieces used for the trilithons range in weight from about twenty-five to fifty tons. These massive stones had to be hauled across sometimes hilly terrain, presumably on log rollers and sledges. Richard Atkinson, one of the foremost authorities on Stonehenge, has estimated that as many as 1,000 people were involved in moving the large stones.

Through the years there has been much debate about the purpose of Stonehenge. Some imaginative traditions have linked its origin to the druids or to Merlin, King Arthur's legendary enchanter. Merlin allegedly brought the stones from Ireland, as mentioned in the splendid fiction of Mary Stewart. Fiction aside, one thing is certain: Radiocarbon dating indicates that the site was built many centuries before the advent of either the druids or Merlin.

Many writers have also noted that Stonehenge had astronomical significance. For example, as long ago as 1771, Dr. John Smith noted that the summer solstice (the first day of summer) sunrise was positioned over the heelstone. About thirty years earlier, Dr. William Stukeley also had called attention to the relationship between Stonehenge and the midsummer sunrise. In 1880 Flinders Petrie, the distinguished Egyptologist who trained Howard Carter, used a surveyor's instrument to test the "popular idea of the sun rising on the longest day behind the Friar's Heel . . ."[4] He concluded that "it seems nearly certain that the point of observation was intended to be from behind the trilithon, to the peak of the Heel stone. . . ." In the years that followed, other writers have noted that Stonehenge was oriented toward the sunrise, and in recent years great multitudes of people, including modern-day druids, have come to watch the sunrise each June.

Despite this general knowledge, the full range of the relationship between Stonehenge and the sky was largely a matter of speculation until research was carried out in the 1960s by Gerald S. Hawkins, an astronomer. Not that Hawkins has answered all the questions, nor are his theories accepted universally. In many ways, though, his research was seminal in that it stimulated a great deal of discussion and promoted interests in archaeoastronomy at a wide range of other sites.[5] Hawkins' involvement began when he was writing an astronomy book and decided to include some comments about Stonehenge.[6] He tells us that after writing "the stone blocks are mute, but perhaps some day, by a chance discovery, we will learn their secrets," it dawned on him that "some day perhaps is now." He went on to note that the time was especially ripe because computers were coming into wide use in the 1960s, enabling researchers to make rapid and complex computations.

As Hawkins puts it, there were thousands of possible alignments given the large number of stones and possible positions of the sun, moon, and planets. Initially, by using a plotting machine called an Oscar, he derived 240 alignments. This told him "where the alignments met the sky, the declinations. The next part of the question was were those declinations celestially significant." In other words, did the alignments correlate with any stars (including the sun), planets, or the moon? In order to evaluate this, the perspective of the sky was adjusted to appear as it would have in 1500 B.C., an acceptable date for Stonehenge. The data was fed into an IBM computer, which produced quick results. Hawkins found no correlations with the planets or the six brightest stars, but there were major correlations with the sun and the moon. The results surprised Hawkins, who remarked, "I was prepared for *some* Stonehenge-sun correlation. I was not prepared for total sun correlation—and I had not at all suspected that there might be almost total moon correlation as well." He announced his finds in the October 1963 issue of the British scientific journal *Nature* with an article called "Stonehenge Decoded." He later published a book of the same title.

As the evidence accumulated, Hawkins argued that Stonehenge was nothing less than an ancient observatory, precisely engineered. Hawkins had found ten significant correlations between Stonehenge alignments and the sun and fourteen between them and the moon. It seemed clear that the ancient Stonehenge peoples were keeping a precise record of the seasons by using the megaliths as sighting points. Apparently they marked the midsummer sunrise and moonrise as well as the midwinter sunrise, sunset, moonrise, and moonset. There were also alignments for the equinoxes, which mark the beginning of the fall and spring seasons. The ancient people used a variety of points for sighting, but perhaps the most striking were the heelstone and the spaces between the trilithons.

As mentioned previously, many scholars have noted that there is a striking view of the summer solstice sunrise directly over the heelstone. Interestingly, in 1929, R. S. Newell suggested that a companion stone to the heelstone must once have existed. As surprising as it might seem, Newell's suggestion has turned out to be more than sheer guesswork. Fifty years later, archaeologists who were doing a salvage dig in an area destined for construction of a telephone cable uncovered the negative impression of Newell's hypothetical missing stone. Hawkins, who was greatly interested in the implications of the new hole, has since shown how the sunrise would initially be framed between the two stones immediately before the sun appeared on top of the heelstone itself.

One of the many puzzles at Stonehenge concerns the function of the fifty-six Aubrey holes. Hawkins argued that they were used as a kind of computer to predict eclipses, which he reasoned happened in fifty-six-year cycles. The Stonehenge people may have kept a record of the cycles by placing posts in the holes at the appropriate times. This interpretation has been disputed vigorously by Atkinson, who noted in a book review of *Stonehenge Decoded* (cryptically entitled "Moonshine on Stonehenge") that the holes were filled up after they were originally excavated.[7] Atkinson also zeroed in on several other aspects of Hawkins' work, including the fact that the margin of error used in Hawkins' calculations might well have had a substantial impact on the sightings, perhaps invalidating some of the basic conclusions. Nonetheless, Hawkins' general views have been very influential and have stimulated much work at other sites.[8] Hawkins himself went on to research other megaliths as well as the previously discussed Nazca lines in Peru.

It is important to realize that archaeological sites such as Stonehenge and other megaliths were not necessarily built with a single purpose in mind. The large size of Stonehenge and its layout is the product of a combination of factors. The political hierarchy, most likely, backed up by powerful religious sanctions, organized the labor for these projects. While most would agree that Stonehenge served as a focal point for important ceremonies, it was also a magnet that helped to keep the society integrated and at the same time served in a symbolic way to justify the authority of the political hierarchy itself. Certainly the building of such sites with massive stones that often weighed over twenty tons each ensured that this symbolism would be perpetuated beyond one's own time.

Stonehenge is one of the most widely visited prehistoric sites in Europe. Interest in the site has often peaked as the midsummer sunrise approaches. During the hippie era very large crowds came to what became known as the "Festival." Stonehenge expert Christopher Chippindale has noted that the annual Festival incorporated rock music, esoteric religious beliefs, drug use, and a range of other activities. The area surrounding the site, which contains valuable archaeological evidence, was increasingly threatened by the thousands of people attending the Festival. In 1985 the Festival was officially banned. This resulted in a major confrontation between the police and those attempting to stage the Festival in spite of the ban. A caravan of Festival-goers led by a nude man was halted at a road block. Chippindale describes the outcome as the "Battle of Stonehenge." The police rushed vehicles of Festival-goers and many were beaten and arrested. It is ironic that some archaeologists who have classified prehistoric societies into stages of evolutionary development have termed the ancient Stonehenge people "barbarians." Such "barbarians" would have been perplexed if they could have witnessed the 1985 events, or even those of 1989 when several hundred more people were arrested.

Stonehenge is not the oldest megalith site that has astronomical significance. The oldest one is the famous Neolithic passage tomb at Newgrange, Ireland. Radiocarbon dates have revealed that this large tomb was constructed in about 3,150 B.C. This is slightly before the first pyramids were built in Egypt. The Newgrange tomb features a narrow passageway a little over sixty feet in length that leads to a chamber with alcoves. There is a spiral design engraved on the wall of the chamber. The tomb was clearly built with the midwinter sunrise in mind. A few minutes after sunrise on midwinter's day, the sun shines through a space in the base of a roof box. According to the careful calculations of T. P. Ray, a narrow beam of light enters through the passage into the burial chamber. While the beam does not focus directly on the spiral, it is generally illuminated by the light.

Other megalithic sites such as the recumbent stone circles of Scotland and the stone alignments in Brittany also have archaeoastronomical significance. While some would credit these Neolithic and Bronze age megalith builders with a precise knowledge of astronomy and engineering, most archaeologists would see this as overkill. On the other hand the monitoring of seasonal changes for ceremonial and agricultural purposes is entirely reasonable.

NAMORATUNGA

I was involved in an archaeoastronomy project in Africa quite by chance while working with Mark Lynch, who was studying the Namoratunga rock art and cemetery sites mentioned in Chapter 2.[9] Local Turkana peoples had told us about another Namoratunga that existed farther to the north, near Lake Turkana, and we decided to investigate. We found a series of basalt pillars that had been placed in the ground at unusual angles. The group of pillars was surrounded by a circle of cobbles, as well as some nearby graves. Some of the pillars had very faint engravings on them, similar to the symbols found at the first Namoratunga site, which was dated to about 300 B.C. The site was quite striking as it stood in isolation, overlooking the bleak desert plain leading to the west shore of Lake Turkana. As part of standard archaeological procedure, we made a map of the site and photographed it. The arrangement and purpose of the stone pillars remained enigmatic.

Later, in the Michigan State University library, Lynch came

across some ethnographic information that provided some possible clues to the meaning of the stone pillars. He had previously established that Namoratunga was related to the remote ancestors of eastern Cushitic-speaking peoples of southern Ethiopia. His library search had revealed that present-day eastern Cushitic people such as the Borana have a complex calendar that divides the year into twelve months with 354 days. This calendar is based on the rising of the following stars or constellations in relation to certain phases of the moon: Triangulum, Pleiades, Aldebaran, Bellatrix, Central Orion, Saiph, and Sirius. The eastern Cushitic peoples monitor the first six months by observing the new moon in conjunction with the above stars and constellations in the order they are listed in above. For the rest of the year, Triangulum is used in relation to various phases of the moon. Lynch was aware of the work at Stonehenge and was intrigued with the idea of seeing whether the Namoratunga pillars were oriented toward the stars and constellations used in the Cushitic calendar. With the help of astronomers at M.S.U., the sky was positioned as it would have been for the Turkana area in 300 B.C., (the date of the site), and the possible alignments were tested. Lynch found a strong correlation between the Namoratunga pillars and the appropriate heavenly bodies. This was the first archaeoastronomical discovery in Africa, and it suggested that some early East African Neolithic peoples had a complex calendar. As in the case of the European megaliths, the interpretation of Namoratunga has not gone unchallenged, and the site has been reinvestigated by several different researchers. Archaeologist Robert Soper has argued strongly against the astronomical interpretation, while Laurance Doyle, an astronomer, has found equally convincing evidence in favor of it. Doyle remeasured the site and ran some statistical programs in a computer before concluding that the alignments cannot be due to chance.

NATIVE AMERICAN SITES

Chaco Canyon

The American Indians also kept track of the sky in ways related directly to their religious beliefs. A Hopi Indian of Arizona who was destined to become sun chief observed his people's dependency on the sky.

> Another important business was to keep track of the time or the seasons of the year by watching the points on the horizon where the sun rose and set each day. The point of sunrise on the shortest day of the year was called the sun's winter home and the point of sunrise on the longest day its summer home. Old Talasemptewa, who was almost blind, would sit out on the housetop of the special Sun Clan house and watch the sun's progress toward its summer home. He untied a knot in a string for each day. When the sun arose at certain mesa peaks, he passed the word around that it was time to plant . . . On a certain date he would announce that it was too late for any more planting. The old people said that there were proper times for planting, harvesting and hunting, for ceremonies, weddings and many other activities. In order to know these dates it was necessary to keep close watch on the sun's movements.[10]

There is a growing body of evidence that the Anasazi ancestors of Pueblo Indian groups such as the Hopi and Zuñi had similar beliefs. The Anasazi left behind the most impressive prehistoric sites in the United States. Because of this, a background sketch is provided before looking at their archaeoastronomy.

The word Anasazi means either "ancient ones" or "ancient enemies" in the language of the Navajo. While Anasazi culture reached its high point between about A.D. 900–A.D. 1300 (when their famous apartmentlike pueblos were built), the roots of the Anasazi can be traced back to the dawn of the Christian era, if not earlier. Some of the best-known sites include the pueblos of Chaco Canyon, New Mexico, as well as cliff dwellings like Cliff Palace and Spruce Tree House at Mesa Verde in southwestern Colorado and Kiet Siel in northern Arizona. Circular underground ceremonial structures called *kivas* (a Hopi word) and black-on-white painted pottery are other hallmarks of classic Anasazi culture. The development of kivas can be traced to earlier pit houses, which were used as dwellings before people began to build the aboveground pueblos. The fact that kivas are currently used for ceremonial purposes by the Hopi is one of the strong ties between past and present in the area. Anasazi sites are numerous in the vicinity of the four corners region where Colorado, New Mexico, Utah, and Arizona meet. This area, which is seen as the "capital" of the Anasazi world, was mysteriously abandoned in about A.D. 1300. This followed an extensive drought that may have been one of the key factors why the Anasazi, who farmed corn, beans, and squash, left the area and eventually moved to the areas now occupied by their Pueblo Indian descendants.

The "discovery" of the Anasazi took place in the last century, beginning somewhat before other landmark finds such as Troy, Java Man, and the cave art of Altamira. A pioneering description of the ruins of Chaco Canyon was made by Lt. James H. Simpson in 1849 during a military campaign against the Navajo. Simpson was fascinated by the building achievements evidenced in the ancient pueblos. Another key discovery was made in the winter of 1888 at Mesa Verde. Two cowboys, Richard Wetherill and Charlie Mason, were following some lost cattle in the snowy terrain of an isolated canyon at Mesa Verde when they came upon the largest cliff dwelling built by the Anasazi. Wetherill named it Cliff Palace. This must have seemed a fitting name to the cowboys, who first saw the ruins from a distance, nestled like a lost city against the natural protection of the canyon wall. Wetherill subsequently spent much of his life in the exploration of Anasazi sites. He died in 1910, the victim of an ambush at Chaco Canyon, where he operated a trading post. Since the pioneering days at the turn of the century, when sites were often haphazardly looted for pots rather than carefully excavated, much informative archaeological work has been done. Currently the Southwest is one of the most thoroughly researched regions in archaeology. Chaco Canyon is one of its key areas.

Situated in a remote part of northwestern New Mexico, Chaco Canyon features a number of the largest and most elaborate of the multistoried pueblos, which are built primarily from sandstone blocks and logs. The latter have provided the basis for an extensive tree-ring dating sequence for the sites, which overall generally fall in the period between 850 and 1150 A.D. Chaco Canyon, like Mesa Verde, is a National Park. The visitor to Chaco Canyon will initially be struck by the pleasing architecture and large size of the buildings known as Great Pueblos. The Great Pueblos bear witness to considerable organizational and technical skills. The best known is Pueblo Bonito (beautiful town). It was originally at least a four- or five-story structure with over 600 rooms and numerous kivas. Shaped like a large letter *D* when viewed from above, Pueblo Bonito was constructed over a total period of about 165 years.

Recent findings summarized by Stephen H. Lekson and his colleagues reveal that Chaco Canyon served as an important focal point of Anasazi culture. It was connected to other areas by a series of carefully laid out roads that covered hundreds of miles. The full extent of the roads was not realized until aerial photos revealed that there were many more miles of them than was previously believed. These roads were traveled on foot, like the Inca roads in Peru. One can imagine that they were used for a variety of purposes such as transporting building materials, and trading goods and food, as well as serving as routes for large groups to attend important ceremonies.

The inhabitants of Chaco Canyon practiced irrigation agriculture in a sensitive environment that featured relatively short growing seasons. Like the present-day Hopi, the Anasazi depended on a very precise knowledge of seasonal changes in order to have a successful harvest. Jonathan Reyman, an archaeologist, found that two of the third-story windows at Pueblo Bonito were positioned purposely so that the winter solstice sunrise would appear in them. Photographs taken from the windows during the December solstices of 1973 and 1975 revealed striking views of the sunrise.[11]

At the south end of Chaco Canyon, Fajada Butte towers about 400 feet above the surrounding landscape like a sentinel. On top of the butte in 1977, Anna Sofaer, an artist, made an unusual discovery while studying two ancient spiral-shaped petroglyphs. She noticed the sun shone on one of the spirals through some adjacent slabs at about noon each day. Further study revealed that the slabs and spirals constitute a sophisticated way of keeping track of the solstices and equinoxes and were, in essence, an Anasazi calendar.

Sofaer and her colleagues kept "records of the patterns of light on the spirals at monthly intervals from 21 June 1978 (summer solstice) to 21 December 1978 (winter solstice) and at some intervening dates."[12] During the summer solstice on 23 June 1978 a spot of sunlight appeared at the top of the spiral shortly after 11:00 A.M. By 11:15 A.M. a knifelike projection of light shone vertically through the middle of the spiral. Within a few minutes the blaze of light had disappeared, the whole process taking about eighteen minutes. The researchers noted that after the summer solstice, "the light pattern follows the same sequence but is displayed increasingly to the right and center of the spiral." During the fall equinox, on 21 and 22 September, the sun highlighted the center of the smaller spiral. During the winter solstice of 22 December 1978, two vertical paths of sunlight framed each side of the larger spiral.

The researchers feel the nineteen lines of the larger spiral may be connected with a nineteen-year cycle of the moon, but this idea has been challenged by Michael Zeilek of the Department of Physics and Astronomy at the University of New Mexico, who argues that the cycle works only partially.[13] He also finds fault with the idea that Fajada Butte served as a calendar. Based on a detailed study of recent Pueblo Indian customs, he concludes that the site was probably a sun shrine, where offerings were placed. There is also some debate regarding who used the Fajada Butte site. Sofaer and her associates feel that it was probably built between A.D. 950 and 1150 by the Anasazi people who lived nearby. Reyman believes that the linkages between the site and the Anasazi are tenuous and that the Fajada Butte site could have been in use either earlier or later than the dates proposed.[14] Unfortunately, petroglyph sites can seldom be directly dated and are often relatively isolated from other types of archaeological data. For this reason arguments such as the above cannot be easily resolved. Whatever the case may have been, the precise relationship between the dagger of sunlight and the engraved spiral at Fajada Butte is very impressive. I think that it is clear that, like their modern descendants, the ancient peoples of the Chaco area were greatly concerned with keeping track of the movements of the sun as it related to the passing of seasons, their agricultural practices, and their ceremonial lives. All of these phenomena were intertwined.

Cahokia

Elsewhere in the United States are other notable prehistoric Native American archaeoastronomical sites. One classic example is associated with the Mississippian culture, during which, between about A.D. 700 and 1200, a series of agriculturally based towns flourished along the fertile Mississippi River bottomlands and along a number of other major river valleys. These sites feature large ceremonial mounds as well as distinctive shell-tempered pottery. The mounds bear witness to a considerable organization of labor and a complex religious and political system. One of the most impressive of them is Cahokia, which is located in the bottom area of East St. Louis.

Cahokia, the largest prehistoric site in the United States, covers about six square miles and contains more than one hundred mounds.[15] Monks Mound, the largest prehistoric Indian mound in the country, dominates Cahokia. It is about 100 feet high, 1,037 feet in length, and nearly 800 feet wide.[16] While these large Mississippian mounds have been termed temple mounds, there is evidence that they were actually the location of "charnel houses," in which the bones of elite individuals were exposed.

Cahokia flourished at about the same time as Chaco Canyon. Population estimates vary, but Michael Gregg has calculated that between A.D. 1050 and 1150, there were about 25,500 people living at Cahokia, with a population density of about 5,000 people per square mile.[17] Cahokia's dense population was supported by maize agriculture, the cultivation of other plants, hunting, fishing, and gathering. Like Chaco Canyon, Cahokia also had its important priests who were concerned with conducting ceremonies and who kept a close watch on the seasons of the year.

Evidence of the astronomical nature of the site began to appear in 1961, when Warren Wittry uncovered some impressions of huge posts, each about two feet in diameter, that had been buried deep in the ground.[18] The post holes formed a series of carefully laid-out circles. One of the latter exceeded 400 feet in diameter and consisted of forty-eight posts, all of which were precisely spaced and must have originally projected a considerable distance above ground level. Interestingly, the circle was laid out with the cardinal directions in mind. Wittry likens this Cahokia circle to the much earlier Woodhenge, a site with posts found near Stonehenge in England. Woodhenge was constructed with wooden posts rather than stone, and it is believed to have had astronomical significance. At Cahokia, the Indians placed one post in the middle, just off center, so that it served as a sighting post for observing the solstice. The sighter could stand in the middle of the circle and use this "center" post to sight the appropriate exterior posts. The alignments marked the summer and winter solstice sunrises and the fall and spring equinoxes. Other evidence in the Midwest occurs near Dayton, Ohio, where very large stone effigies of snakes have been excavated; they were positioned to mark the summer and winter solstices.[19] They appear to date to between the twelfth and fifteenth centuries A.D. It is interesting that midwestern Indians apparently kept track of many of the same events as did the Chaco Canyon people, while employing very different means. The archaeological evidence would support the opinion of Jon D. Muller, who states that all Indian "religious beliefs share certain basic features, including emphasis on four-part division of the world and universe with stress on cardinal directions and celestial objects."[20] The contention that such religious beliefs were widespread and ancient is supported by many other archaeological examples, from the stone circles known as "medicine wheels" found as far north as Canada to the buildings of the Mayas of Mesoamerica.

PALEOLITHIC CALENDARS

The idea of using solar events to keep track of time and the passing of seasons could be very old. In 1962 Alexander Marshack, then a general-science writer, made a significant breakthrough in understanding the origins of mankind's concern with time. (Marshack's ideas were mentioned earlier in connection with the idea that certain cave paintings reflect seasonal concerns of Upper Paleolithic peoples.) While writing a book on the history of space exploration, Marshack became interested in how the ancient peoples reckoned time, but much to his surprise, there was very little hard evidence about this prior to the age of the earliest civilizations such as ancient Egypt. In researching the question further, Marshack came across a journal article on Ishango, a Late Stone Age site in Zaire about 7,000 years old. The site produced a unique artifact: a small piece of quartz set in the end of a bone handle, which was incised with a series of small marks. Jean de Heinzelin, the Belgian archaeologist who excavated Ishango, argued that the lines were evidence of a numbering system and suggested such systems may have first developed in central Africa and then spread north to Egypt via the upper Nile Valley.[21] Marshack writes how, puzzled by the bone, he followed a "hunch based on ideas suggested by the book I was writing. In fifteen minutes I had cracked the code of the Ishango bone . . . I was dizzied."[22]

Marshack found a close match between the number and sets of engraved marks and phases of the moon. This evidence suggested that the Ishango peoples had a form of lunar calendar, as well as a system for keeping track of time, some 3,000 years before the dawn of Egyptian civilization. Marshack promptly put his book aside and proceeded to investigate older engraved bones from Upper Paleolithic times (ca. 39,000–10,000 B.C.). Some of these bones, which date to the time and cultures of the cave artists in France, had similar markings on them. For years, most of these specimens had been ignored in comparison to some of the finely carved art objects. Many experts thought the lines were little more than a kind of doodling. Marshack studied each specimen microscopically and noted that the profiles, or shapes, of the cut marks varied, indicating that different stone tools had been used to make the marks and, importantly, that the lines must have been cut at different times. Marshack's analysis of cut marks has been disputed.[23] It has been argued that the variation in the profile of the cut marks may have been due to the dulling of the edge on the stone tool as it was used on a single occasion rather than the use of different tools over an extended period of time. Marshack has countered by noting that the significant variation is between different sets or groupings of marks. In other words, he sees each varying set as having been made by a different tool with unique edge characteristics rather than resulting from the dulling of the edge of only one tool. According to Marshack, the work clearly was not done at random. Marshack also discovered close correspondences between the series of marks and phases of the moon. He concluded that upper Paleolithic peoples kept records of lunar cycles with a kind of notation system.

Marshack has also examined even earlier evidence from Neandertal sites and one specimen from the pre-Neandertal levels of Pech de l'Azé in France. This earlier evidence is much less persuasive, but the idea that Upper Paleolithic peoples kept close track of the moon is consistent with the fact that hunting and foraging peoples also must keep abreast of seasonal changes in order to predict when animal migrations, rains, and the like would take place. As Marshack points out, this knowledge was important in the scheduling of rituals and ceremonies. Marshack's evidence for an Upper Paleolithic lunar notation system also has been seen as a form of "pre-writing" that, in some ways, provides a remote conceptual background to the development of writing, a subject considered in the next chapter.

7

THE WRITTEN FRONTIER

The Origin of Writing

The archaeological record is fickle. Finds usually consist of durable items, like potsherds or bones, that were people's discarded trash. It is a tribute to archaeologists that so much can be learned from so little. There have been dramatic exceptions: the frozen Siberian tombs and wet sites such as the "lake dwellings." But even these rare finds almost never allow for significant penetration into the thoughts of ancient peoples and their perceptions of the world. This is why the discovery of written texts piques our interest in the past. Of course, what the ancient scribes wrote was not necessarily an accurate or unbiased portrayal of reality, but it does carry us beyond the limitations of stones, bones, and potsherds. The written frontier in archaeology is fascinating and complex. There are three main areas of concern: the origins of writing, the decipherment of dead languages, and the discovery and impact of key texts. Here are some famous examples.

THE DEVELOPMENT OF WRITING ON CLAY TABLETS

A recurring theme in history is that inventions often appear independently in widely separated areas but in the same general cultural milieu. This is certainly true for writing, which was probably invented at least four times in the Old World (Egypt, Mesoptamia, the Indus Valley, and China) and also in the New World among the Mayas and Zapotecs of Mesoamerica. In each case, the dawn of writing is first associated with the emergence of "civilizations." To some scholars, writing is seen as one of the necessary ingredients of civilization, yet civilized societies such as that of the Incas lacked writing, though the Incas themselves did keep records by using an elaborate system of knotted cords.

The use of abstract symbols and primitive notation can be traced back to at least the Upper Paleolithic, as evidenced by the abstract signs in cave art and Alexander Marshack's research on engraved bones. I do not feel, however, that these Stone Age efforts were systematic attempts to codify a language. Most available evidence suggests that the impetus for writing occurred during the development of the first bureaucracies, when there was a need to keep records of economic transactions, to codify the rules that kept the state functioning, and to document religious ideas and records.

Cuneiform, the famous wedge-shaped writing on clay tablets that was used widely by scribes in ancient Mesopotamia, first appears at about 3500 B.C. at the ancient city of Uruk, not far from the Euphrates River in southern Iraq. Here, about fifty years ago, large numbers of illegible clay tablets were found. Cuneiform was eventually deciphered by several scholars, most notably Henry Rawlinson, an Englishman, who dangled precariously over a sheer cliff face while copying the trilingual Behistun inscriptions in Iran. The Behistun inscriptions, which glorified the Persian ruler Darius, represented an important key for Rawlinson because he could use the inscriptions from a known language to decipher the unknown cuneiform.

Insights into the distant origins of this ancient language have been revealed through the research of Denise Schmand-Besserat. In 1969 she began to investigate not the origins of writing but "when and in what ways clay first came to be used in the Near East."[1] As an aside, the earliest evidence for the use of baked clay is at the Upper Paleolithic site of Dolni Věstonice in Czechoslovakia, where numerous lumps of clay and animal figurines date back to approximately 23,000 B.C. After this time there is very little evidence of the use of baked clay until the first pots are found that possibly date to as early as 10,000 B.C. in Japan. In the Near East, pottery begins to appear between roughly 7,000 and 6,000 B.C. Along with the pots were a wide variety of other clay objects, such as figures of animals and amulets that are found in early farming sites. Although the pottery has been studied, no one had systematically reviewed and compared the other kinds of clay artifacts from the many different sites. Among the collections Schmandt-Besserat studied were a series of enigmatic clay objects that she dubbed "tokens," ranging in shape from disks to cones. Like the engraved bones Marshack studied, these objects had been discounted and treated as miscellaneous finds by the excavators. No one knew what, if any purpose, they served. Schmandt-Besserat's comparative study revealed that the tokens were not isolated finds but were distributed all the way from Turkey to the Nile Valley in Sudan. For this reason, she felt that they were not produced at random but must have had some general use. Furthermore, she learned that the tokens were first used in early Neolithic times, about 9,000 years ago, and continued to be used up to the time of the first city-states in Mesopotamia.

What were they used for? A close look at Neolithic lifestyles provides important clues. Between 7000 and 6000 B.C., early Neolithic villagers at sites such as Ali Kosh in Iran and Jarmo in Iraq raised emmer wheat and herded sheep and goats. No doubt grain and livestock were important in the economic life of these communities. If present-day pastoralists can provide insights, the value of livestock may fluctuate according to the kind of animal, its quality, size, age, sex, color, and relative abundance in a particular area. Possibly similar variables may have been important in the Neolithic period, and certainly keeping track of the amount of grain harvested and stored was critical. This was also a time when trade networks were developing among the nascent village communities. For example, obsidian (volcanic glass) from sources in Turkey was being exchanged throughout the Near East. The obsidian, excellent for making sharp blades, can be traced to specific sources through trace-element studies and other kinds of analysis. Some communities, such as pre-biblical Jericho, were rising to prominence because they were located strategically with respect to trade routes or raw materials. It is clear that the roots of complex economic relationships were present in these communities. Because of this, Schmandt-Besserat believes that the tokens were used initially for keeping records of grain and that other items were gradually incorporated into the system. She has noted that the utility of Neolithic tokens increased when middlemen came on the scene and negotiated trades.

In such cases the owners, who may not have been in the immediate area, needed to have a way of ensuring that the specific terms of an agreement were followed. Much later, laws would be written to prevent trade disputes, such as one of Hammurabi's laws (1700 B.C.):

> If a merchant lent grain, wool, oil, or any goods at all to a trader to retail, the trader shall write down the value and pay (it) back to their merchant, with the trader obtaining a sealed receipt for the money which he pays to the merchant.[2]

Schmandt-Besserat postulates that the tokens were at first used as a method of reckoning, but gradually the system became more complex, mirroring the growth in sociopolitical organization. As the state began to emerge, tokens appeared that had incised marks in various set patterns. Many of these patterns have been shown to resemble closely the incised designs that appear on the earliest clay tablets. For example, the symbol for sheep is a circle divided by a cross. This is identical to what is found on those early clay tablets from which the meaning of sheep has been deciphered. Eventually the tokens were placed in clay envelopes, which were sealed. The number and kinds of tokens inside were inscribed on the clay surface of the envelope. According to Schmandt-Besserat, this meant that all parties to the transaction knew what was in the envelope, and in the event there was no deal, the envelope did not have to be broken to reveal the contents. In time the tokens themselves became insignificant because the signs on the envelopes conveyed the necessary meanings. Schmandt-Besserat concludes that the envelopes developed subsequently into the first clay tablets.

Interestingly, she has carried her research further by deciphering some of the earliest cuneiform tablets from the perspective gained through her analysis of clay tokens.[3] She has found evidence of eighteen signs on the clay tablets that represent tokens. A clear example of this continuity is seen in the shallow circles on the tablets, which are derived from disk-shaped tokens. In her reading of the earliest tablets, she concludes that they were receipts for taxes paid in grain and livestock. This serves to underscore the theory that economic forces led to the genesis of Mesopotamian writing. In retrospect, it is remarkable to see how seemingly insignificant, simple clay disks, cones, triangles, and other tokens were, in reality, the seeds of a complex system of writing.

THE ROSETTA STONE

Most of the best known of ancient writing systems have been deciphered, though researchers are still hard at work decoding Mayan hieroglyphics and the puzzling script of Indus civilization. Although all of the cases of decipherment are intrinsically interesting because of the puzzlelike aspect of the work, the most fascinating story centers on Egyptian hieroglyphics. Their decipherment was the key that unlocked much of the history of one of the unique civilizations of the ancient world.

The Egyptians began to write in about 3000 B.C. This is roughly the time when the first Pharaoh, Menes, began to rule. The Egyptians left behind a rich body of hieroglyphic writing painted on the walls of tombs and represented on monuments. They also used a cursive form of the writing known as *hieratic*, which was used to write on papyri, a kind of paper made from the papyrus plants that thrived along the Nile. After the eventual collapse of Egyptian civilization, the active use of hieroglyphs faded out gradually and was forgotten. Luckily at about 196 B.C., during the reign of King Ptolemy V, some unknown scribe wrote a trilingual document on a piece of basalt nearly four feet high and almost a foot thick. The message itself was really not that important: It announced that honors had been granted to King Ptolemy by the priesthood. What was significant was that the same message was repeated in Egyptian hieroglyphs, *demotic* (a kind of neo-Egyptian shorthand), and Greek. This was the Rosetta Stone, which would become one of the most important finds ever made in Egypt. The stone would one day offer the unparalleled opportunity for scholars to work from a known language, Greek, to an unknown, the mysterious hieroglyphics. But as the centuries rolled by, the stone was lost, along with the knowledge of hieroglyphics. Nearly 2,000 years would pass before the stone would reemerge from the sun-scorched Nile delta.

In 1798 Napoleon, accompanied by thousands of troops, invaded Egypt. Napoleon was curious about life in ancient Egypt and brought with him nearly 200 scholars to record as many details as possible about the remains of the ancient civilization.[4] A year after the invasion, when the French were constructing a fort at Rosetta, a town in the Nile delta area, a soldier working on the project discovered the trilingual stone buried in the debris of a wall. Fortunately he recognized its potential importance and saved it for future study by the scholars. Not long afterward, however, the British defeated the French and gained rights to Egyptian antiquities. A British major-general, Tomkyns Hilgrove Turner, relates how he carried off the stone in an artillery cart amid the jeers of the French and took it to his house. There he allowed some of the French scholars to make a cast of the stone and copy the trilingual writing for their own use. In 1802, when the stone was shipped to the British Museum, General Turner described his confidence in the stone's significance.

> I trust it will long remain a most valuable relic of antiquity, the feeble but only yet discovered link of the Egyptian to the known languages, a proud trophy of the arms of Britain (I could almost say spolia opima), not plundered from defenceless inhabitants, but honourable acquired by the fortune of war.[5]

Today the Rosetta Stone continues to stand in a prominent position in the British Museum, where it provides a testimonial of the events of 1802 and the general period when Egypian antiquities were blatantly removed to Europe. Another important stone, the obelisk of Philae, also had writing in Greek and hieroglyphics. The obelisk was found on the island of Philae on the Nile in 1815 and removed to England. For years, it has been used as a decoration at the Kingston-Lacey estate in England.

As the relics of ancient Egypt were emerging from the Nile Valley, there was much curiosity and speculation about the hieroglyphs. Some thought that they were picture writing, and there were elaborate attempts to decipher them, some of which resulted in utter nonsense cast in the image of scholarship. It was a Frenchman, Jean François Champollion, who finally deciphered hieroglyphics. Champollion fit the mold of other scholarly pioneers described in this book who, through exceptional dedication to an elusive goal, were able to fulfill their youthful dreams.

Champollion was only eleven years old when he was first shown some hieroglyphics on stone tablets and papyrus. He was fascinated immediately and asked, "Can anyone read them?" When he was told that no one had a clue to their meaning, he declared, "I am going to do it. In a few years I will be able to. When I am big."[6] Champollion indeed became a gifted linguist who, even as a youth, mastered a variety of Middle Eastern languages, including Coptic, an exotic language developed in Egypt at the time when Christianity was spreading. Coptic contained aspects of Egyptian and Greek and, because of this, was an important tool in some of the early decipherment efforts.

Later an Englishman, Thomas Young, made another important breakthrough by deducing that hieratic was a kind of cursive for hieroglyphics. He found that certain words enclosed by ovals, or *cartouches*, were in fact names. This key point enabled Champollion to crack the code by systematically comparing the names in the different languages. A comparison of a cartouche on the Rosetta Stone with one on the Kingston-Lacey obelisk revealed that two cartouches in question were the names for Cleopatra and Ptolemy respectively. It was a matter of matching up the symbols that stood for common meanings, such as the squares indicating *p* and the lions meaning *l* in both of these names. From that point on, it was a case of making further comparisons and deductions. During this endeavor, there was much competition and animosity between Champollion and his rival, Young, as indeed, there have been bitter rivalries between scholars in almost all landmark areas of discovery. After ten years of meticulous work on the Rosetta Stone, Champollion announced his conclusions in September 1822 in a formal letter that was publicized widely. Then he fulfilled another dream by going to Egypt, where he saw the sites first hand and further advanced his knowledge of hieroglyphics.

By deciphering hieroglyphics, Champollion single-handedly opened the door to the understanding of many significant aspects of Egyptian history. First, there was the establishment of chronologies, so that the various dynasties could be dated in calendar years. Egyptologists could then determine when specific Pharaohs reigned and which ones were associated with the pyramids, other great monuments and works of art, and military conquests. Equally important, the hieroglyphics unlocked a vast amount of information on Egyptian customs, ranging from religion and funerary beliefs to economics. Because of this rich information, Champollion's breakthrough was a discovery of far greater magnitude than Carter's uncovering of King Tutankhamen's tomb. The former had a major scholarly impact, while the latter, though of exceptional public interest, was of lesser consequence from the scientific point of view.

THE DEAD SEA SCROLLS

The Great Rift Valley is an enormous geological trough that cuts through much of eastern Africa. It has figured prominently in the latest research into the question of human origins, revealing the 3.7-million-year-old footprints at Laetoli in Tanzania and the relatively complete skeleton of Lucy in Ethiopia. The valley continues on from Ethiopia, extending under the Red Sea and into the Middle East, where it reaches one of the world's unique features, the Dead Sea. The saltiest and the lowest body of water on earth, the Dead Sea is situated 1,300 feet below sea level. Its extremely dry conditions in the cliffs on its west side have preserved one of the most extraordinary finds ever made: the Dead Sea Scrolls.

Shortly before and after the turn of the Christian era, some

Jewish sects began to store Hebrew manuscripts on sheepskin in some caves by the Dead Sea. Among their manuscripts were extensive writings from the Old Testament and other religous literature. Little did those people know that some of their work would survive in those caves as a "time capsule" for over 2,000 years and one day astonish the world of scholars.

The initial find was accidental. Three nomadic Bedouins were herding their sheep and goats near the northwest end of the Dead Sea early in 1947, when one of them found two holes in the cliff and threw a stone into the lower one. When the stone apparently hit an earthen jar, the herdsman's curiosity was aroused, but it was already too dark to investigate, since evening was approaching. The next day the Bedouins returned from watering their flocks, and early the next morning the youngest one "ventured into the [larger] hole and fell into a cave," as he told it, where he found several large pottery jars (7–10, according to his different acounts).[7] From one he removed three scrolls which he carried down to their camp at the base of the cliff. The older shepherds took the scrolls from their cousin, and one of them took them to their main center, east of Bethlehem, where they hung in a bag from a tent pole for about a month. Thinking that the scrolls might be worth selling, one of the Bedouins took them to a shopkeeper in Bethlehem, who advised him not to try to sell them. When the Bedouins returned a few weeks later, they were advised to take them to another antiquity dealer, known as Kando, an Assyrian Orthodox Christian who had ties with St. Mark's Monastery in Jerusalem.

At the monastery, the scrolls came under the scrutiny of the Metropolitan (Archbishop) Mar Athanasius Y. Samuel of the Syrian Orthodox Church of Jerusalem and Transjordan. He had been told that the scrolls might be ancient Syriac documents but was surprised to discover that the largest one "was not Syriac . . . but Hebrew. It was a light yellow color and quite brittle."[8] He "broke off a small piece from the margin and burned it," concluding from the odor that "it must be leather or parchment." Metropolitan Samuel later purchased the four scrolls for $97.20, of which $64.80 was paid to the Bedouins. He assumed they were old, in spite of the doubts of others. One person in the antiquities service bluntly told him, "They are worthless."

It is clear that the main interest in the scrolls was in their monetary value rather than in their archaeological importance. The Metropolitan needed expert opinions but did not want to arouse any suspicions about the origin of the scrolls. Meanwhile, Kando and his sidekick had found out from the Bedouins the location of the cave and secretly looted the site, as did Metropolitan Samuel later on.[9] This was strictly illegal according to the antiquities laws and was devastating from the archaeological viewpoint. Nevertheless, the number of scrolls retrieved reached seven.

On November 25, 1947, E. L. Sukenik, the professor of archaeology at the Hebrew University, was shown a small piece of another scroll by a Jerusalem antiquities dealer, who told him there was more of the material, and that it had been found by some Bedouins. Sukenik wrote in his diary, "I saw four pieces of leather with Hebrew writing. The script seems ancient to me . . ."[10] Sukenik bought what was available and two months later learned via librarians at Hebrew University that similar scrolls were at St Mark's Monastery. Sukenik was excited by this news and wanted to see them. Palestine had just been partitioned, however, and St. Mark's was in the Old City, which was off limits to Sukenik. Travel in the area was dangerous, as there was much violence and loss of life. St. Mark's itself was eventually shelled, killing the head monk. Nevertheless, Sukenik was able to arrange a meeting with a prominent layman of St. Mark's in the local YMCA, which was in a safe area. Sukenik tells us that as soon as he saw the scrolls from the monastery he was "convinced that they were part and parcel of the same group of scrolls" that he had recently bought for the Hebrew University Museum. He offered to buy them, but without success, for the Syrians decided to get another opinion about their value. Later, when American biblical scholars scooped him and released the news about the scrolls, Sukenik was understandably upset.

Within a few days of Sukenik's YMCA meeting, a monk from the monastery contacted the American School of Oriental Research in Jerusalem, a major center of research in biblical archaeology. The monk was careful to cover up the real story about the origin of the scrolls, claiming that they had been in the monastery for about forty years, which, of course, was not true. At the American School, the scrolls were shown to a Fellow, John C. Trever, who was acting director for two weeks. When he opened the largest scroll he was startled to see evidences of great antiquity in its Hebrew writing. When he compared the script to a photograph he had of a small piece of papyrus with a script that had been dated to the second century B.C., he was excited to think that the scroll might be from such an early time. He copied a few lines from it. After the monk left he consulted a Hebrew dictionary for occurrences of a word that appeared twice on the first line copied and checked several references. Trever noted in his diary,

> The next reference showed two occurrences in Isaiah 65:1. With growing expectancy, I hastily turned to it. There, word for word, and almost letter for letter, was exactly what I had copied from the manuscript! It was a scroll of Isaiah, without a doubt.[11]

This was very exciting, but many questions remained: Could the scrolls really be that old? Could they be forgeries? A more careful examination was essential.

Trever arranged to get a pass into the Old City and visit the monastery the next day. Closer scrutiny of the Isaiah Scroll soon proved to him that it could not be a forgery, and that it must be at least 2,000 years old, the oldest version of any part of the Old Testament known. As soon as some photographs could be made, he sent two to Dr. W. F. Albright, one of the foremost biblical scholars of the time, for verification. He replied in a letter to Trever, "My heartiest congratulations on the greatest MS discovery of modern times!"[12] Albright suggested that it might be older than the papyrus, probably from about 100 B.C.

In May 1948 *The Biblical Archaeologist*, published by the American Schools of Oriental Research (Jerusalem and Baghdad), came out with an article titled "A Phenomenal Discovery." Its praise of the find was hardly subtle.

> The most important discovery ever made in Old Testament manuscripts was officially announced on

> April 11. . . . The entire Book of Isaiah in Hebrew was found on a well preserved scroll of parchment and the date—*first century* B.C., says Dr. Burrows! [the head of the Oriental School]. This is amazing, for complete Hebrew manuscripts of Isaiah, or for that matter of any part of the Old Testament, have hitherto been unknown before the 9th century A.D.[13]

This particular scroll was important because it filled a significant gap in knowledge of Biblical history falling between the Old and New Testaments, near the time of the appearance of Christianity.

It became obvious that the scrolls were exceedingly valuable, but of course as academic treasures they were priceless. Early in 1949, Metropolitan Samuel took the four scrolls that he had out of the country and attempted to sell them in the United States. He relates that he wanted to use the money to rebuild the war-torn monastery in Jerusalem and to aid refugees who were members of his church. The scrolls were exhibited in the U.S. and received much publicity. Surprisingly, the Metropolitan experienced considerable difficulty in attempting to sell them. They were, in fact, "hot" items. One authority noted that because they were taken out of Jordan illegally, prospective purchasers might have been subject to an international lawsuit. The government of Israel, however, one of the most interested of possible buyers, would almost certainly not be sued. According to Hershel Shanks: "To sue Israel would imply recognition and Jordan would never do this."[14] The Metropolitan Samuel has noted that neither Jordan nor Israel were nations when the scrolls in question were discovered. Even so, the scrolls, like other archaeological finds, should not have been considered as private property to be bought and sold. Eventually, the Metropolitan placed an ad in the *Wall Street Journal* in the miscellaneous column. While the Metropolitan did not intend to sell the scrolls to Israel, they were, in fact, sold for $250,000 to a man who secretly represented Israel. These original finds are now housed as a national treasure in a specially built part of the Israeli Museum called the Shrine of The Book.[15] This building features carefully controlled atmospheric and light conditions designed to prevent the scrolls from deteriorating. For example, there is no natural light, since ultraviolet rays are destructive. The artificial light is minimal and can be turned on for only fifty seconds at a time. Scientists monitor the scrolls for deterioration by a method known as X-ray diffraction. This measures the amount of gelatin forming in the scrolls as a result of heat and moisture.

Eventually the Syrians at the monastery decided it was in their best interests to tell the truth about the origin of the scrolls, although they were not very specific about the location of the cave. It was only through some patient inquiry and astute investigation that the source of the scrolls was finally found. Once political conditions were relatively stable, intensive searches got underway for more documents. Through the years, a large number of other scrolls were found at other sites by Bedouins and archaeologists. There may be 800 manuscripts available now, nearly half of which came from one cave.[16]

In 1967, during the Six Day War, the Israelis captured Arab territory that included the area where a certain antiquities dealer lived and worked. This gave Yigael Yadin the chance to follow up on a lead that this man might have a new scroll. Yadin, a deputy prime minister of Israel and the son of Eliezer Sukenik, is also well known for his archaeological work at the Fortress of Masada. In an engrossing account Yadin relates how the first clue to the existence of an important new scroll was revealed in a letter to him in 1960. Years of on-and-off-again secret negotiations for the purchase of the scroll by Yadin and the anonymous Mr. Z, a middleman, and Mr. X, the dealer, failed. However, during this process Yadin received two small fragments. Surprisingly, Yadin found out that one of them was actually the piece of a scroll that had been previously discovered. However, the other one was from an unknown scroll. During the war Mr. X was located by an intelligence officer. The dealer produced the Temple Scroll, which was hidden in a shoe box beneath the floor of his house. Other pieces were found behind pictures on the wall.[17] Eventually Yadin negotiated the purchase of the new scroll for Israel for $105,000. When unrolled, it proved to be twenty-seven feet long (the longest scroll), and it contained elaborate plans for building a temple as well as many parts of the Old Testament. All in all, the Dead Sea Scrolls contain almost all of the books of the Old Testament and a variety of other religious writings.

Who wrote the Dead Sea Scrolls? Not far from the original Dead Sea Scroll cave there is an impressive archaeological site known as Khirbet Qumran. Most authorities strongly believe that the inhabitants of Qumran were the authors of the scrolls and that they had placed them in the nearby caves, a kind of library, for safekeeping. Furthermore, it is accepted widely that the people of Qumran belonged to an isolated Jewish sect known as the Essenes, who lived during the time of Roman domination, had very strict rules governing their community, and believed in the coming of a Messiah. One of the basic building blocks in this reasoning is a historical account by Pliny the Elder, who died in the fiery volcanic blast of Vesuvius.

> On the west side of the Dead Sea, but out of range of the noxious exhalations of the coast, is the solitary tribe of the Essenes, which is remarkable beyond all other tribes in the whole world, as it had no women, and has renounced all sexual desire, has no money, and has only palm-trees for company.[18]

This must indeed have seemed remarkable to a Roman like Pliny, judging from the pornographic artwork and licentious handwriting on the walls at Pompeii. The linkage between the Essenes, the Dead Sea Scrolls, and the site at Qumran was established early in the research on the scrolls. Not only was there Pliny's description of such a people existing in the area, but one of the original scrolls known as the Manual of Discipline contained various rules governing a community like the Essenes. In addition, pottery found in the caves matches material excavated from the settlement at Qumran. There have also been more unusual ways of demonstrating the Essene connection. Yadin, for example, has supported the linkage in a discussion of the placement of outhouses as documented in the Temple Scroll. They are referred to by the word "hand." According to Yadin, the hand had to be located a specified distance outside of the city walls. Apparently, this distance exceeded the limits that the Essenes were allowed to walk on the Sabbath. Therefore, the outhouses could not have been used on the Sabbath. Yadin notes that this deduction is consistent with the description provided by the early Jewish historian Flavius Josephus, who reported that the Essenes were not allowed to defecate on the Sabbath. If this was true, the morning after the Sabbath must have witnessed a rapid exit from the city! Humor aside, there are other reasons cited by Yadin and numerous researchers supporting the connection and it is undoubtedly the prevailing view presented by biblical scholars in accounts of the Dead Sea Scrolls.

Still, this widely accepted theory that the Essenes were the authors of the Dead Sea Scrolls has been challenged recently. Norman Golb, an expert on Jewish History at the University of Chicago, maintains that there is insufficient evidence to confirm that this linkage really exists. When the scrolls were first found and the sample was small, the link between Essenes and the scrolls seemed clear, but now that the sample is much larger, it is more difficult to support this connection. Golb feels the vast majority of the new scrolls that have been described cannot be related specifically to the Essenes or their customs. The scrolls seem too varied in content to be linked to a single isolated group. Moreover, additional scrolls are now known from a much wider area than the original caves near Qumran where they were first discovered. According to Golb, the pottery link between Qumran and the caves is also not so specific as early investigators believed. The particular kind of pottery found in the caves has now been shown to be more widespread. Golb also observes that some of the interpretations of the Qumran site have been stretched to suit the Essene-Scrolls-Qumran connection. For example, the tables found in the scribe's room at Qumran do not seem to be the right kind to have been used for writing manuscripts. There were no artifacts or pieces of parchment that might have proved that the room was, in fact, used by scribes. Finally, Qumran's was not an all-male society such as that described by Pliny; graves of females have been excavated there. For these and other reasons, Golb makes the case that the Dead Sea Scrolls did not come from Qumran.

These manuscripts stem from first-century Palestinian Jews and are remnants of a literature showing a wide variety of practices, beliefs and opinions which was removed from Jerusalem before or during the siege,

> brought down to the Judaean wilderness and adjacent areas, and there, with the aid of inhabitants of the region, successfully hidden away for long periods of time.[19]

The threat of a Roman invasion must have been a great concern to the residents of Jerusalem. It is reasonable to postulate, as Golb has done, that many valuables, including religious writings and other documents, would have been removed and hidden from the approaching Roman army. The remote caves along the Dead Sea were ideal places to store these treasures safely. Indeed, it is interesting to note that a unique copper scroll found in one of the caves actually contains a list of where various treasures were hidden. Eventually, as feared, Jerusalem was invaded and taken by the Romans in approximately A.D. 70.

Regardless of the narrowness or diversity of their origin, the Dead Sea Scrolls remain of great significance. They have provided a wealth of unprecedented texts from a period ranging from about 200 B.C. to roughly A.D. 70. Other documents found in the caves have extended this time range slightly. Initially controversial, these dates are now widely accepted. The dating estimates are based on comparative studies of the development of Hebrew writing, radiocarbon-dating, and historical considerations. The initial dating of the linen wrapping of the Isaiah Scroll to A.D. 33 +/−200 years was one of the exciting early applications of the radiocarbon technique. As mentioned previously, this period (200 B.C. to A.D. 70) was poorly known to biblical scholars. The scrolls contained the earliest known examples of the Old Testament. One of the interesting findings was that the sum of the basic parts of the Old Testament have not changed much since at least the first century B.C. Nonethess, the scrolls have also revealed that Jewish religious practices of the time were quite varied. In the years following the initial discovery, much popular interest in the scrolls was stimulated by references to the coming of a messiah. While this is true, it is clear that the scrolls do not make any specific reference to the coming of Jesus. In addition, it has been pointed out that the nature and expectations of the messiah referred to in the Dead Sea Scrolls contrasts considerably with the early Christian conceptions. What is interesting is that the data from the scrolls reveals that the belief in the coming of a messiah was both widespread and varied at the turn of that era. From an anthropological perspective it is significant to point out that messianic movements and the appearance of prophets are common occurrences in societies that are under stress, especially as a result of "foreign" domination. Perhaps one of the better-known cases happened in the late 1800s among the Plains Indians when the Ghost Dance religion swept through the area in response to the destruction of the traditional ways of life of the Indians. The movement was started by a prophet who promised that if certain ritual procedures were followed their ancestors along with the great herds of buffalo would return and the white people would be destroyed. In a like manner, the messianic writings of the Dead Sea Scrolls may be a reflection of the turbulent era associated with the advent of the Romans as well as other factors. One of the scrolls known as the "War of the Sons of Light against the Sons of Darkness" is concerned with an ultimate war of salvation against the key biblical enemies of Israel. In this war, the Sons of Light, with the assistance of God, were destined to win. Like the Ghost Dance, proper rituals and procedures had to be followed to ensure success. Another scroll called the "Manual of Discipline" contains the very strict rules and rituals of a religious sect, presumed to have been the Essenes. This sect despised the Sons of Darkness. Violation of the rules resulted in long periods of isolation. Even a relatively minor infraction such as inappropriate laughter could result in a month of isolation. More severe punishment for serious offenses such as slander could include banishment from the community.

While the Dead Sea Scrolls are widely considered among the most important archaeological finds ever made, the complete significance of the scrolls will not be fully understood until the basic data are made available to a wide range of scholars. As surprising as it may seem, a great many of them are simply unavailable for scrutiny by scholars.[20] This is remarkable, given the great amount of time that has elapsed since the discoveries were made. Following the discoveries, an international committee of scholars was charged with the publication of the scrolls. This committee had exclusive rights to publication, even to the point where a member could will his rights to another scholar after death! Other qualified researchers could not see the unpublished material housed in the Rockefeller Museum in Jerusalem. Most members of the committee have moved at a snail's pace in publishing the finds. Ironically, one of the scholars who forged ahead and published his results quickly was heavily criticized for making significant errors. This situation has received much attention in the press and there seems to be some gradual movement toward rectifying the problem. By contrast, imagine what our knowledge of human evolution might be like if Dart had not allowed anyone to see *Australopithecus* and debate the issues!

HAMMURABI'S LAWS

Next to the Dead Sea Scrolls, the law code of King Hammurabi of Babylon is probably one of the best known of ancient documentary finds. In it is the famous passage about "an eye for an eye, a tooth for a tooth." The Code of Hammurabi was written in cuneiform about 1750 B.C. on a black piece of diorite about seven feet long. These types of standing stone monuments are called *stelae*. At the top, above the columns of writing, there is a bas-relief of the king receiving instructions directly from the sun-god and guardian of justice, Shamash, to establish a code of laws. In addition to the laws there is a prologue and an epilogue. The prologue extols the power and virtues of Hammurabi, while the epilogue blesses those who follow the laws and resoundly curses those who violate them or who attempt to change them. The curses include hunger, destruction, and death. Hammurabi was a very influential king who was successful in warfare. Quite possibly, the stele with the law code was erected in one of the conquered areas as a testimony of his power. In any event, it is assumed to have been taken by the Elamites as war booty during one of their military campaigns into Babylon and was brought back to their capital at Susa in southwestern Iran. This was about 500 years after Hammurabi's reign. It is uncertain why the Elamites bothered to carry this heavy Babylonian monument across many miles of desert. Perhaps an answer to this question is reflected in the fact that some of the lines on the monument have been deliberately removed. I wonder if the Elamites did this in order to demonstrate publically their own power over their enemies. On the other hand, it is possible that they brought it back out of interest and curiosity, much in same way that Egyptian monuments were taken back to Europe following Napoleon's campaign.

While the specific site where the stele was originally erected is unknown, it was eventually discovered during December of 1901 and January of 1902 when Susa was being excavated by the French archaeologist M. de Morgan. This was during the general time when biblical sites were beginning to be unearthed in the Near East. Ironically, the law code, which was originally moved from Babylonia to the Elamite capital, was once again moved, this time to the Louvre in Paris, where it remains.

The discovery of the law code of Hammurabi was a sensational find. For many years, it was the oldest law code known. It is now known that there are even earlier Mesopotamian law codes that go back to about 2100 B.C.,[21] but the Code of Hammurabi is the most complete of the early codes. The discovery was especially exciting because it extended the knowledge of early legal systems to the period before the ancient Greeks and Romans. As such, the find was of major importance to scholars interested in the nature and development of law in early civilizations. For the first time, they could closely scrutinize what the laws were like in a pre-Classical civilization. In addition, the law code provided the first comparative data base for the study of biblical laws. It was immediately apparent that there were some close parallels with certain of the laws in the Old Testament. The fact that Hammurabi's laws were earlier meant that scholars could now explore some of the roots of the biblical laws as well as see how they contrasted with those of the Babylonians. Shortly after the law code was discovered, it was translated by Father Vincent Scheil and several other workers. The quickness with which the basic data was made available contrasts sharply with the situation described for the Dead Sea Scrolls. As early as 1903, the year following the discovery, there was already a major comparative study by the English biblical scholar Stanley A. Cook. His book was titled *The Laws of Moses and the Code of Hammurabi*. In it, Cook examined one of the major questions engendered by the discovery of the law code: Were the laws of Moses directly derived from the Babylonians? After extensive comparisons, he concluded that the similarities were due to a common Semitic heritage, rather than that the biblical laws were derived directly from the Babylonians.

Altogether, there are about 300 laws on the stele, of which about 262 are well enough preserved to be classified.[22] The laws cover an array of topics, ranging from adultery to medical malpractice. A casual analysis reveals that about 65 percent of the classified material can be grouped into one of the following categories:

- rental of property and hiring (boat rentals, hiring an ox, etc.): 34 laws
- marriage, divorce, adultery, incest: 29
- inheritance of property: 20
- interest payment, borrowing, and debt: 20
- fights, beatings: 19
- theft: 16
- farming, irrigation: 12
- medical operations (human and veterinary): 11

This summary gives us a quick impression of some of the chief legal concerns of the state. Of course there are many other areas covered by the laws, such as murder, military problems, business disputes, and the purchase of slaves.

The consequences of breaking the law were also quite varied, ranging from death and mutilation to fines of grain or money and loss of property. The particular punishment not only depended upon the crime, it was also influenced strongly by the relative status of both the person committing the crime and the victim. For instance, if a nobleman struck and killed another nobleman's daughter who was pregnant, his own daughter would be killed. If, however, the nobleman struck and killed the pregnant daughter of a commoner, he paid five shekels of silver. This is also seen in medical malpractice laws. "If a physician performed a major operation on a seignior [free man] with a bronze lancet and has caused the seignior's death or he opened up the eye-socket of a seignior and has destroyed the seignior's eye, they shall cut off his hand." However, if the physician killed a slave during an operation, "He shall make good slave for slave."

In spite of the popularity of the phrase "an eye for an eye and a tooth for a tooth." only 0.5 percent of Hammurabi's laws are based literally on paying back physical mutilation in kind. On the other hand, about 14 percent of the laws resulted in capital punishment. The pertinent section on the "eye for an eye" punishment begins with, "If a son had struck his father, they shall cut off his hand." Interestingly, this is less severe than its Old Testament counterpart, which, in Exod. 21:15 states, "Whoever strikes his father or his mother shall be put to death." As suggested in the passage on medical malpractice, Hammurabi was specific.

> If a seignior has destroyed the eye of a member of the aristocracy, they shall destroy his eye. If he has broken a [nother] seignior's bone, they shall break his bone. If he has destroyed the eye of a commoner or broken the bone of a commoner, he shall pay one mina of silver. If he has destroyed the eye of a seignior's slave or broken the bone of a seignior's slave, he shall pay one-half his value. If a seignior has knocked out a tooth of a seignior of his own rank, they shall knock out his tooth. If he has knocked out a commoner's tooth, he shall pay one-third mina of silver.

This sample further illustrates how the law and the various punishments were linked closely to social status. James B. Pritchard, an authority on ancient Near Eastern texts, has made some very interesting points about the Old Testament parallels to this section. In Lev. 24:18–21, the Lord instructs Moses that

> when a man causes a disfigurement in his neighbor, as he has done it shall be done to him, fracture for fracture, eye for eye, tooth for tooth; as he has disfigured a man he shall be disfigured.

But in Exod. 21:26–27, we note that

> when a man strikes the eye of his slave, male or female, and destroys it, he shall let the slave go free for the eye's sake. If he knocks out the tooth of his slave, male or female, he shall let the slave go free for the tooth's sake.

In other words, biblical punishments were also related to one's status in the community.

Returning the the question posed by Stanley Cook in 1903, we may ask whether there was a direct influence between the Babylonian law code and the Old Testament. Were some of the basic legal ideas developed originally in ancient Babylon? Many writers believe so. On the other hand, some workers are now suggesting that the ideas were introduced even earlier by western Semitic peoples who moved into the area about three centuries before Hammurabi's laws were written.[23]

GILGAMESH AND THE FLOOD STORY

Through the years, archaeologists and biblical scholars have found many similarities in the societies of the ancient Near East, as reflected in comparisons between clay tablets and portions of the Old Testament. Just as some ideas in the Code of Hammurabi were restated in the Bible, the Gilgamesh Epic contains a flood story that is strikingly similar to the account in Genesis. (There are also many significant differences as well.) The Gilgamesh Epic was discovered in the library of King Ashurbanipal (ca. 669–663 B.C.) of Assyria at the site of Kouyounjik. This site is recognized currently as the famous Biblical city of Nineveh. Nineveh's military power was much feared, and the prophet Zephaniah in the Old Testament (Zephaniah 2:13) forecast that the city would be destroyed and turned into "a dry waste like the desert."

Archaeology's role in transforming mounds on the desert landscape from "dry waste" into biblical cities such as Nineveh must be seen as one of its great contributions. These identities are made possible largely by reference to kings' names on clay tablets and cuneiform writing associated with palace sculptures. Archaeology has made the Bible lands come to life in an academic way, even though it cannot prove that the specific miraculous events described in the Bible took place. This is an important distinction.

Sir Austen Henry Layard, one of the most colorful personalitities in the history of Near Eastern archaeology, excavated at Nineveh during the middle of the last century. He followed on the heels of Paul Botta, a Frenchman, who did some initial work at Kouyounjik without much success. Layard was another adventurer-archaeologist, a real-life Hollywood character. At an early age he was influenced by reading the *Arabian Nights*, just as young Heinrich Schliemann had been fascinated with the Troy of the *Iliad*. Layard traveled all over the Middle East sometimes disguised in local attire. His adventures were wild, if indeed they took place in the way he described them. He was robbed at knifepoint and nearly killed on several occasions.

One of my favorite Layard adventures recounts how he was crossing the Tigris River on the local ferry during the flood stage. It was the last boat of the day, and when he noticed some people had arrived at the riverbank after the ferry had left, he urged the boatman to return to pick them up. This act of good will turned out to be a grave mistake. The stranded party consisted of the Cadi of Mosul and his men. Layard relates that he took his customary seat next to the steersman, while the cadi sat below him. The cadi saw this as an insult and said, "Shall the dogs occupy the high places, whilst the true believers have to stand below?"[24] Layard lost his temper and hit the cadi on the head with a stick—harder than he had intended. He was "surprised to see the blood streaming down his face." As the cadi's men started to draw their swords and pistols, Layard jumped into the middle of the crowded boat with split-second timing and grabbed the cadi "by the throat threatening to throw him into the river." The water was flowing at a great rate, so the bluff, backed up by some of Layard's laborers, worked. After this foolhardy crossing of the Tigris, the Pasha of Mosul urged Layard to keep a low profile, but he refused, mounted his horse, and rode through the town. For some time, the situation was very tense and his life was in danger. Luckily, as time passed, the incident was forgotten and Layard continued digging at Kouyounjik.

Many artifacts in the Assyrian Room of the British Museum are the products of Layard's activities at the sites of Nineveh and Nimrud (the biblical Calah). These include huge winged bulls and other Assyrian palace sculptures. The finds created great public interest and were featured items in the British press. Regrettably, however, the colorful Layard was an extemely destructive excavator and, like some others of his time, was interested mainly in recovering spectacular finds as quickly as possible. Nonetheless the biblical landscape began to come to life as the result of his work.

Layard's efforts at Nineveh were followed by further excavations conducted by a variety of teams. As Glyn Daniel, one of the leading authorities on the history of archaeology, has noted, the Middle East soon became fraught with competing archaeological interests, most of them intent on the rapid recovery of sculpture. According to Daniel's description, the work at Kouyounjik epitomizes this deplorable situation. Like a microcosm of part of the colonial world, the site was divided into a British and French section. At one point Hormuzd Rassam, who was working in the British sector in 1853, realized that the French were approaching one of the most promising parts of the site. In a clandestine fashion, he went to the French area at night and worked his men "without stopping, one gang assisting the other," until he beat the French to the discovery of the palace and library of Ashurbanipal.[25] Rassam notes triumphantly, "It was an established rule that whenever one discovered a new palace, no one else could meddle with it, and thus, in my position as the agent of the British Museum, I had secured it for England." (Layard had previously found some tablets at the site.)

Although Rassam did not know this, the clay tablets in the library included the Gilgamesh Epic, which is one of the earliest known hero stories. Other versions found at different sites show that the roots of the Gilgamesh Epic go back to much earlier times in ancient Mesopotamia, at least to the second millennium B.C. In other words, the main theme of the epic was often modified and rewritten to suit the needs of changing times.

When the tablets were first excavated, no one knew how significant they would be. Only a handful of experts could read cuneiform, so the tablets were shipped to the British Museum, where they were studied and translated by George Smith. Smith was a self-educated scholar who came into the exotic field of reading texts from a completely unrelated profession: He had been a bank-note engraver with a flair for the ancient Near East and had worked his way into the job at the British Museum. Smith writes how in 1872, while working in the museum, he had "the good fortune to make a . . . discovery, namely, that of the tablets containing the Chaldean (Babylonian) account of the deluge."[26] While Smith was translating the document, he found that a significant portion of the flood story was missing. Was the missing piece still buried in the dusty layers at Nineveh?

Because the find was of such great interest, a London newspaper funded an expedition headed by Smith to try to locate the missing section. Smith went to the site in 1873 and, almost unbelievably, found the missing piece in less than a week. He tells us how he "sat down to examine the store of fragments of cuneiform inscriptions from the day's digging, taking out and brushing off the earth from the fragments to read their contents." Much to his "surprise and gratification," he found the missing piece, which fit "into the only place where there was a serious blank in the story." (The jealous Rassam later downplayed the find by noting that Smith found it in his "abandoned trenches."[27] Furthermore, he notes that the tablet was not really the missing piece because the writing was in the third person instead of the first person.) After taking his trophy back to England, Smith returned to the area for further digging. This proved to be his undoing, however, as he was stricken by fever and died on the return trip to England. He joins the ranks of Carl Mauch and Lord Carnarvon, both of whom died as a result of their pioneering work.

According to James B. Pritchard, the story of Gilgamesh is the first heroic epic known. In it, Gilgamesh seeks the secret of immortality from Utnapishtim, the counterpart to the biblical Noah. Gilgamesh asks him, "How joinedst thou the Assembly of the gods, in thy question of life?" to which Utnapishtim replies with an account of the great flood.[28] The hero of the flood tells how the gods instructed him to build a ship in order to save his life. "Aboard the ship take thou the seed of all living things." Utnapishtim is then given specific instructions on how to build the ship, including its measurements and the kind of caulking to be used. While its specific details differ from those in the Genesis account (e.g. six decks versus three in the biblical version), the general similarities are so striking that they cannot be due to chance. The number seven figures prominently in both accounts. Utnapishtim's boat took seven days to build, while Noah was warned that the flood would come in seven days. Utnapishtim, just like Noah, relates that he took all of his "family and kin" and the "beasts of the field, the wild creatures of the field." The gods unleashed the heavens and the flood waters destroyed everything. Utnapishtim's ship stopped eventually at Mount Nisr. This, of course, runs parallel to Noah's Ark landing on Mount Ararat. Both Noah and Utnapishtim released birds to see if the flood waters had receded and land were present. Both men released a raven and a dove, though Utnapishtim also released a swallow. Utnapishtim's dove "went forth, but came back; since no resting-place for it was visible, she turned round." Noah "sent forth a dove from him, to see if the waters had subsided from the face of the ground; but the dove found no place to set her foot, and she returned to him to the ark, for the waters were still on the face of the whole earth" (Gen. 8:8–10). Following the voyage, Utnapishtim pours a libation to the gods and sets up cult vessels, while Noah "offered burnt offerings on the altar" (Gen. 8:20). "After the flood Noah lived three hundred and fifty years; and he died" (Gen. 9:28–29). Utnapishtim got a better deal. Enlil, one of the prominent gods, was "filled with wrath" to learn that Utnapishtim survived the flood. He thundered, "No man was supposed to survive the destruction." The solution to this oversight was to grant Utnapishtim immortality.

The Babylonian flood story is substantially older than the biblical account in terms of its ultimate roots. In fact most authorities believe that the Old Testament version is based on the earliest Babylonian account and was modified to suit the new monotheistic beliefs of the time. This naturally raises the questions of whether there really was a flood and, if so, whether it can be identified archaeologically.

Some of the key evidence centers on the ancient Babylonian site of Ur and the excavations of Sir Leonard Woolley. Ur is situated not far from the lower Euphrates valley, about 200 miles from the Persian Gulf. Woolley was keenly interested in relating Ur to the Bible. A list of Sumerian kings refers to "the flood" as a major event in the history of the area, accounting for a significant break in the sequence of rulers. In the list is found the passage, "The flood came. After the flood came, kingship again was sent down from on high."[29]

According to Max Mallowan, the Mesopotamian flood is best dated to about 2900 B.C. in this list.[30]

One of the many interesting problems that the work at Ur could shed light on was whether there were any traces of this flood. The evidence was first uncovered in 1929, when one of Woolley's workmen was excavating below the Royal Cemetery of Ur (famous for its gold and human sacrifices) in an effort to get to the bottom of the deeply stratified mound, or tell (about sixty-four feet thick). The small test pit exposed a thick layer of "only clean water-laid mud . . ." which was sterile but had other cultural material underlying it.[31] Woolley, interested in the reaction of others, showed the evidence to his wife, who replied, "Well, of course, it's the Flood." Woolley responded, "That was the right answer."

During the next season, he expanded the excavation area to get a better view of the flood deposits and see if he was really correct in his interpretation. The silt layer that was exposed was "about eleven feet in thickness" and was identified as resulting from an overflow of the Euphrates River, currently about eleven miles from the site. Woolley concluded that such a great thickness of silt would have been produced by "a flood not less than twenty-five feet deep; in the flat, low-lying land of Mesopotamia a flood of that depth would cover an area about three hundred miles long and a hundred miles across . . ." He goes on to note that this would have leveled virtually everything in the area, causing massive loss of life. If such a flood did occur, it certainly would have provided a basis for writing the famous account.

Yet the interpretation and dating of the sediments at Ur have been questioned seriously, and there is really no convincing archaeological evidence that a flood covered the whole region. In order to demonstrate that such a flood took place, it would be necessary to correlate the stratigraphy and dating from many sites spread throughout the area. This is a standard archaeological procedure used in demonstrating regional, or large-scale, geological sequences. Such widespread paleoenvironmental correlations simply do not exist for the period concerned in Mesopotamia or for other parts of the biblical world. On the other hand, there is evidence for local flooding at different sites and at different times.[32] Perhaps some unknown localized flood along the Euphrates valley was the basis for the ancient Mesopotamian flood story, which, in turn, gave rise to the biblical account. An important point to stress here is that, while locally devastating floods must have occurred, there is no archaeological support for those particular events described in the flood stories such as the launching of an ark loaded with all living things.

The story of a great flood is not restricted to the Ancient Near East. Flood myths are found in Asia, in the Pacific islands, among Native American groups, and in many other societies. Explanations for the widespread occurrence of flood myths have been both varied and imaginative. Folklore expert Alan Dundes of the University of California at Berkeley has noted that some early workers believed that the stories diffused from a single source, while others argued that the widely distributed myths were the result of what has been called the psychic unity of humankind. This concept holds that certain underlying psychological themes are shared in common by all peoples. Thus, unusual similarities seen in the myths of culturally distinct and geographically separated peoples can be explained. Dundes also points out that some explanations have been psychologically based. Roheim, for example, saw the flood myths rooted in dreams where the flood water, in some cases, is actually described as urine. In this theory, the basis of the dream is the prevalent experience of nocturnal bladder pressure while sleeping! In a different approach, Dundes has argued that the flood myths are almost exclusively dominated by males. In other words, the stories often center on men such as Noah and Utnapishtim, the Babylonian hero, as well as males in other versions. According to Dundes, the stories feature the destruction and the re-creation of the world. He concludes that they can be interpreted as male creation myths.

Many people have interpreted the biblical flood story literally and have searched for the remains of the biblical ark, but no one has produced indisputable evidence that it exists.[33] The lure of the ark continues to attract people who are neither archaeologists nor historians. For example, in 1986 James Irwin, a former astronaut and veteran moon-walker, launched his fourth expedition to Mt. Ararat, the landing place for the ark. News reports have stated that he was detained and released by Turkish police, who were suspicious that he was using the Noah's Ark search as a front for spying in a politically sensitive area.[34] Subsequently, Irwin decided not to continue his quest for the ark. However, others have continued the search. In September

1989 two people, while flying past Mt. Ararat, sighted what they believed was the remains of the ark lying at an elevation of over 14,000 feet. Mt. Ararat, a 16,950-foot rugged, snow-capped peak (actually, there are two peaks) in Armenia, is situated near the border of the Soviet Union and Turkey. *Ararat* may, in fact, have originally been a word that meant "highlands."[35] Later the name was given to the specific mountain in Armenia in an ex post facto way in order to fit the biblical story. There is no direct, unbroken, ancient historical tradition that clearly links and identifies that particular mountain as the one described in Genesis.

Of the many "expeditions" in search of the ark, those led by Fernand Navarra, a Frenchman, are the most interesting from an archaeological point of view. From out of the glacial ice, just a few hundred feet from the top of windswept Ararat, Navarra recovered some pieces of wood above the timberline, where they could not have occurred naturally. Subsequently he wrote a book entitled *Noah's Ark, I touched it*. Did he really find the ark? Navarra's wood samples were radiocarbon-dated by some of the most widely used and respected labs in the business. Unfortunately five of the dates cluster to between the sixth and ninth centuries A.D., while another one (the earliest) dates to between the third and fourth centuries A.D.[36] Of course these dates are all far too recent to pertain to events generally assumed to have taken place prior to the second millennium B.C. What, then, is the origin of the wood? R. E. Taylor and Rainer Berger, two radiocarbon-dating experts, speculate that the wood might actually have come from a religious memorial, built in the years prior to the Islamic conquest of the area to commemorate where people thought the ark landed.

CONCLUSION

In these pages, I have followed the frontier beneath the earth in many directions. The journey has been quite varied, and no doubt some interesting cases have been missed. Along the way there have been some unusually interesting and strong-willed personalities, most notably pioneers such as Dubois, Schliemann, Leakey and others, who pursued their dreams relentlessly in the face of great opposition. In some cases, such as those of Schlieman, Champollion, and Layard, the seeds of the discoveries were sown at an early age; it seems remarkable that any one discipline can boast so many outstanding examples of this happening. The story of these discoveries has been replete with amazing adventures, ranging from confrontations with rattlesnakes and bandits to being lost in the jungle. Fortunately for archaeologists, such adventures are the exception. Most of our work goes on with relatively few mishaps.

In telling the tales of these scientific pioneers, I have diligently tried to capture the actual *moment* of discovery. Wherever possible, I have done this by letting the discoverers speak for themselves. In most cases, there was great excitement, ranging from Howard Carter's first view of "wonderful things" in King Tutankhamen's tomb to Hiram Bingham's view of Machu Picchu and the comment, "Would anyone believe what I had found." At the discovery of Lascaux cave, it was Marcel Ravidat exclaiming, "Our joy was beyond description." Then there was the find of Lucy, with Donald Johnanson and Tom Gray "jumping up and down" and "howling and hugging" in the desert heat of the Afar. This is only a partial recapitulation, but it serves to highlight the feeling of awe that was coupled with such exuberance that it seems to freeze time for the discoverer.

Another major concern of mine was the *process* of discovery, ranging from sheer accident, as at Altamira and Little Salt Spring, to the deliberate following of clues, as in the King Tut adventure. In some cases, as in the research on the origins of cuneiform, it was refreshing to see how investigators working in one area unintentionally shed important new light on other areas. Of course most of the day-to-day discoveries made in archaeology do not occur in such ways. They are usually the result of carefully planned surveys.

Lastly, in addition to the processes and moments of discovery, the *impact* of the finds was of great significance, too. In almost every frontier area, ranging from human-origins research to manuscript discoveries, there have been outstanding examples of major controversies regarding the interpretations of finds. Heated arguments surrounded Altamira, *Australopithecus afarensis*, Zimbabwe, and a host of other finds. In some cases, such as in the early interpretations of the Neandertals and the lake dwellings, erroneous points of view became so widely accepted that they persisted for years before they were challenged effectively and demonstrated as being obsolete. It is always easy to look back and ask how people could have been so stubborn and irrational, yet old ideas are often made of surprisingly strong stuff. Thus it is encouraging to note that archaeological work proceeds in an atmosphere conducive to open debate, an atmosphere in which ideas will be verified, rejected, or modified on the basis of how well they are supported by evidence.

I have found it especially satisfying to have begun *Stones, Bones, and Ancient Cities* with an account of human origins and to have finished it with the great flood story in Gilgamesh. This order contains an ironic twist that I did not anticipate originally but that fell into place quite naturally. It was Boucher de Perthes, the persistent French customs agent, who provided one of the greatest breakthroughs in human-origins research by demonstrating, in the face of great opposition, that stone tools were associated with extinct animals in the

Somme River deposits at Abbeville. De Perthes had essentially challenged the literal acceptance of the flood story in the Book of Genesis. No longer could science accept that the world was created in 4004 B.C. and that the flood followed somewhat later. This conclusion paved the way for the discovery of the many human-fossil finds that would follow, culminating in such finds as Lucy and *Homo habilis*. At the other end of the frontier, archaeology has discovered the roots of the Genesis flood story in the Gilgamesh Epic and earlier Mesopotamian accounts. The fact that archaeology could be instrumental in demolishing the chronological context of the biblical flood while discovering its literary origins by employing the same critical methods stands as a powerful testimony to the extreme breadth of its contributions.

Which discoveries have been the greatest? Was it de Perthes' breakthrough, the discovery of King Tutankhamen's tomb, the use of flotation methods, the decipherment of Egyptian hieroglyphics, the discovery of *Australopithecus*, or some other find? No doubt all of these would rank high for good, but varied, reasons. It could be argued, for example, that flotation is making a much greater contribution to archaeology than King Tut's tomb, yet this would be an outrageous statement to make from the point of view of public impact. Quite obviously, no long lines will form to see mud and fragments of wheat and barley grains. As just implied, however, the significance of finds depends on the interests and attitudes of whoever is making the judgments. Thus, in human-origins research, de Perthes' breakthrough and the discovery of *Australopithecus* would surely top my list. Both have revolutionized the state of the art. But I would be hesitant to compare them to finds in Egyptology or some other area.

Some of the greatest discoveries that are made may, in fact, be the day-to-day mundane finds that are "bagged" by archaeologists, which generally excite only a small audience and are featured in obscure journals that are great dust collectors in libraries. These finds are the real building blocks of information through which normal advances in knowledge are made. In final analysis, what is important is that the respective discoveries have had a profound influence on advancing the state of knowledge in a particular area. And what is more important is that the work is still going on. The frontiers remain wide open.

Some Key Discovery Dates

1763	Ruins of Pompeii identified
1822	Rosetta Stone deciphered
1854	Swiss lake dwellings discovered
1859	De Perthes' associations between stone tools and extinct animals verified
1868	Troy located
1871	Ruins of Zimbabwe found
1872	Flood story in Gilgamesh Epic deciphered
1874	Work begins at Mycenae
1879	Altamira cave art discovered
1891	*Pithecanthropus erectus (Homo erectus)* first found in Java
1899	Ancient Chinese oracle bones discovered
1901	Code of Hammurabi discovered
1902–03	Cave art of Altamira accepted as authentic
1904–11	Chichén Itzá Well of Sacrifice probed
1911	Ruins of Machu Picchu discovered
1911	Olduvai Gorge discovered
1923	Tomb of Tutankhamen discovered
1924	Frozen Scythian tombs investigated
1925	Dart describes the Taung child, *Australopithecus africanus*

1928	Shang Dynasty capital at Anyang discovered
1929	First Peking skull found
1939	Sutton Hoo ship burial excavated
1940	Lascaux cave art discovered
1943	Aqualung invented
1946–47	Dead Sea Scrolls discovered
1949	Radiocarbon-dating technique invented
1951	Shanidar Cave discovered
1956	Skudelev Viking ships excavated
1959	Little Salt Spring Paleoindian site discovered
1959	*Zinjanthropus (A. boisei)* discovered at Olduvai
1963	Flotation method applied to Neolithic sediments in Iran
1963	Stonehenge astronomical implications "decoded"
1969	Oldest African rock art discovered at Apollo 11 cave, Namibia
1970	*Mary Rose* rediscovered
1972	East Turkana *Homo habilis* (skull 1470) discovered in Kenya
1974	Skeleton of Lucy found in Afar Triangle, Ethiopia
1974	Buried clay army of Qin-Shi-Huang found
1977	Oldest hominid footprints found, Laetoli, Tanzania
1984	Most complete *Homo erectus* skeleton found, west of Lake Turkana
1985	Oldest *Australopithecus boisei* skull found, west of Lake Turkana

Time Perspective

A.D. DATES

1548	Sinking of the *Mary Rose*
1450	Machu Picchu
1380	Zimbabwe
900–1200	Cahokia, Mississippian culture
850–1150	Chaco Canyon, Anasazi culture
950–1050	Skudelev Viking ships
800–1539	Chichén Itzá, Well of Sacrifice
624	Sutton Hoo ship burial
79	Destruction of Pompeii and Herculaneum

B.C. DATES

A.D. 70– 200 B.C.	Dead Sea Scrolls
196	Rosetta Stone
206	Buried clay army of Qin-Shi-Huang
300	Namoratunga
430	Pazyryk, frozen Scythian tombs

669–663 and earlier versions	Gilgamesh Epic, flood story
1250	Troy, Homeric city
1350	Tutankhamen's tomb
1111–1384	Shang Dynasty capital at Anyang
1750–1792	Code of Hammurabi
1111–2900	Stonehenge
1500–3000	Gwisho hot springs
2000–3000	Swiss lake dwellings
3500–7500	Neolithic clay tokens
6000–7500	Early Neolithic wheat at Deh Luran, Iran
12,300	Little Salt Spring
13,550	Altamira cave art
15,000	Lascaux cave art
27,000	Apollo 11 art
60,000	Shanidar Neandertal burials (flower burial)
400,000	Peking skulls (*Homo erectus*) at Zhoukoudian, earliest
900,000	*Pithecanthropus erectus (Homo erectus)* of Java
1,500,000 (continues to at least **200,000)**	Acheulian stone-tool tradition
1,600,000	West Turkana *Homo erectus* skeleton
1,750,000	*Zinjanthropus (A. boisei)*, Olduvai Gorge
1,800,000	East Turkana *Homo habilis* skull 1470
2,000,000	Taung child, *Australopithecus africanus*
2,000,000	Oldowan stone tools
2,500,000	Oldest *Australopithecus boisei* skull, west Turkana
2,900,000	Lucy, *Australopithecus afarensis*
3,700,000	Laetoli hominid footprints
4,000,000	Awash hominid fossil fragments
5,500,000	Lothagam hominid fragment

Notes

CHAPTER 1

1. Boucher de Perthes, 1860, in Heizer, 1969: 103.
2. Darwin, 1871: 521.
3. Dubois, 1898.
4. Hrdlicka, 1930, page 45.
5. The following quotes are from G.H.R. von Koenigswald, 1947, page 15.
6. Rukang and Shenglong, 1983. For a discussion of dating techniques, see B.M. Fagan, 1985, *In the Beginning* (ch. 7), Little, Brown and Co., Boston.
7. Brain, C. K. and A. Sillen, 1988.
8. Dart, R. A., 1925, quotes from pages 195 and 198.
9. Keith, Arthur, 1925, quotes from page 11.
10. The quotations on Broom's work are from Broom and Schepers, 1946, page 46.
11. Reck, Hans, 1933, quotes from pages 20, 46, and 49.
12. Leakey, 1937, page 297.
13. See Pat Shipman, 1986, "Scavenging or Hunting in Early

Hominids: Theoretical Framework and Tests," *American Anthropologist*, 88:27–43.

14. The cranial capacity of the 1470 skull is from Walker and Leakey, 1978.

15. Wilford, J.N., 1984, provides an initial account of the find. For more complete data see Brown et al., 1985.

16. Johanson and Edey, 1981, quotes from pages 155, 16–17.

17. For detailed discussion, see Johanson and White, 1979.

18. Lewin, 1983b.

19. Lewin, 1983a; see also Johanson and Edey, 1981: 166 for background.

20. Johanson et al., 1987.

21. Leakey, M. D. and J. M. Harris, 1987.

22. Robbins, L. M., 1987.

CHAPTER 2

1. Radiocarbon-dating, the most important dating method used in archaeology, was discovered by Willard Libby at the University of Chicago in 1949. It is based on the principle that all organisms take in radioactive carbon from the atmosphere. When they die, the radiocarbon decays at a known and measurable rate. When the technique was being developed, samples included wood from an Egyptian boat of known age. The radiocarbon date and the historically known age for the boat were in close agreement. Charcoal from hearths is the most commonly used substance for dating; only a small amount is necessary. The technique can provide dates as old as about 70,000 years ago, though most dates are within the last 45,000 years. For further reading, see Brian M. Fagan, *In The Beginning*, 1985 (ch. 7), Little, Brown and Co., Boston.

2. Graziosi, 1960, page 17.

3. Breuil and Obermaier, 1935, page 5.

4. Rivière, 1897: 313–14.

5. Cartailhac, the following translated quotes are from pages 350 and 354.

6. Conkey, 1981.

7. See Leroi-Gourhan, 1982, pages 12–13.

8. See Leroi-Gourhan, 1982, pages 46–50, for percentages of other animals.
9. Leroi-Gourhan, 1968.
10. Marshack, 1972.
11. Forbes and Crowder, 1979.
12. See P. Ucko and A. Rosenfeld, 1967.
13. Breuil, 1952, page 176.
14. See Ucko and Rosenfeld, 1967.
15. Casteret, 1924, page 131.
16. Ucko and Rosenfeld, 1967.
17. Bataille, 1955, quotes from page 137.
18. Arlette Leroi-Gourhan, 1982.
19. Bataille, 1955, page 136.
20. Arlette Leroi-Gourhan, 1982.
21. Leroi-Gourhan, 1968.
22. Barrow, 1802, page 226.
23. Wendt, 1976.
24. Thackeray et al., 1981.
25. Lewis-Williams, 1981.
26. Lewis-Williams, 1981, page 93.

CHAPTER 3

1. Trinkaus, 1978.
2. Solecki, 1971, quotes from pages 68 and 196.
3. Arlette Leroi-Gourhan, 1975, quotes from pages 562 and 563.
4. Radloff, 1893, translated quotes from pages 108–109.
5. Rudenko, 1970, is the primary reference on Pazyryk in English.
6. Rudenko, 1970, page 221.
7. Artamonov, 1965, page 239.
8. Herodotus, Book IV, page 264.
9. Herodotus, Book IV, page 266.
10. See Phillips, 1965.
11. See Hopkirk in Bruce-Mitford, 1975.
12. Quotes from Brown in Bruce-Mitford, 1974, pages 156, 158.

13. Phillips quotes are from his excavation diary contained in Bruce-Mitford, 1975, pages 737 and 741.

14. Quotes from Munro Chadwick, 1940, page 76.

15. Bruce-Mitford, 1979.

16. Blackstone, 1765–69, book 1, page 285.

17. Bruce-Mitford, 1975, ch. xi describes the Inquest. Phillips quote is from this section on page 722.

18. Tung in K. C. Chang, 1980, page 45 for both quotes. See Chang, 1980, and Li Chi, 1977, for additional reading on the Shang dynasty.

19. Chang, 1980.

20. Zheng, 1984; the following quote is from page 69.

21. Chou, 1979, page 149.

22. Zheng, 1984.

23. Qian description is from Swart and Till, 1984.

24. Stature estimates from Audrey Topping and Yang Hsein-Min, 1978, "China's Incredible Find," *National Geographic*, Vol. 153:439–59.

25. Nianlun, 1984, page 39 for both quotes.

26. Carter and Mace, 1977, pages 58–59.

27. Quote from Carter and Mace, 1977, pages 26–27.

28. Quotes from Carter and Mace, 1977, pages 82 and 83.

29. Hoving, 1978.

30. Carter and Mace, 1977, quotes from pages 85, 86, 89, and 96.

31. See Carter, 1963, Vol. 2, ch. vi, for a description of the process as recorded by Herodotus.

32. Carter, 1963, Vol. 2, quotes from pages 45 and 78.

33. Leek, 1972.

34. Hoving, 1978.

35. See Hoving, 1978, page 227 for the quotes regarding the curse and an excellent discussion of it.

36. See Hoving's 1978 masterful discussion of the political turmoil.

37. Hoving, 1978, page 299.

38. Carter, 1963, Vol. 2, page xii.

CHAPTER 4

1. Schliemann, 1880, contains his autobiography; quotes are from pages 3 and 9.

2. See Brackman, 1974, for an interesting discussion of this point.

3. Schliemann, 1880, page 17.

4. Quotes are from Schliemann, 1880, pages 19 and 20.

5. See Lilly, 1961, and Brackman, 1974, for further discussion.

6. Quotes from Schliemann, 1880, pages 22, 23, and 25.

7. Schliemann, 1875, page 203.

8. See Wood, 1985, for a comprehensive review of the issue. Dörpfeld also believed that Troy VI was the Homeric city.

9. Quotes are from Schliemann, 1875, pages 323 and 332–33. See Brackman, 1974, for discussion.

10. Meyer, 1936, page 132; quoted in Easton, 1981.

11. Brackman, 1974.

12. Quote from Schliemann, 1878, *Mycenae*, page 296.

13. See Michael Wood, 1985, page 70, for further discussion.

14. Pliny quotes are from Brion, 1960, pages 29–30.

15. Prinz, 1979.

16. Corti, 1951.

17. Deiss, 1966.

18. Deiss, 1966; Corti, 1951.

19. Gore, 1984.

20. Corti, 1951.

21. Corti, 1951.

22. See Corti, 1951, for discussion of this during the year 1826.

23. Grant, 1971.

24. See Gore, 1984, or ch. xvii of the revised version of J.J. Deiss, *Herculaneum*, Harper & Row, N.Y., 1985.

25. References to the graffiti follow in the order quoted, Corti, 1951, page 60; Lindsay, 1960, pages 181 and 184; Corti, 1951, pages 42 and 58; Lindsay, 1960, pages 30–31; D'Avino, n.d., page 16. The final quote regarding the nettle was slightly modified from Lindsay, 1960, page 244.

26. Bibby, 1956, page 4.

27. For further description of Zimbabwe, see Garlake, 1973.

28. Elkiss, 1979, page 20.

29. Haggard, 1964, page 20.

30. Mauch quotes are from E. E. Burke, 1969, *The Journals of Carl Mauch 1869 to 1872*, National Archives of Rhodesia, Salisbury.

31. News quote from Edward Bacon, *The Great Archaeologists*, Bobbs-Merrill Co., N.Y., 1976, page 43 ("The Ophir of Scripture").

32. Mauch in E. E. Burke, page 234.

33. See Summers, 1963, for discussion.

34. Bent, 1893, quotes from pages, v–vi, 5, 95, 184, and 244.

35. Wallace, 1936, page 10.

36. The poster is reproduced in Garlake, 1973.

37. Gayre, 1972.

38. Garlake, 1973.

39. See Huffman, 1981.

40. Garlake, 1982, page 13.

41. Jett, 1978.

42. Von Däniken, 1972, page 17 for this quote and the next one.

43. Quotes are from Kosok, 1947, pages 202 and 203.

44. Prescott, 1847, Vol. 1, page 370.

45. S. Chávez, personal communication.

46. Bingham, 1948, page 102.

47. Bingham, 1948, page 166.

48. Hemming, 1981.

49. Dearborn et al., 1987.

50. Hammer, 1984.

CHAPTER 5

1. Keller, 1878, quotes from pages 489 and 490.

2. Heer, 1878.

3. Keller, 1878, page 469.

4. Chantres discussion is found in Keller, 1878.

5. Bocquet, 1979.

6. Bocquet, 1979.

7. De Landa quote is found next to the frontispiece in Thompson, 1932.

8. Thompson, 1932, page 271.

9. Stephens, 1843, page 182.

10. Quotes are from Thompson, 1932, pages 40, 105, 269, 270, and 272.

11. Coggins et al., 1984.

12. Morley, 1938.

13. Thompson, 1932, pages 281–82.

14. Romero, 1972.

15. Coggins et al., 1984.

16. Cappuzzo, 1984.

17. Clausen et al., 1979; Holman and Clausen, 1984.

18. Clausen et al., 1979.

19. Quotes from Olsen and Crumlin-Pedersen, 1978, page 20.

20. Olsen and Crumlin-Pedersen, 1978.

21. Account of P. Carew in M. Rule, 1982, page 38.

22. See McKee, 1982.

23. The quotes that follow are found in McKee, 1982, pages 44, 73 (Clark), 64, 70–71 (Bullivent), and 85.

24. Evershed et al., 1985.

25. Rule, 1982, page 189.

26. Rule, 1982.

27. Fagan and Van Noten, 1971.

28. Struever, 1968, page 353.

29. Helbaek, 1969, quotes are on page 385 (in Hole, Flannery, and Neely, 1969).

30. Conard et al., 1984, page 444.

31. Chomko and Crawford, 1978.

CHAPTER 6

1. Renfrew, 1973.

2. Pitts, 1982.

3. See Atkinson, 1981, for details of periods of construction and dating.

4. Quotes from Petrie, 1880, pages 18, 19.

5. For criticism of Hawkins' views, see C. Chippindale's *Stonehenge Complete*, 1983, Cornell University Press.

6. Hawkins and White, 1965, quotes from pages 92, 105, and 107.

7. Atkinson, 1966.

8. For another example of a megalithic site with astronomical alignments, see A. Burl, "The Recumbent Stone Circles of Scotland," *Scientific American*, 245: 66–72.

9. Lynch and Robbins, 1978.

10. Simmons, 1942, pages 58–59.

11. Reyman, 1976.

12. Quotes from Sofaer et al., 1979, pages 284 and 286.

13. Zeilek, 1985.

14. Reyman, 1980.

15. Fowler, 1969.

16. Reed, 1969.

17. Gregg, 1975.

18. Wittry, 1977.

19. White, J. R., 1987.

20. Muller, 1978, page 317.

21. Heinzelin, 1962.

22. Marshack, 1972, page 16.

23. See Lewin, 1989 and Marshack, 1989.

CHAPTER 7

1. Schmandt-Besserat, 1978, page 53.
2. Pritchard, 1958, page 149.
3. Schmandt-Besserat, 1981.
4. Bratton, 1967.
5. Turner quote from Budge, 1929, page 28.
6. Ceram, 1980, page 103.
7. Quote from Trever, 1965, page 170.
8. Quotes are from Samuel, 1949, pages 26–27 and 28.
9. See Allegro, 1956.
10. Quotes are from Sukenik, 1955, pages 15, 16, and 17.
11. Trever, 1965, page 26.
12. Albright quote from Trever, 1965, page 85.
13. *Biblical Archaeologist* quote is from Wright, 1948, page 21.
14. Shanks, 1985, page 4. Shanks also notes that the purchase

of the scrolls, which took place in New York, was a "cloak and dagger" operation in which there was an attempt to deceive Metropolitan Samuel regarding who was buying the scrolls.

15. See Shenhav, 1981, for details on the museum. Other scrolls are kept in the Rockefeller Museum in Jerusalem.

16. Golb, 1980.

17. Yadin, 1984.

18. Pliny quote from Golb, 1980, page 12.

19. Golb, 1980, page 11.

20. See Shanks, 1985, for further information and discussion of the issues.

21. See Frymer-Kensky, 1980.

22. All of the laws of Hammurabi quoted here are from Pritchard, 1965 (pages 139–67). I have not broken the laws down by individual numbers as done in Pritchard.

23. See Frymer-Kensky, 1980.

24. Layard, 1903, Vol. 2, page 169.

25. Quotes from Rassam, 1897, pages 25 and 26.

26. Quotes from Smith, 1875, pages 13 and 97.

27. Rassam, 1897, page 53.

28. All of the Gilgamesh quotes are from Pritchard, 1958 (pages 40–75).

29. From Woolley, 1965, Appendix, page 251.

30. Mallowan, 1964, 1977.

31. Woolley, 1965, quotes from pages 27 and 35.

32. Mallowan, 1964.

33. Teeple, 1978.

34. *Lansing State Journal*, 31 August and 15 September 1986.

35. Taylor and Berger, 1980.

36. The radiocarbon dates are in Taylor and Berger, 1980.

Bibliography

CHAPTER 1

Brain, C. K. and A. Sillen. 1988. "Evidence from the Swartkrans cave for the earliest use of fire." *Nature* 336:464–466.

Broom, Robert. 1947. "A new missing-link skull from South Africa." *Natural History* 56:320–23.

Broom, Robert, and G. W. H. Schepers. 1946. *The South African Fossil Ape-Men, The Australopithecinae.* Transvaal Museum Memoir, no. 2. Pretoria.

Brown, Frank, John Harris, Richard Leakey, and Alan Walker. 1985. "Early *Homo erectus* skeleton from West Lake Turkana, Kenya." *Nature* 316:788–92.

Clark, J. D., Behane Asfaw, Getaneh Assefa, J. W. K. Harris, H. Kurashina, R. C. Walter, T. D. White, and Maj. Williams. 1983. "Paleoanthropological discoveries in the Middle Awash Valley, Ethiopia." *Nature* 307:423–28.

Dart, R. A. 1925. "*Australopithecus africanus* The man-ape of South Africa." *Nature* 115:195–99.

Darwin, Charles. 1871. *The Descent of Man.*

Day, M. H. and E. H. Wickens. 1980. "Laetoli Pliocene hominid footprints and bipedalism." *Nature* 286:385–387.

de Perthes, Jacques Boucher. 1850. "On antediluvian man and his works." Translated by R. F. Heizer. 1969. *Man's Discovery of His Past.* Palo Alto, Calif.: Peek Publications. Pg. 103.

Gould, S. J. 1980. "The Piltdown conspiracy." *Natural History* 89: 8–28.

Gowlett, J. A. J., J. W. K. Harris, D. Walton, and B. A. Wood. 1981. "Early archaeological sites, hominid remains and traces of fire from Chesowanja, Kenya." *Nature* 294:125–29.

Haeckel, E. 1866. *Natural History of Creation.*

Hay, R. L. and M. D. Leakey. 1982. "The Fossil Footprints of Laetoli." *Scientific American* 246:50–57.

Howell, F. C., and Y. Coppens. 1976. "An overview of Hominidae from the Omo." *Earliest Man and Environments in the Lake Rudolf Basin.* Chicago: Univ. of Chicago Press.

Hrdlicka, A. 1930. "Skeletal remains of early man." *Smithsonian Miscellaneous Collections* 83:29.

Isaac, G. Ll. 1978. "The food sharing behavior of protohuman hominids." *Scientific American* 238:90–108.

Johanson, D. C., and Maitland Edey. 1981. *Lucy: The Beginnings of Humankind.* New York: Simon and Schuster.

Johanson, D. C., and T. D. White. 1979. "A systematic assessment of early African hominids." *Science* 203:321–29.

Johanson, D. C., F. T. Masao, G. G. Eck, T. D. White, R. C. Walter, W. H. Kimbel, B. Asfaw, P. Manega, P. Ndessokia, and G. Suwa. 1987. "New Partial skeleton of *Homo habilis* from Olduvai Gorge, Tanzania. *Nature* 327:205–209.

Keith, Arthur. 1925. "The Taungs skull." *Nature* 116:11.

Keeley, L. H., and Nicholas Toth, 1981. "Microwear polishes on early stone tools from Koobi Fora, Kenya." *Nature* 297:464–65.

Leakey, L. S. B. 1937. *White Africans.* London: Hodder and Stoughton Ltd.

Leakey, M. D. 1971. *Olduvai Gorge.* Cambridge: Cambridge Univ. Press.

Leakey, M. D., R. L. Hay, G. H. Curtis, R. E. Drake, M. K. Jackes, and T. D. White. 1976. "Fossil hominids from the Laetoli Beds." *Nature* 262:461–66.

Leakey, M. D. And J. M. Harris. 1987. *Laetoli, A Pliocene Site in Northern Tanzania*. Oxford. Clarendon Press.

Lewin, R. 1981. "Ethiopian stone tools are the world's oldest." *Science* 211:806–7.

Lewin, R. 1983a. "Fossil Lucy grows younger, again." *Science* 219: 43–44.

Lewin, R. 1983b. "Ethiopia halts prehistory research." *Science* 219: 147–49.

McHenry, H. M., and R. S. Corruccini. 1980. "Late Tertiary hominoids and human origins." *Nature* 285:397–98.

Reck, Hans. 1933. *Oldoway, die schlicht des urmenschen, die entdeckung des altsteinzeitlichen menschen in Deutsch-ostafrika*. Leipzig: F. A. Brockhaus.

Shipman, Pat, 1986a. "Scavenging or hunting in early hominids: theoretical framework and tests," *American Anthropologist*, 88: 27–43.

Shipman, Pat. 1986b. "Baffling limb on the family tree." *Discover* 87–93.

Theunissen, Bert. 1989. *Eugene Dubois and the Ape-Man from Java*. Dordrecht, Boston, London: Kluwer Academic Publishers.

Robbins, L. H. 1972. "Archeology in the Turkana district, Kenya." *Science* 359–66.

Robbins, Louise, M. 1987. "Hominid footprints from Site G" (pgs. 496–501) in M. D. Leakey and J. M. Harris, eds., *Laetoli, A Pliocene Site in Northern Tanzania*. Oxford: Clarendon Press.

Rukang, Wu, and Lin Shenglong. 1983. "Peking Man." *Scientific American* 248:86–94.

Von Koenigswald, G. H. R. 1947. "Search for Early Man." *Natural History* 56:8–15, 48.

———. 1952. *Meeting Prehistoric Man*. London: Thames and Hudson.

Walker, Alan, and R. E. F. Leakey. 1978. "The hominids of East Turkana." *Scientific American* 239:54–66.

Walker, Alan, R. E. Leakey, J. M. Harris and F. H. Brown. 1986. "2.5 MYR *Australopithecus boise* from west of Lake Turkana, Kenya." *Nature* 322:517–22.

White, T. D. 1980. "Evolutionary implications of Pliocene hominid footprints." *Science* 208:175–76.

Wilford, J. N. 1984. "A strapping youth of eons ago." *The New York Times*, Oct. 19, pg. 1.

CHAPTER 2

Bacon, Edward. 1976. *The Great Archaeologists.* Four *London Illustrated News* articles cited. Indianapolis: Bobbs Merrill Co.

Barrow, J. 1802. *An Account of Travels into the Interior of Southern Africa in the Years 1797 and 1798*, New York: G. F. Hopkins.

Bataille, Georges. 1955. *Lascaux, or, the Birth of Art: Prehistoric Painting.* Switzerland.

Bégouën, Le Comte. 1912. "Les statues d' Argile de la Caverne du Tuc d'Audoubert." *L' Anthropologie* 23:657–65.

Bégouën R., and Jean Clottes. 1987. "Les Trois-Frères after Breuil." *Antiquity* Vol. 61:180–187.

Breuil, Henri. 1952. *Four hundred centuries of Cave Art.* Montignac: Centre d'études et de documentation prehistoriques.

Breuil, H., and Hugo Obermaier. 1935. *The Cave of Altamira at Santillana del Mar, Spain.* Junta de las Cuevas de Altamira. The Hispanic Society of America and the Academia de la historia. Madrid: Tipografia de Archivos.

Carcauzon, C. 1988. "Decouverte de quatre grottes ornees en Perigord," *Archaeologia* 235:16–24.

Cartailhac, Émile. 1902. "Les Cavernes Ornées de dessins, La Grotte d'Altamira, Espagne. Mea culpa d'un sceptique." *L'Anthropologie* 13:348–54.

Casteret, Norbert. 1924. "Discovering the oldest statues in the world." *National Geographic* 46, 2:124–52.

Conkey, M. W. 1980. "The Identification of Prehistoric Hunter-Gatherer Aggregation sites: The Case of Altamira." *Current Anthropology* 21:609–630.

———. 1981. "A century of Paleolithic cave art." *Archaeology* 34:20–28.

De Quiros, F. Bernaldo, and V. Cabrera Valdes. 1982. *El Arte Paleolitico En La Cornisa Cantabrica.* Madrid: Ministerio De Cultura.

Delluc, Brigitte, and Gilles Delluc. 1984. "Lascaux II: a faithful copy." *Antiquity* 58:194–96.

Forbes, Allan Jr., and T. R. Crowder. 1979. "The problem of Franco-Cantabrian abstract signs: agenda for a new approach." *World Archaeology* 10, 3:350–66.

González Echegaray, J. 1985. *Altamira Y Sus Pinturas Rupestres*. Madrid: Ministerio De Cultura.

Graziosi, P. 1960. *Palaeolithic Art*. New York: McGraw Hill.

Lee, R. B. 1967. "Trance cure of the !Kung Bushmen." *Natural History* 86, 9:31–33.

Leroi-Gourhan, André. 1968a. "The evolution of Paleolithic art." *Scientific American* 218, 2:58–70.

———. 1968b. *The Art of Prehistoric Man in Western Europe*. London: Thames and Hudson.

———. 1982. *The Dawn of European Art*. Cambridge: Cambridge University Press.

Leroi-Gourhan, Arlette. 1982. "The archaeology of Lascaux Cave." *Scientific American* 246:104–12.

Lewis-Williams. J. D. 1981, 1983. *Believing and Seeing: Symbolic Meanings in Southern San Rock Paintings*, London: Academic Press.

Lewis Williams, J. D. and T. A. Dowson. 1988. "The Signs of All Times, Entoptic Phenomena in Upper Palaeolithic Art." *Current Anthropology*. Vol. 29, 2:201–245.

Lynch, B. Mark, and R. Donahue. 1980. "A statistical analysis of two rock art sites in northwest Kenya." *Journal of Field Archaeology* 7:74–85.

Marshack, Alexander. 1972. *The Roots of Civilization*. New York: McGraw-Hill.

Rice, P. C., and A. L. Paterson. 1986. "Validating the cave art-archeofaunal relationship in Cantabrian Spain." *American Anthropologist* 88:658–67.

Rivière, Émile. 1897. "La Grotte de la Mouthe (Dordogne)," *Bul. et Mem. de la société d'anthropologie de Paris*. Vol 8, Series 4:302–29.

Thackeray, A. I., J. F. Thackeray, P. B. Beaumont, and J. C. Vogel. 1981. "Dated rock engravings from Wonderwerk Cave, South Africa." *Science* 214:64–67.

Ucko, P. J., and A. Rosenfeld. 1967. *Palaeolithic Cave Art*. New York: McGraw-Hill.

Wendt, W. E. 1976. "Art mobilier from the Apollo 11 Cave, South

West Africa: Africa's oldest dated works of art." *South African Archaeological Bulletin* 21, parts 1 and 2:5–11.

CHAPTER 3

Artamonov, M. I. 1965. Frozen tombs of the Scythians." *Scientific American* 212:101–9.

Brackman, A. C. 1976. *The Search for the Gold of Tutankhamen*. New York: Mason/Charter.

Bruce-Mitford, Rupert. 1974. *Aspects of Anglo-Saxon Archaeology, Sutton Hoo and Other Discoveries* London: Gollancz.

———. 1975. *The Sutton Hoo Ship-Burial*. Vol. 1. Trustees of the British Museum, London: British Museum Publications Ltd.

———. 1979. *The Sutton Hoo Ship-Burial, Reflections after Thirty Years*. Univ. of York, Medieval Monograph Series, 2. York: Ebor Press.

Burghclere, Winifred. 1923. "Introduction." In *The Discovery of the Tomb of Tutankhamen*, by H. Carter and A. C. Mace. Reprint.: New York: Dover Publications, Inc. 1977.

Cann, R. L., Stoneking, M. and A. C. Wilson. 1987. "Mitochondrial DNA and human evolution." *Nature* 325:31–36.

Carter, Howard. 1963. *The Tomb of Tut-Ankh-Amen*. Vols. 2–3. New York: Cooper Square publishers.

Carter, Howard, and A. C. Mace. 1923. *The Discovery of the Tomb of Tutankhamen*. Reprints. New York: Dover Publications, Inc., 1977.

Chang, K. C. 1980. *Shang Civilization*. New Haven: Yale Univ. Press.

Chêng Tê-k'un. 1960. *Archaeology in China*, Vol. II. Shang China, Cambridge: W. Heffer & Sons LTD.

Chou, Hung-hsiang. 1979. "Chinese oracle bones." *Scientific American* 240:135–45.

Gowlett, J. A. J. 1987. "The coming of modern man," *Antiquity* 61:210–219.

Harrold, F. B. 1980. "A comparative analysis of Eurasian Palaeolithic burials." *World Archaeology* 12:195–211.

Herodotus. *The Histories, Book IV*. Translated by Aubrey de Selicourt. 1955. Edinburgh: R. R. Clark Ltd.

Hopkirk, Mary. 1975. "Edith May Pretty: A biographical note." In *The Sutton Hoo Ship Burial*, Vol. I, by R. Bruce-Mitford. London: British Museum Publications Ltd.

Hoving, Thomas. 1978. *Tutankhamen: The Untold Story*. New York: Simon and Schuster.

James, T. G. H. 1979. *An Introduction to Ancient Egypt*. London: British Museum Publications.

Leary, W. E. "Tomb in Peru Yields Stunning Pre-Inca Trove," *The New York Times*. Sept. 14, 1988, pg. 1.

Leek, F. Filce. 1972. *The Human Remains from the Tomb of Tutankhamen*. Tutankhamen Tomb series, vol. 5. Oxford.

Leroi-Gourhan, Arlette. 1975. "The flowers found with Shanidar IV, a Neanderthal burial in Iraq." *Science* 190:562–64.

Li Chi. 1977. *Anyang*. Seattle: Univ. of Washington Press.

Munro, Chadwick, H. 1940. "Who was he?" *Antiquity* 14:76–87.

Nianlun, Hua. 1984. "The first emperor's chariot." *China Reconstructs* 33:34–39.

Phillips, E. D. 1965. *The Royal Hordes: Nomad Peoples of the Steppes*. New York: McGraw-Hill.

Radloff, Wilhelm. 1893. *Aus Siberien*. Leipzig. T. O. Weigel.

Rudenko, S. I. 1970. *Frozen Tombs of Siberia*. London: J. M. Dent Sons.

Solecki, R. S. 1971. *The First Flower People*. New York: Alfred A. Knopf.

Swart, Paula, and Barry D. Till. 1984. "Bronze carriages from the tomb of China's first emperor." *Archaeology* 37:18–25.

Trinkaus, E. 1978. "Hard times among the Neanderthals." *Natural History* 87:58–63.

Zhenxiang, Zheng. 1984. "Yin ruins—grandaddy of Chinese archaeology." *China Reconstructs* 33:66–69.

Zhongyi, Yuan, 1983. *Terra-Cotta Warriors in Armour and Horses at the Tomb of Qin Shi Huang*. Beijing: Cultural Relics Publishing House.

CHAPTER 4

Aveni, A. F. 1986. "The Nazca Lines: patterns in the desert." *Archaeology* 39:33–39.

Bent, T. 1893. *The Ruined Cities of Mashonaland*. 2d ed. London: Longmans, Green and Co.

Bibby, Geoffrey. 1956. *Testimony of the Spade.* New York: Mentor.

Bingham, Hiram. 1913. "The discovery of Machu Picchu." *Harpers Monthly Magazine* 126:709–19.

———. 1930. *Machu Picchu, a Citadel of the Incas.* Report of the explorations and excavations made in 1911, 1912, and 1915. Memoirs of the National Geographic Society. New Haven: Yale Univ. Press.

———. 1948. *Lost City of The Incas* New York: Duell, Sloan and Pearce.

Blegen, C. W. 1963. *Troy and the Trojans.* New York: Praeger.

Book of Kings references are from the *Old Testament,* Revised Standard Version, Thomas Nelson and Sons, N.Y. (1953).

Brackman, A. C. 1974. *The Dream of Troy.* New York: Van Nostrand Reinhold Co.

Brion, Marcel. 1973. *Pompeii and Herculaneum.* London: Elek Books Ltd.

Burke, E. E. 1969. *The Journals of Carl Mauch, 1869 to 1872.* Salisbury: National Archives of Rhodesia.

Calder, W. M., III. 1972. "Schliemann on Schliemann: A study in the use of sources." *Greek, Roman and Byzantine Studies* 13:335–53.

Chávez-Ballón, Manuel. 1971. "Cuzco y Machu-Pijchu." *Wayka* 4–5:1–4. Translated by S. J. Chávez.

Corti, E. C. 1951. *The Destruction and Resurrection of Pompeii and Herculaneum.* London: Routledge and Kegan Paul Ltd.

D'Avino, Michele. (n. d.) *Pompeii Prohibited.* Naples: Edizioni Proccini.

Dearborn, D.S.P., K. J. Schreiber, and R. E. White, 1987. "Intimachay: A December Solstice Observatory at Machu Picchu, Peru." *American Antiquity,* 52:346–352.

Deiss, J.J. 1966. *Herculaneum.* New York: T. Y. Crowell Co.

———. 1985. *Herculaneum.* New York: Harper & Row (Revised and Updated Edition).

Denbow, J. R. 1984. "Cows and kings: a spatial and economic analysis of a hierarchical Early Iron Age settlement system in eastern Botswana." *Frontiers: Southern African Archaeology Today.* BAR Internat. Series, no. 207. Cambridge: Monographs in African Archaeology.

Deuel, Leo. 1977. *Memoirs of Heinrich Schliemann.* New York: Harper and Row.

Easton, D. F. 1981. "Schliemann's discovery of 'Priam's treasure,' two enigmas." *Antiquity* 55:179–83.
Elkiss, Terry. 1979. The quest for an African Eldorado: Sofala, Southern Zambezia and the Portuguese, 1500–1865. Ph. D. diss., Dept. of History, Michigan State Univ., East Lansing.
Garcilaso de la Vega. 1966. *El Inca, Royal Commentaries of The Incas, Part 1.* (Translated by H. V. Livermore). Austin: University of Texas Press.
Garlake, P. S. 1973. *Great Zimbabwe.* London: Thames and Hudson.
———. 1978. "Pastoralism and Zimbabwe." *Journal of African History* 19:479–93.
———. 1982. *Great Zimbabwe Described and Explained.* Harare: Zimbabwe Publishing House.
———. 1984. "Ken Mufuka and Great Zimbabwe." *Antiquity* 58:121–23.
Gasparini, Graziana and Luise Margolies 1980 *Inca Architecture* (Translated by P. J. Lyon) Bloomington: Indiana Univ. Press.
Gayre, R., and Robert Nigg. 1972. *The Origin of the Zimbabwean Civilization.* Salisbury: Galaxie Press.
Gore, Rick. 1984. "The dead do tell tales at Vesuvius." *National Geographic* 165:557–613.
Grant, Michael. 1971. *Cities of Vesuvius: Pompeii and Herculaneum.* London: Michael Grant Pubs. Ltd, George Weidenfeld and Nicholson Ltd.
Haggard, H. Rider. 1964. London: Macdonald. *King Solomon's Mines.*
Hammer, Signe. 1984. "Surprise discovery at Machu Picchu." *Science Digest* 53–57.
Hall, R. N. 1905. *Great Zimbabwe.* London: Methuen and Co.
Hemming, John. 1981. *Machu Picchu.* New York: Newsweek Book Division.
Huffman, T. N. 1972. "The rise and fall of Zimbabwe." *Journal of African History* 13:353–66.
———. 1981. "Snakes and birds: expressive space at Great Zimbabwe." *African Studies* 40:131–50.
Isbell, W. H. 1978. "The prehistoric ground drawings of Peru." *Scientific American* 239:140–53.
Jett, S. C. 1978. "Pre-Columbian transoceanic contacts." Chap. 13

in *Ancient Native Americans* ed. by J. D Jennings. San Francisco: W. H. Freeman and Co.

Kosok, Paul. 1947. "The mysterious markings of Nazca." *Natural History* 56.

Kraft, J. C., Ilhan Kayan, and Oguz Erol. 1980. "Geomorphic reconstuctions in environs of ancient Troy." *Science* 209:776–82.

Lattimore, Richmond. 1951. *The Iliad of Homer.* Chicago: Univ. of Chicago Press.

Lilly, Eli. 1961. *Schliemann in Indianapolis.* Indianapolis: Indiana Historical Society.

Lindsay, Jack. 1960. *The Writing on the Wall.* London: Fredrick Muller Ltd.

Lumbreras, L. Y. 1974. *The People and Cultures of Ancient Peru.* Translated by B. J. Meggars. Washington, D. C.: Smithsonian Institution Press.

Moseley, M. E. 1978. "The evolution of Andean civilization." In *Ancient Native Americans*, ed. by J. D. Jennings. San Francisco: W. H. Freeman and Co.

Phillipson, D. W. 1977. *The Later Prehistory of Eastern and Southern Africa.* London: Heinemann.

Prinz, Martin. 1979. "Pompeii AD 79." Ed. by A. M. Cunningham. *Natural History* 88:41–48.

Prescott, W. H. (n.d.) *History of the Conquest of Peru.* 2 vols. Philadelphia: David McKay Publishers.

Reiche, M. 1980. *Mystery on the Desert.* Stuttgart: Heinrich Fink GmbH + Co.

Rowe, J. H. 1963. "Urban settlements in ancient Peru." *Nawpa Pacha* 1. (Institute of Andean Studies, Berkeley, Calif.).

———. 1967. "What kind of settlement was Inca Cuzco?" *Nawpa Pacha* 5:59–76.

Schliemann, Heinrich. 1875. *Troy and Its Remains.* Reissue, 1968. New York: Benjamin Blom.

———. 1878. *Mycenae: A Narrative of Researches and Discoveries at Mycenae and Tiryns.* London: John Murray.

———. 1880. *Illios: The City and Country of the Trojans.* London: John Murray.

Sheridan, M. F., F. Barberi, M. Rosi, and R. Santacroce. 1981. "A

mode for Plinian eruptions of Vesuvius." *Nature* 289:282–85.
Sheridan, M. F., and K. H. Wohletz. 1981. "Hydrovolcanic explosions: the systematics of water-pyroclast equilibration." *Science* 212:1387–89.
Summers, Rogers. 1963. *Zimbabwe—A Rhodesian Mystery*. Johannesburg: Nelson.
Traill, D. A. 1979. "Schliemann's mendacity: fire and fever in California." *The Classical Journal* 74:348–55.
———. 1982. "Schliemann's American citizenship and divorce." *The Classical Journal* 77:336–42.
———. 1983. "Schliemann's 'discovery' of 'Priam's Treasure.' " *Antiquity* 57:181–86.
Von Däniken, Erich. 1972. *Chariots of the Gods?* New York: Bantam.
Wallace, St. C. A. 1936. *The Great Zimbabwe Ruins, Mashonaland Southern Rhodesia* London: Rhodesia House.
Wood, Michael. 1985. *In Search of the Trojan War*. New York: New American Library.

CHAPTER 5

Adovasio, J. M., and R. C. Carlisle. 1984. "An Indian hunter's camp for 20,000 years." *Scientific American* 250:130–36.
Bass, G. F. 1966. *Archaeology Under Water*. New York: Praeger.
———. 1967. "Cape Gelidonya: a Bronze Age shipwreck." *Transactions of the American Philosophical Society*. New Series 57, pt. 8.
Bocquet, Aimé. 1979. "Lake-bottom archeaology." *Scientific American* 240:56–64.
Handouts from: *The Mary Rose Exhibition*. Cleveland Museum of Natural History. Oct. 11–Dec. 8, 1985.
Cappuzzo, Mike. 1984. "Return from the bog." *Tropic Magazine (Miami Herald)*. 26 Aug.
Chomko, S. A., and G. W. Crawford. 1978. "Plant husbandry in prehistoric eastern North America: new evidence for its development." *American Antiquity* 43:405–08.
Clausen, C. J., A. D. Cohen, Cesare Emiliani, J. A. Holman, and J. J. Stipp. 1979. "Little Salt Spring, Florida: a unique underwater site." *Science* 203:609–14.

Coggins, C. C., G. R. Willey, and L. H. Wren 1984. *Cenote of Sacrifice.* Austin: Univ. of Texas Press.

Conrad, Nicholas, D. L. Asch, N. B. Asch, David Elmore, Harry Gove, Meyer Rubin, J. A. Brown, M. D. Wiant, K. B. Farnsworth, and T. G. Cook. 1984. "Accelerator radiocarbon dating of evidence for prehistoric horticulture in Illinois." *Nature* 308: 443–46.

Dillehay, T. D. 1984. "A late Ice-Age settlement in southern Chile." *Scientific American* 251:106–117.

Evershed, R. P., K. Jerman, and G. Eglinton. 1985. "Pine wood origin for pitch from the *Mary Rose.*" *Nature* 314:528–30.

Fagan, B. M., and E Van Noten. 1971. *The Hunter-Gatherers of Gwisho.* Tervuren, Belgium: Musée Royal de l'Afrique Central.

Gallenkamp, Charles. 1981. *Maya, The Riddle and Rediscovery of a Lost Civilization.* 2d ed. Middlesex: Penguin Books.

Heer, Rev. Dr. Oswald. 1878. "Plants of the lake dwellings." In *The Lake Dwellings of Switzerland and Other Parts of Europe,* ed. by F. Keller. London: Longmans, Green and Co.

Helbaek, Hans. 1969. "Plant collecting, dry-farming and irrigation agriculture." In *Prehistory and Human Ecology of the Deh Luran Plain,* by Frank Hole et. al. 383–426.

Hole, Frank, K. V. Flannery, and J. A. Neely. 1969. *Prehistory and Human Ecology of the Deh Luran Plain.* Memoirs of the Museum of Anthropology. No. 1. Ann Arbor: Univ. of Michigan.

Holman, J. A., and C. J. Clausen. 1984. "Fossil vertebrates associated with Paleo-Indian artifacts at Little Salt Spring, Florida." *Journal of Vertebrate Paleontology* 4:146–54.

Hurtado, E. D. 1961. "Return to the sacred cenote." *National Geographic* 120:543–61.

Keller, Ferdinand. 1878. *The Lake Dwellings of Switzerland and Other Parts of Europe.* 2d ed. 2 vols. Translated by J. E. Lee. London: Longmans, Green and Co.

McKee, Alexander. 1973. *King Henry VIII's Mary Rose.* London: Souvenir Press.

———. 1982. *How We Found The Mary Rose.* New York: St. Martin's Press.

Morley, S. G. 1938. "Yucatan, home of the gifted Maya." *National Geographic* 70:623.

Olsen, Olaf, and Ole Crumlin-Pedersen. 1959. "The Skudelev Ships." *Acta Archaeologica* 29:161–74.

———. 1978. *Five Viking Ships from Roskilde Fjord.* Translated by Barbara Bluestone. Copenhagen: National Museum.

Romero, P. B. 1972. "The sacred well of Chichén Itzá and other fresh water sites in Mexico." Chapter 11 in *Underwater Archaeology, A Nascent Discipline.* Paris: UNESCO.

Rule, Margaret. 1982. *The Mary Rose.* London: Conway Maritime Press Ltd.

Stephens, J. L. 1841. *Incidents of Travel in Central America, Chiapas and Yucatan.* 2 vols. New York: Harper & Brothers.

Struever, Stuart. 1968. "Flotation techniques for the recovery of small-scale archaeological remains." *American Antiquity* 33:353–62.

Thompson, E. H. 1932. *People of the Serpent.* Boston: Houghton Mifflin.

Weaver, M. P. 1981. *The Aztecs, Maya and Their Predecessors.* 2d ed. New York: Academic Press.

CHAPTER 6

Atkinson, R. C. J. 1966. "Moonshine on Stonehenge." *Antiquity* 40:212–16.

———. 1981. *Stonehenge and Neighboring Monuments.* London: Her Majesty's Stationery Office.

Aveni, A. F. 1981. "Tropical archaeoastronomy." *Science* 213:161–71.

Baity, Elizabeth. 1973. "Archaeoastronomy and ethnoastronomy so far." *Current Anthropology* 14:389–449.

Chippindale, C. 1986. "Stoned Henge: events and issues at the summer solstice, 1985." *World Archaeology* 18:38–58.

Daniel, Glyn. 1980. "Megalithic monuments." *Scientific American* 243:77–90.

Doyle, L. R. 1984. "Astronomy In East Africa." *Anthroquest.* No. 29.

Fowler, M. L., ed. 1969. *Explorations into Cahokia Archaeology.* Illinois Archaeological Survey, bul. 7. Urbana: Univ. of Illinois.

Gregg, M. L. 1975. "A population estimate for Cahokia." In *Perspectives in Cahokia Archaeology,* ed. by J. A. Brown. Illinois Archaeological Survey, bul. 10. Urbana: Univ. of Illinois.

Hawkins, G. S. 1963. "Stonehenge decoded." *Nature* 200:306–08.

———. 1973. *Beyond Stonehenge*. New York: Harper & Row
———. 1983. *Mindsteps to the Cosmos*. New York: Harper & Row.
Hawkins, G. S., and J. B. White. 1965. *Stonehenge Decoded*. New York: Dell.
Heinzelin, Jean de. 1962. "Ishango." *Scientific American* 206:105–16.
Kendrick. 1986. *People of Chaco, a Canyon and Its Culture*. New York, London: W. W. Norton.
Lekson, S. H., Windes, T. C., Stein, J. R., and W. James Judge. 1988. "The Chaco Canyon Community." *Scientific American*. 259:100–109.
Lewin, R 1989. "Ice Age Art Idea Toppled." *Science* 17 March: 1435.
Lipe, W. D. 1978. "The Southwest." Chap. 8 in *Ancient Native Americans*, ed. by J. D. Jennings. San Francisco: W. H. Freeman and Co.
Lynch, B. M., and L. H. Robbins. 1978. Namoratunga: The first archeoastronomical evidence in sub-Saharan Africa." *Science* 200:766–68.
Marshack, Alexander. 1972. *The Roots of Civilization*. New York: McGraw-Hill.
Marshack, A. 1989. "Ice Age Art Analysis." *Science* 244: 1029.
McNitt, Frank. 1966. *Richard Wetherill: Anasazi*. Albuquerque: Univ. of New Mexico Press.
Muller, J. D. 1978. "The Southeast." Chap. 7 in *Ancient Native Americans*, ed. by J. D. Jennings. San Francisco: W. H. Freeman and Co.
Noble, D. G. *New Light on Chaco Canyon*. 1984. Santa Fe, New Mexico School of American Research.
Petrie, W. M. 1880. *Stonehenge*. London: Stanford.
Pitts, M. W. 1982. "On the road to Stonehenge." *Proceedings of the Prehistoric Society* 48:129–30.
Ray, T. P. 1989. "The winter solstice phenomenon at Newgrange, Ireland: accident or design?" *Nature* 337:343–345.
Reed, N. A. 1969. "Monks and other Mississippian mounds." In *Explorations into Cahokia Archaeology*," ed. by M. L. Fowler Illinois Archaeological Survey. Urbana: Univ. of Illinois.
Renfrew, Colin. 1973. *Before Civilization*. New York: Alfred A. Knopf.
Reyman, J. E. 1976. "Astronomy, architecture, and adaptation at Pueblo Bonito." *Science* 193:958–62.
———. 1980. "An Anasazi solar market?" *Science*, 299:858–60.
Simmons, L. W. 1942. *Sun Chief*. New Haven: Yale Univ. Press.

Sofaer, Anna, Volker Zinser, and Rolf M. Sinclair. 1979. "A unique solar marking construct." *Science* 206:283–92.
White, J. R. 1987. "The Sun Serpents." *Archaeology* 40:52–57.
Wittry, W. L. 1977. "The American Woodhenge." In *Explorations into Cahokia Archaeology*, 2d rev. ed., ed. by M. L. Fowler. Illinois Archaeological Survey, bul. 7:43–48. Urbana: Univ. of Illinois.
Zeilik, Michael. 1985. "The Fajada Butte solar marker: a reevaluation." *Science* 228:1311–13.

CHAPTER 7

Allegro, J. M. 1956. *The Dead Sea Scrolls*. Harmondsworth: Penguin Books.
Bratton, F. G. 1967. *A History of Egyptian Archaeology*. London: Hale.
Budge, E. A. Wallis. 1929. *The Rosetta Stone in the British Museum*. London: The Religious Tract Society.
Ceram, C. W. 1980. *Gods, Graves, and Scholars*. New York: Bantam.
Champollion, Le Jeune (J.F.). 1824. *Précis du Système Hieroglyphique ou Recherches*. 2d ed. Paris: L'Imprimerie Royale.
Cook, S. A. 1903. *The Laws of Moses and the Code of Hammurabi*. London: Adam and Charles Black.
Daniel, Glyn. 1983. *A Short History of Archaeology*. New York: Thames and Hudson.
Dundes, A. 1988. *The Flood Myth*. University of California Press. See Dundes, "The Flood as Male Myth of Creation," pgs. 167–182.
Frymer-Kensky, Tikva. 1978. "What the Babylonian flood stories can and cannot teach us about the Genesis flood." *Biblical Archaeology Review* 4:43–41.
———. 1980. "Tit For tat: The principle of equal retribution in Near Eastern and Biblical law." *The Biblical Archaeologist* 43:230–34.
Golb, Norman. 1980. "The problem of origin and identification of the Dead Sea Scrolls." *Proceedings of the American Philopsophical Society* 124:1–24.
Golb, N. 1989. "The Dead Sea Scrolls." *The American Scholar*. Spring issue.
Lansing State Journal. Sept. 24, 1989. Pg. 3D.

Larue, G. A. 1968. *Old Testament Life and Literature.* Boston: Allyn and Bacon, Inc.

Layard, A. H. 1949. *Nineveh and the Remains.* Vols. I and II. London: John Murray.

Layard, Sir Henry. 1903. *Autobiography and Letters.* Vol. 2, Ed. by W. N. Bruce. London: J. Murray.

Mansoor, M., 1983. *The Dead Sea Scrolls.* Grand Rapids, Michigan: Baker.

Mallowan, M. E. L. (Max). 1964. "Noah's flood reconsidered." *Iraq* 26:62–82.

———. 1977. *Mallowan's Memoirs.* New York: Dodd, Mead and Co.

Pritchard, J. B. 1965. *The Ancient Near East, An Anthology of Texts and Pictures.* Princeton: Princeton Univ. Press.

Rassam, Hormuzd. 1897. *Asshur and the Land of Nimrod.* New York: Eaton and Mains.

Samuel, A. Y. 1949. "The purchase of the Jerusalem Scrolls." *The Biblical Archaeologist.* 12:26–32.

Samuel, Athanasius Yeshue. 1966. *Treasure of Qumran.* Philadephia: Westminister Press.

Schmandt-Besserat, Denise. 1978. "The earliest precursor of writing." *Scientific American* 238:50–59.

———. 1981. "Decipherment of the earliest tablets." *Science* 211:238–95.

———. 1986. "An ancient token system: the precursor to numerals and writing." *Archaeology* 39:32–39.

Shanks, Hershel. 1984. "Yigael Yadin, 1917–1984." *Biblical Archaeology Review* 10:24–29.

———. 1985. "Bar view, failure to publish Dead Sea Scrolls is leitmotif of New York University scroll conference." *Biblical Archaeology Review* II:4–6, 66–70.

———. 1989. "Dead Sea Scrolls Scandal." *Biblical Archaeology Review.* XV, No. 4, July/Aug: 18–21.

———. 1989. "What Should Be Done About the Unpublished Dead Sea Scrolls?" *Biblical Archaeology Review.* XV, No. 5, Sept/Oct: 18–22.

Simpson, W. K. 1978. "The gift of writing" In *Ancient Egypt, Discovering its Splendors,* ed. by J. B. Billard. Washington, D. C.: National Geographic Society.

Shenhav, D. J. 1981. "Saving the Dead Sea Scrolls for the next 2000 years." *Biblical Archaeology Review* 7:44–49.

Smith, George. 1875. *Assyrian Discoveries.* New York: Schribner, Armstrong and Co.

Sukenik, E. L. 1955. *The Dead Sea Scrolls of The Hebrew University.* Jerusalem: Magnes Press.

Taylor, R. E., and Rainer Berger. 1980. "The date of Noah's Ark." *Antiquity* 44:34–36.

Teeple, H. W. 1978. *The Noah's Ark Nonsense.* Evanston, Ill: Religion and Ethics Institute, Inc.

Trever, J. C. 1965. *The Untold Story of Qumran.* Westwood, N. J.: F. H. Revell Co.

Woolley, Sir Leonard. 1965. *Excavations at Ur.* New York: T. Y. Crowell.

Wright, G. E. 1948. "A phenomenal discovery." *The Biblical Archaeologist* 11:21–23.

Yadin, Yigael. 1984. "The Temple Scroll—The longest and most recently discovered Dead Sea Scroll." *Biblical Archaeology Review.* 10:33–49.

———. 1985. *The Temple Scroll.* London: Weidenfeld and Nicolson.

Photograph Credits

View of Olduvai Gorge	Lawrence H. Robbins
Zinjanthropus skull from Olduvai	Courtesy the Wenner-Gren Foundation for Anthropological Research, Inc., New York, and with permission of the owners of the original specimens
View of Lothagam	Lawrence H. Robbins
Lucy	After N. J. Sauer and T. W. Phenice, 1977, *Hominid Fossils,* copyright W. C. Brown Co., with permission of Wm. C. Brown and Dr. Lillian Phenice
Comparison of Laetoli footprint contour patterns with modern human female	Reprinted by permission from *Nature,* Vol. 286, 385–387, copyright 1980, Macmillan Journals Ltd., courtesy of Dr. M. H. Day
Les Trois Frères cave	Courtesy of the Field Museum, Chicago
Sorcerer of Les Trois Frères	Courtesy of the American Museum of Natural History, New York
Lascaux Cave, Hall of the Bulls	Courtesy of Caisse Nationale des Monuments Historiques et des Sites, Paris (Arch. Phot. Paris/SPADEM)

Lascaux, dead man scene	Courtesy of Caisse National des Monuments Historiques et des Sites, Paris (Arch. Phot. Paris/SPADEM)
Rock art from Africa: Tsodilo hills, Botswana	Lawrence H. Robbins
The oldest art in Africa: Painted slabs from Apollo 11 Cave, Namibia	Courtesy of Dr. W. E. Wendt, copyright Dr. W. E. Wendt
South African rock art, Kamberg	From J. D. Lewis-Williams, 1981, *Believing and Seeing: Symbolic Meanings in Southern San Rock Paintings*, with permission of Academic Press and Dr. J. D. Lewis-Williams
The Sutton Hoo ship	After R. Bruce-Mitford, 1979, *The Sutton Hoo Ship-Burial*, Vol. 1, British Museum Publications Ltd., London, Courtesy of the Trustees of the British Museum
Buried life-size army of Qin-Shi-Haung	After Yuan Zhongyi, 1983
Outer gold shrine of Tutankhamen's tomb	Courtesy of Lehnert & Landrock, Fine Arts Publishers, Cairo
Throne from Tutankhamen's tomb	Courtesy of the Egyptian Museum, Cairo
Gold coffin containing mummy of Tutankhamen	Courtesy of Lehnert & Landrock, Fine Arts Publishers, Cairo
Gold mask from Tutankhamen's tomb	Courtesy of the Egyptian Museum, Cairo
View of Hissarlik	Lawrence H. Robbins
View of Pompeii	Lawrence H. Robbins
Great Zimbabwe hill ruin	Courtesy of the Department of Information, Photographic Section, Harare, Zimbabwe
Great Zimbabwe: great enclosure	Courtesy of the Department of Information, Photographic Section, Harare, Zimbabwe

View of Machu Picchu	Courtesy of Sergio Chavéz
Machu Picchu	Courtesy of Sergio Chavéz
The Well of Sacrifice at Chichén Itzá	Courtesy of Dr. Karen L. Mohr-Cahvez
Gold faces from the Well of Sacrifices, Chichén Itzá	Courtesy of the Peabody Museum. Harvard University, photograph by Hillel Burger
Heavily encrusted cannon from the *Mary Rose*	After Alexander Mckee, 1973, *How We Found the Mary Rose*, reproduced with permission of Souvenir Press, Ltd., London
The *Mary Rose* in a new home	Courtesy of the Mary Rose Trust
View of Stonehenge showing sarsen circle and trilithons	Courtesy of David Barondess
Stonehenge showing the heelstone centrally framed	Courtesy of Dr. G. S. Hawkins, copyright by Dr. G. S. Hawkins
The Rosetta Stone	Courtesy of the Trustees of the British Museum
Comparison of Ptolemy and Cleopatra as used by Champollion	After F. G. Bratton, 1967, *A History of Egyptian Archaeology*, courtesy of Robert Hale, London
Dead Sea cave at Qumran	Courtesy of the Israel Museum, Jerusalem
The Isaiah Scroll	Courtesy of the Israel Museum, Jerusalem
Stelae of King Hammurabi	Courtesy of Caisse Nationale de Monuments Historiques et des Sites, Paris (Arch. Phot. Paris/SPADEM)
Clay tablet with the Gilgamesh epic	Courtesy of the Trustees of the British Museum

Index